PAUL TILLICH
AND PENTECOSTAL THEOLOGY

PAUL TILLICH
AND PENTECOSTAL THEOLOGY

Spiritual Presence & Spiritual Power

EDITED BY

NIMI WARIBOKO & AMOS YONG

INDIANA UNIVERSITY PRESS
Bloomington and Indianapolis

This book is a publication of

INDIANA UNIVERSITY PRESS
Office of Scholarly Publishing
Herman B Wells Library 350
1320 East 10th Street
Bloomington, Indiana 47405 USA

iupress.indiana.edu

Manufactured in the United States of America

Library of Congress Cataloging-in-Publication Data

Paul Tillich and pentecostal theology : spiritual presence and spiritual
power / edited by Nimi Wariboko and Amos Yong.
     pages cm
  Includes bibliographical references and index.
  ISBN 978-0-253-01802-1 (cloth : alk. paper) — ISBN 978-0-253-01808-3
(pbk. : alk. paper) — ISBN 978-0-253-01812-0 (ebook) 1. Tillich, Paul,
1886-1965. 2. Pentecostalism. 3. Pentecostal churches—Doctrines.
I. Wariboko, Nimi, 1962- editor.
  BX4827.T53P295 2015
  230.092—dc23
                          2015017066

1 2 3 4 5 20 19 18 17 16 15

To
Harvey G. Cox

CONTENTS

PREFACE

All pre-faces to edited volumes appear to have two "faces," two ways of pre-speaking. One introduces readers to the story the editors want to tell about how the idea for the volume was conceived. This is a story they are eager to persuade readers to own as theirs, as if to bring the readers and authors to a shared moment of inspiration that appreciates the book's thesis, argument, and goals. This story also serves to establish the need for their volume. The other "face" is an afterthought, a reinterpretation, a retrospective take, a retroactive examination by the editors of the various processes that worked to bring the book to completion. Usually, it is on this *face* of the discourse that the editors squeeze meanings out of random events, surprises, and unexpected turns that are inevitable when many scholars are brought together to work, individually and collectively, on a joint project. We want to tell both stories.

Paul Tillich (1886–1965) wrote a great deal about the *Spiritual Presence*, the immanent presence of the transcendental God amid history. Pentecostal theology accents the Holy Spirit as actively moving, working, and personally transforming human beings, institutions, and communities in the world. While resolutely Christ-centered in its piety, pentecostal theology has nevertheless been intuitively and consistently at work in the formulation of a pneumatological approach to the theological task as well as in the forging of a pneumatological theology focused on the work of the Holy Spirit. By doing so, pentecostal theologians have been major contributors to the articulation and elaboration of the doctrine of the Holy Spirit that has emerged in the last generation in the wider theological academy. So it appears pentecostal theology and Tillichian thought have common ground on which to engage one another and, in so doing, also expand the frontiers of pneumatological theology. Yet a critical conversation between pentecostal theology and the legacy of Tillich has not occurred in any significant way. Thus the need for this book.

On January 21, 2010, we exchanged emails on this shortcoming. Before the end of the day we had identified not only most of the potential contributors to a possible volume on Tillich and pentecostal theology, but also its possible signature character. We decided that the overall thrust of the volume would be around Tillich's *Systematic Theology*, volume 3, and that his idea of the Spiritual

Presence would serve as the springboard to the rest of his oeuvre. The volume would provide a series of pentecostal critical dialogues with Tillich's ideas and Tillichian scholarship, with a fourfold goal: (a) expanding the scope and horizon of pentecostal dialogue partners; (b) contributing further to the contemporary renaissance in pneumatological theology in dialogue with Tillich; (c) critically engaging with contemporary Tillich scholarship in particular; and (d) creatively providing pentecostal engagements with a broad range of contemporary theological topics in dialogue with Tillich.

While the various chapters in this volume critically and adequately engage with Tillich and his ideas, the dialogue with Tillich does not mean that the terms of the engagement are always Tillichian; putting an emphasis on Pentecostalism and pentecostal theology while incorporating or appropriating Tillichian theology is one way of engaging with Tillich's theology. Similarly we are hoping that this dialogue with Tillich helps to generate creative impulse when Tillich is read from a Pentecostal vantage point such that pentecostal theology in turn provides insights for Tillichian scholars.

This volume was conceived amid and against the backdrop of the ongoing development and maturation of pentecostal scholarship as it enters its next phase. The first generation of pentecostal scholars focused on the history of the movement. The generation that came after was concerned with laying the groundwork for pentecostal biblical scholarship. The third wave of scholarship has produced scholars who have developed pentecostal theologies increasingly set within a broad ecumenical, pneumatological, and trinitarian framework. In this latest phase, the dialogue partners for pentecostal theologians have been dominated by the Wesleyan tradition, especially in light of the trajectories of conversation launched by the work of Don Dayton and Stephen Land in the late 1980s. Insofar as pentecostal theologians have engaged the broader tradition of Protestant theology at all, this has been limited to a very small circle dominated by Karl Barth (e.g., in the work of Frank Macchia and Terry Cross, most explicitly). But recently there have been indications that the circle is widening, especially to include Catholic charismatic theology, non-Christian theologies, science, and continental philosophy. This volume on Tillich and pentecostal theology denotes the expanding scope and horizon of pentecostal dialogue partners in today's theological landscape. Its goal is, at least, in part to deepen and strengthen pentecostal theology in the twentieth-first century and re-cognize its enduring insights as it interfaces with the thought of one of the twentieth-century greatest theologians. Now, that is the story that we want you, the reader, to own as definitely yours.

The other story also needs to be briefly mentioned. It was a delight to work with all the contributors who made this volume possible. The significance of the project was easily grasped by all of them in January 2010 when we invited them to consider writing for the book, and they approached it with dedication, care, and commitment. There were even more who initially responded positively to our proposal and invitation, but they were prevented by the unpredictable circumstances of life from realizing their chapters here. Each of our contributors in the pages to come creatively provides a pentecostal engagement with a contemporary topic by arguing *with and against* Tillich and his ongoing theological legacy. We say a big thank-you to all of you for your hard work, dedication, and the great patience you exercised throughout many rounds of editing, cutting, revisions, and delays.

At the 2012 meeting of the American Academy of Religion (AAR), Wolfgang Vondey presented, of his own initiative, an earlier version of his essay in this volume as part of a panel of the Paul Tillich: "Issues in Theology, Religion, and Culture Group." Enthusiastic reception by group members inspired Russell Re Manning, co-chair of the group, to work with Vondey and Wariboko to organize a full panel at the 2013 meeting of the AAR where Frank Macchia, Nimi Wariboko, and Lisa Stephenson presented versions of the papers published here. (Note: Unlike books that have come out of conference presentations, this collection was commissioned as a set of essays out of which a number of conference papers were presented.) John J. Thatamanil (Union Theological Seminary) and Mark Lewis Taylor (Princeton Theological Seminary) responded to the papers. Thatamanil had agreed from the time the volume had been commissioned to contribute a response, and the editors are thankful for his careful interaction with the essays. The editors are also grateful that Taylor agreed, following the meeting, to rework and develop his response for inclusion in this volume, and what he produced stands on its own as a constructive exposition of Tillich's pneumatology (which itself confirms the book's capacity to inspire original thinking). Both write as respected Tillichian scholars and established theologians in their own right. Part of this other story is that Nimi studied Tillich with and under Taylor at Princeton Theological Seminary, while Amos read Tillich, among other topics, as a doctoral student with Thatamanil in the mid-1990s when both were studying under Robert Cummings Neville at Boston University.

Dee Mortensen, senior sponsoring editor at Indiana University Press (IUP), deserves also our salute and thanks for believing in the project and for staying with us from conception to publication. David Miller and Candace McNulty at IUP, among others helped with the various phases of copyediting, production, and marketing. Vince Le, Amos's former graduate assistant, standardized the manuscript according to IUP preferred style and format, and Ryan Seow, Amos's present graduate assistant, helped with final corrections and created the volume index. We thank our spouses (Alma and Wapaemi) for their wonderful support and encouragement and acknowledge the blessings that are our children (Annalisa, Alyssa, and Aizaiah—and his wife Neddy—and Nimi, Bele, and Favor).

We dedicate the book to Harvey Gallagher Cox, Hollis Research Professor of Divinity at Harvard University. Cox has been a friend to us and a sturdy bridge between Tillichian thought and pentecostal scholarship for decades. He was a student and teaching assistant of Tillich at Harvard in the early 1960s. In keeping with Tillich's interest in the theology of culture, the Spiritual Presence, and the impact of Spirit-movements on cultures and their criticism of established religious life and creeds, in 1995 Cox published a remarkable book on global Pentecostalism, *Fire from Heaven: The Rise of Pentecostal Spirituality and the Reshaping of Religion in the 21st Century*. This was a time when high caliber, world-class theologians had not yet taken the pentecostal-charismatic movement seriously, to engage it academically. We think, therefore, it is befitting to dedicate to him the first book that deals with the reception of Tillich in pentecostal theology.

Reference Note

All references to Paul Tillich, *Systematic Theology*, 3 vols. (Chicago: University of Chicago Press, 1951–1963), will be made parenthetically in text as *ST* followed by volume and page number.

PAUL TILLICH
AND PENTECOSTAL THEOLOGY

Why Is the "Correlation" between Paul Tillich and Pentecostal Theology Important, and Who Cares?

AMOS YONG

The last generation has seen the explosion of pentecostal-type churches at the vanguard of the world Christian movement, at least across the global South,[1] and the last twenty years or so have seen also a gradual emergence of pentecostal theology in the wider academic discussion.[2] Although nurtured and deeply informed by Wesleyan Holiness roots and close relationships with conservative evangelical theological traditions, the growth and development of pentecostal theology as a scholarly enterprise has forced consideration of the nature of pentecostal self-understanding.[3] Part of the result has been the rise of efforts to articulate a distinctive pentecostal theological identity. To be sure, there is consensus about neither what that identity is nor the most promising way forward for pentecostal theological reflection. Those associated with the so-called Hollenweger School (initially at Birmingham, England, now centered at the Free University of Amsterdam and in relationship with the European Research Network on Global Pentecostalism [Glopent]) are more global and elastic in their approach, while the Center for Pentecostal Theology (Cleveland, Tennessee) focuses much more on the Wesleyan Holiness connections and the "Full Gospel" (four-fold or five-fold) framework. There is also more recently the Center for Renewal Studies associated with the Regent University School of Divinity, which is oriented toward a more interdisciplinary self-understanding including pentecostal, charismatic, and other renewal movements. Other schools are emerging and will no doubt be actively engaged in the discussion by the time this volume is published. This book seeks to explore the contours of more-or-less conservative pentecostal theology in dialogue with what is now probably best known as one of major strands of contemporary liberal theology, the liberal Lutheran tradition charted by the legacy of Paul Tillich (1886–1965).[4]

Why liberalism in general, and why Tillich in particular? These are valid questions, to which more complete responses cannot be comprehended apart from the remainder of this introductory chapter as well as the rest of the chapters in this volume. Preliminarily, however, three interrelated sets of justification can be offered. First, pentecostal theology springs not from a major theological figure (like Lutheranism, Calvinism, or Wesleyanism) but from a set of spiritual encounters. This means that Pentecostalism is first and foremost less a creed or an *ism* than it is a spirituality.[5] Liberalism as a theological tradition, it is well known, is also experientially based, at least in part, with its recognized patriarch being the Pietist theologian Friedrich Schleiermacher (1768–1834), especially his religious philosophy centered on the feeling of absolute dependence. Of course, there are similarities but also major differences between the Tillichian and liberal theological tradition in regard to religious experience, not the least of which concerns the contrast between Tillich's more dialectical theology, forged in the continental context, and the progressive and evolutionary impulses characterizing American theological liberalism. The rest of this book will explore some of the dynamics involved and also demonstrate how pentecostal theology's intervention might further complicate the already complex spectrum of Tillichian-liberal thought.

Second, Pentecostalism continues to be known in some quarters primarily as an "enthusiastic movement." The theological tradition has by and large considered such movements—from the ancient Montanists through the Reformation *Schwärmerei* to the early modern revival movements[6]—in a pejorative sense. Yet Tillich himself confessed that "the present system is essentially, but indirectly, influenced by the Spirit-movements, both through their impact on Western culture in general (including such theologians as Schleiermacher) and through their criticism of the established forms of religious life and thought" (ST 3.126). The remainder of this volume will explore to what degree Tillich can be considered an "enthusiastic theologian" on the one hand while also investigating how pentecostal theological instincts compare and contrast with Tillich's Spirit movement–motivated theological system.

The preceding confession of Tillich suggests a third line of justification for this project: the emphasis on pneumatology and the doctrine of the Holy Spirit. As is well known, Tillich's pneumatology in volume 3 was the largest part of his *Systematic Theology;* but his doctrine of the Spiritual Presence—a rearticulation of traditional pneumatology—was also the culmination and apex of his theological system. Constructive pentecostal theology, in the meanwhile, has at least in some of its dominant tributaries in the last decade been consciously, intentionally, and substantively pneumatological, seeking to articulate what some have called a theology of the Third Article (of the creed, on the Holy Spirit).[7]

This book proceeds from the conviction that the experience of the Spirit, the shape of Spirit-movements, and the theology of the Spirit provide bridges that hold potential for a productive dialogue between pentecostal theology and the legacy of Paul Tillich. More precisely, the wager motivating this work is that important questions related to the tasks of *pneumatology* (theology of the Holy Spirit) and *pneumatological theology* (theologies of the Third Article shaped by the doctrine of the Spirit) can be explored precisely by bringing into mutually critical conversation pentecostal and Tillichian theologies. The results, we aver, will contribute both to the contemporary renaissance of the doctrine of the Spirit in particular and to the wider theological discussion in general.[8] The remainder of this introduction clarifies more explicitly the methodological framework for this conversation. We look first at Tillich's method of correlation and then at pentecostal theological methods, before discussing the convergences and divergences vis-à-vis contemporary developments in pneumatology and pneumatological theology. The concluding section summarizes how the rest of the chapters in the book build off these methodological ramparts.

Tillich's Method of Correlation: Pneumatological Implications

We begin with Tillich's method of correlation because our own overall task in this volume is a correlational one between his theological legacy and the emerging pentecostal theological tradition. Part of the challenge here is that the notion of correlation in Tillich has received fairly extensive discussion already, so space constraints mean that our exposition and analysis have to be selective. We proceed therefore right to the heart of Tillich's own definition of the method driving his theological system:

> Symbolically speaking, God answers man's questions, and under the impact of God's answers man asks them. Theology formulates the questions implied in human existence, and theology formulates the answers implied in divine self-manifestation under the guidance of the questions implied in human existence. . . . [Systematic theology] makes an analysis of the human situation out of which the existential questions arise, and it demonstrates that the symbols used in the Christian message are the answers to these questions (*ST* 1.61–62)

Two major observations can be registered from the foregoing. First, the theological task arises out of the human situation or condition. More specifically, theology emerges from the questions posed by human existence. Even theology's answers are shaped by—Tillich indicates they are crafted "under the guidance of"—human questions. In a real sense, then, divine revelation is dependent upon, in the sense of respondent to, the human condition. But it should also be noted that the human questions themselves are asked not merely on their own terms but "under the impact of God's answers." There is therefore a dialectical relationship between the questions and the answers—this is at the heart of Tillich's method of correlation.

Beyond this more abstract definition, however, Tillich's notion of correlation can also be exemplified in how it functioned in relationship to its competitors. Tillich contrasted the correlational method with supranaturalism, in which divinely revealed truths were believed to be deposited amid the human condition; naturalism or humanism, in which the human state itself produces salvific answers; and dualism, which recognizes both the gap between divinity and humanity on the one hand but also a "positive relation between them" (*ST* 1.65). Supranaturalism was incoherent particularly in its monophysitic view of the Bible, and naturalism or humanism was similarly impotent since the answers could be neither revelatory nor, then, salvific. With regard to dualism, Tillich insisted on avoiding any form of natural theology that identified the revelatory answers with the human questions; instead, the questions and answers are correlated as was his own theological method (form) and system (content) (*ST* 1.60).

What more specifically did this mean? Correlation, for Tillich, was based on three types of theological correspondence: between symbols and the realities to which they pointed or in which they participated; between finite human realities and infinite divine ones; and between "man's ultimate concern and that about which he is ultimately concerned" (*ST* 1.60). These were, respectively, epistemological, existential, and ontological correlations. Put another way, then, human epistemic concerns arose under the ambiguity of existential life, but were always already informed by the ontological realities of estrangement and the desire for reunion. This is the dialectical or correlational character of the theological endeavor. The three volumes of Tillich's *Systematic Theology* thus explore the correlations between the questions of human existence and the answers of divine revelation from theological, christological, and pneumatological perspectives respectively.

There are many possible assessments of Tillich's method of correlation. One can take a more historical approach and identify various correlative projects in the development of Tillich's thinking, including that of the cultural angst of the 1920s and the religious socialism of the early Tillich.[9] Alternatively, Lutheran theologians have characteristically observed that Tillichian correlation was always between existence and essence, between doubt and assurance, between sin and grace, and between law and gospel—all in that order.[10] The emphasis here is, finally and not surprisingly, on the last two correlational pairs: sin and law providing the questions and grace and gospel responding with the answers. In this view, Tillich "formulates the answers which are contained in these revelatory events by working *from* the *sources* (the Bible, church history, and the history of religion and culture), *through* the *medium* of theology (experience), and *under* the *norm* of Christian theology (the 'New Being in Jesus as the Christ')."[11]

More critical assessments, however, have involved asking whether or to what degree Tillich's method of correlation accomplishes its task. There are both formal and theological modes of analyzing this issue. The former is best observed, for example, in John Clayton's inquiry about whether Tillich's theological system finally succeeds as a mediating theology for the modern world.[12] If the norms for successful mediation are that Christian faith and modernity should both be thoroughly reciprocal on the one hand and yet remain relatively autonomous on the other hand—these are the two criteria by which Clayton, following Schleiermacher, defines a successful mediating theology, and which Tillich himself also affirms in terms of both the "independence" and the "mutual dependence" of existential questions and theological answers (*ST* 2.14)—then the conclusion is that Tillich's method of correlation is not up to the task. Either the terms correlated are too closely related (thus losing their autonomy) or they are too disparate (so that correlation is forced). Clayton puts it this way:

> While not directly competitive, neither of the two models [Tillich's question-and-answer and form-and-content correlations] on its own satisfies both the conditions of a correlative relation laid down above. . . . Although it might satisfy the reciprocity condition, "questioning and answering" is by itself too shapeless to be an adequate model of correlationship; and, although it might satisfy the autonomy condition, the dialectic of "form and content" as developed in Tillich's later writings on correlation cannot be regarded on its own as sufficiently dialectical to satisfy the reciprocity condition. It might therefore be thought that, although each on its own is insufficient, in combination the two metaphors would meet both conditions. I shall argue that this, regrettably, is not the case.[13]

Those who might be motivated to counterargue Clayton's conclusions may think either that his criteria are inadequate or that Tillich's achievements are more robust than on Clayton's examination; but they will by and large question neither the need for a correlational method nor the value of developing the kind of mediating theological system characteristic of the tradition from Schleiermacher through Tillich.

A more theological assessment, however, would worry that in the end the correlational dialectic at the heart of Tillich's method does not allow divine revelation to come through clearly. Shortly after the completion of the *Systematic The-*

ology, Alexander McKelway raised a number of important and critical questions along these lines.[14] 1) By starting with being and existence, is Tillich's system finally more anthropologically oriented than theologically substantive? 2) With regard to Tillich's doctrine of revelation, "What are we to take more seriously, his abhorrence of natural theology [clearly registered at various places in his *System*], his sense of the estranged and fallen state of creation, or his concept of the depth of reason and his use of the *analogia entis?*"[15] 3) When christology does appear in the third part (volume 2) of the *System,* Jesus of Nazareth's self-sacrificing to Jesus as the Christ is presented as the formal norm of theology (1.135); yet "what is not certain at all is that this sacrifice can be correlated or even paralleled with what Tillich calls the necessity of sacrificing the finite medium,"[16] especially in terms of minimizing the central importance and particularity of the incarnation in the Jesus of history. And perhaps most important for our concerns, 4) What is the Spiritual Presence in part 4 of the *System,* and how is the "Spirit" there related to Jesus of Nazareth as the Christ? Put another way: "Is there not the greatest danger that this Spirit will become confused with man?"[17] McKelway thus concludes that in the end, Tillich's philosophical existentialism and ontological theology betray the more specific christological center of Christian theology, and so: "We cannot but feel that if Tillich had allowed the object of theology to be the object which as subject creates the conditions for its own reception, his intention to present both a kerygmatic and an apologetic theology would have been better served."[18]

McKelway's criticisms certainly begin not quite where Tillich himself did—which thus exacerbates the disjuncture felt in McKelway's analyses—even as there may be resources internal to Tillich's system that can begin to respond to these questions. Our suggestion, and the thought experiment motivating this volume, is that starting with what Tillich called the Spiritual Presence helps to raise anthropological, christological, and theological questions simultaneously, which may have sustained Tillich's correlational enterprise while avoiding the pitfalls alleged by McKelway. In other words, rather than relegating pneumatology to the fourth part (and third volume) of the system, beginning with the Spirit would have afforded Tillich the opportunity to ask all of the anthropological and existential questions he was motivated to pursue on the one hand, but would also have invited more specific christological considerations as well. There is of course no predicting how pursuing christological issues would have redirected the *System.*[19] Our task, however, is not to revise Tillich's system but to approach it from a pneumatological angle. How might the correlations differ and what might be the theological cash value of such an enterprise, not in place of the *System* as it is but *after* the *System,* in the sense of shining upon it a new—pentecostal—light?

Pentecostal Theology: Is There a "Method" in This "Madness"?

In contrast to the explicitly formulated method of correlation deployed by Tillich, there is neither any one form of Pentecostalism nor one type of pentecostal theological method. So to ask about the theological methodology of the global renewal movement may itself finally be a futile exercise. Nevertheless we may chart a number of trends and, through these, begin to explore a dialogue with Tillich on method.

The earliest pentecostal scholars to begin reflecting self-critically at a theological level were biblical scholars. For many of these, the most pressing question is how, if at all, a pentecostal biblical hermeneutic differed from a more evangelical approach. Pentecostals had been most closely aligned with evangelicals at least since the establishment of the National Association of Evangelicals in North America in the early 1940s and thus resonated most with those working in this arena. Yet evangelical theological instincts were dominated by the epistles of St. Paul, especially the letter to the Romans, which was at the heart of the Protestant Reformation, while Pentecostals gravitated first and foremost to narrative genres, in particular the book of Acts. From this arose two initial hermeneutical sensibilities: that Luke could provide just as much of a point of entry as could Paul into the New Testament specifically and the biblical canon in general,[20] and that the scriptural revelation could be understood as an invitation to affectively embrace, imaginatively participate in, and faithfully inhabit a certain form or way of life (this is how narrative genres function) and not just as providing cognitive information for the orientation of our minds (which is what didactic genres communicate primarily through various types of propositions). Along with this shift was the recognition of the central role of the Holy Spirit. The book of Acts itself could just as well be read as unfolding the work of the Spirit in the early Christian community, and hermeneutically, the authority and guidance of the Spirit was already appealed to in reading scripture (the Hebrew Bible in this one case) and in seeking solutions to theological questions (Acts 15:28). In short, Pentecostals intuitively began thinking about theirs as a distinctively pneumatic hermeneutic, one in which the Spirit plays a central role not only in the formation of the scriptural witness but in enabling readers and reading communities to enter into and experience the saving work of God for themselves.[21]

In other words, pentecostal engagements with scripture, while compatible in many ways with those of their evangelical counterparts, differed considerably—some might say radically—in emphasizing the role of the Spirit. In its most conservative aspects, Pentecostals would agree with evangelicals that the Spirit only illuminates and applies biblical truth to contemporary human lives, in that sense bridging the scriptural and the present horizons; but in its more radical forms, Pentecostals insist that the revelatory work of the Spirit manifest in and through the apostolic experience remains ongoing today, and in that sense there is the possibility of new truths that the Spirit will unfold through new experiences and in different times and places (even if some might then draw back in saying such new truth will neither contradict nor be inconsistent with what the Bible says). In any case, the ongoing role of the Spirit cannot be denied, including the horizon of lived experience that pentecostal readers and reading communities bring to the Bible.

In part for this reason Harvey Cox, in his book on Pentecostalism, has suggested that this revival movement is a specifically Christian expression of a primordial *homo religiosus*.[22] What Cox means is that the pentecostal emphasis on the encounter with the Holy Spirit invites consideration of Pentecostalism first and foremost as a spirituality rather than as a creed or theological movement. More precisely, pentecostal spirituality is a species of a more primordial religiosity that is found in indigenous traditions around the world and is what enables the successful expansion and adaptation of Pentecostalism as a portable Christian movement. Thus the attractiveness of Pentecostalism—the motor that drives its explosion as the new form of global Christianity—lies in is its primal speech (multilinguality), its primal piety (healings, signs, wonders, and other charismatic manifestations and expressions), and primal spirituality (spontaneity in ritual and liturgy, pneumacentric religiosity, and ecological sensitivity). For these among other reasons, then, Cox believes that pentecostal experientialism, as he calls it,[23] has more in common with liberal Christian traditions and their valuation of religious experience than it does with those evangelical movements that are focused on the more rational, cognitive, or doctrinal expressions of Christian faith. Further, the prevalence of ecstatic and demonological phenomena in Pentecostalism also provides explicit points of entry for the encounter between pentecostal theology and the legacy of Tillich.[24]

There is no space for any thorough interaction with Cox's thesis.[25] For our immediate purposes, I would merely note the parallels between the evangelical pietism that informs pentecostal spirituality and the similar Moravian pietism underneath Schleiermacher's feeling of absolute dependence. Yet my own methodological proposals for pentecostal theologians have sought not an anthropological starting point (not even in pietistic experience) but an explicitly theological one. More precisely, pentecostal theological method ought to follow pentecostal biblical interpretation so that the latter's pneumatic hermeneutics should be developed into a pneumatological methodology, or a theology of the Third Article. In short, pentecostal theology starts with the Holy Spirit and with what I have called a pneumatological imagination.[26]

This pneumatological approach, however, is resolutely theological in the Christian trinitarian sense: the Spirit of Pentecost is none other than the Spirit of Jesus as the Christ (to use Tillich's formulation) and the Spirit of God the Father of Jesus. In that sense, pentecostal theology is already deeply anchored in the particularity of the Christian theological tradition. On the other hand, however, the Spirit of God in Christ is also the breath of Yahweh given to all living being in the primordial creation and the Spirit who has been poured out upon all flesh at Pentecost. In this other sense, then, the line between human spirit and divine Spirit, while clear in some respects, is also blurred in other respects.[27] The theological task thus continuously has to navigate this tension between the divine and the human, but does so from this pneumatological perspective within which we participate both at the creational and at the redemptive levels.

The Pneumatological Imagination and Tillichian Correlation: Who Cares?

The preceding sketches of Tillich's method of correlation and pentecostal theological method suggest that a mutual conversation should be of interest to Tillichian scholars and to pentecostal theologians. Beyond these two circles, however, the discussion should also be relevant to Christians engaged in the broader theological task. Let me briefly address these three audiences.

First, those interested in the theology of Tillich and in his theological legacy are probably convinced that Christian theology cannot ultimately avoid some kind of correlational enterprise, whatever that might be called. Of course, unless one lapses into a mere humanism,[28] the dilemma that persists is the one registered above, albeit in different ways, by Clayton and McKelway. If one overemphasizes the autonomy of the human questions, theology is reduced to anthropology; but if one secures the divine initiative too strongly, then the terms of correlation dissolve.

Tillich strove to distinguish the questions and the answers by beginning with the existential questions of being (volume 1) before proceeding to the christological answers of revelation (volume 2). Our solution is to start with the Spirit, who is both the Spirit of God in Christ and the breath of life in every living creature. Might such a pneumatological approach open up new venues to think about theological method in general and about a correlational or mediating theology in particular? Arguably, Tillich himself attempted to make such a new beginning with his pneumatology in the final volume of the *Systematic Theology,* but he was too far into the system then and did not have the energy to make a fresh start. Perhaps such an effort now, initiated by pentecostal theologians, can precipitate a reengagement with these matters.

Second, for pentecostal theologians, Tillich's normative christological principle of Jesus as the Christ who is the New Being has profound implications yet to be considered. Surely, the risk of disconnecting Jesus of Nazareth from Jesus as the Christ should be noted, but the pentecostal pneumatological imagination will usually involve some kind of Spirit-christology that will minimize the risks involved.[29] But what Tillich's christological imperative enables, through what he calls the *Protestant principle*, is critical resistance against any self-absolutizing claims of finite realities.[30] Such a critical perspective can bolster and reinvigorate the prophetism that is arguably intrinsic to pentecostal spirituality but has, in the upward social mobility of the global renewal movement, become domesticated and less willing to challenge the status quo in many respects and on many fronts. If the concern, though, is that in Tillich's hands the Protestant principle severs the relationship between Jesus of Nazareth and Christ as the New Being, then a Spirit-christological and pentecostal perspective would simply add that Jesus neither raises himself from the dead nor anoints himself as the Christ, but both are works of the Holy Spirit (a point Tillich also recognized in his pneumatology).

In that case, Tillich's Protestant principle needs what Nimi Wariboko calls the "Pentecostal principle."[31] What Wariboko means is both that whereas the Protestant principle is a principle of opposition and negation, the Pentecostal principle is a principle of generation and regeneration, and also that the former's deconstruction needs the latter's reconstruction. When conjoined with the pneumatological imagination, then, the Pentecostal principle harnesses the potentiality of the human *imago Dei* to actualize the normative values of the New Being of Jesus as the Christ. Yet as deeply pentecostal in terms of the pluralism observed in the Day of Pentecost narrative, the dynamic power of creativity after the "Protestant no!" is pluralistic in its expressions.[32] In short, pentecostal theologians can receive valuable impetus from the Tillichian Protestant principle even as they might able to contribute something of value to the contemporary discussion in Tillich scholarship and indeed the larger theological task.[33]

Last but not least, a dialogue between Tillich and pentecostal theology has implications for the Christian theological enterprise at large, in particular for trinitarian theological reflection. It is well known that Tillich followed in the Schleiermacherian tradition in relegating the doctrine of the Trinity to an a posteriori position in his theological system (*ST* 3.283–294), even if he did so for reasons other than did the father of modern liberal theology. Tillich certainly affirmed the importance of the trinitarian symbols, although he also insisted that previous formulations should not simply be reiterated in the present time. Pentecostals, however, are similarly divided, although for very different reasons. Trinitarian Pentecostals will struggle at various levels to reconcile the Tillichian doctrine of the Trinity with classical orthodoxy; however, if the dialogue can proceed from a firm pneumatological foundation, then the intricacies of traditional trinitarian thinking need not bog down the conversation. In that sense, pentecostal trinitarians will resonate with Tillich's methodological intuitions about not starting out with the doctrine of the Trinity, although they may wish to have a much tighter link between the Son and the Spirit than exists across the last two volumes of the *Systematic Theology*.[34]

Oneness Pentecostals, on the other hand, will be intrigued by the Tillichian approach precisely inasmuch as both view the trinitarian relations in less than personalistic terms.[35] But if Tillich insists that the trinitarian doctrine is one type of second order reflection on first order Christian experience, oneness theologians will counter that the Nicene articulation betrays the biblical revelation of the unity of God. Interestingly, however, both Tillich and oneness theologians have high christologies and robust pneumatologies, although Tillich is not wedded to the classical orthodox articulations and oneness Pentecostals wholly reject the Nicene tradition. Steven Studebaker's and Frank Macchia's chapters below pick up on some of these issues.

An Overview of the Volume: Methodological Ramifications for Contemporary Theology

The contributors to this volume include both established and younger pentecostal theologians. The organization of the chapters follows a basic order that moves from broader more philosophical and foundational trinitarian themes to other more specific doctrinal topics. My introductory chapter's discussion of the methodological convergences and divergences is thus complemented by Veli-Matti Kärkkäinen's overall mapping of the contemporary landscape of pneumatology (the doctrine of the Spirit). Together, our chapters can be read as establishing, respectively, the formal/methodological and material parameters for the chapters to follow.

The next five chapters encompass the broad scope of Tillich's philosophical and trinitarian theology. Wolfgang Vondey's includes historical perspective on how Tillich's synthesis of Schelling and Schleiermacher provides a pneumatological ontology from which pentecostal pneumatology can build, even as he shows how the concrete manifestation of the charismatic and demonic in pentecostal life presses Tillich's attempted union of spirit and nature to its most radical conclusion. The next chapter, by Rhys Kuzmič, straddles Tillich's ontology and doctrine of God. The argument is that Pentecostal prayer invites transcending the subject/object structure of theological symbol and ontological reality, since it envisions God praying through human creatures even as pentecostal theology ought to critically appropriate elements of Tillich's ontological theology, in particular those foregrounding God as living, personal, and spirit. The chapter on the Trinity by Steve Studebaker indicates how pentecostal oneness and trinitarian theology sets in relief Tillich's trinitarianism as simultaneously both surprisingly orthodox (with regard to dialectic differentiation as internal to the life of God) and yet also heterodox (in principalizing the three dialectic movements rather than in recognizing them as subsisting persons) compared to classical orthodoxy. Terry Cross's chapter on Tillich's christology depicts how, for Tillich, the Spirit enables faith in Christ beyond the uncertainties of history but through the history of sacramental effects, whereas for Pentecostals, the Spirit enables christological faith immediately through her "inner word" in human hearts. (I would further suggest that the "mediation" of the Spirit is not necessarily limited to such inner words but is carried through re-presentation, in embodied experience, of the deeds and words of the first-century carpenter from Nazareth in each subsequent generation.) Frank Macchia next provides a pentecostal reading of Tillich's *Systematic Theology,* albeit one that is not only from the standpoint of the modern classical pentecostal movement but rather from a pneumatological and Day-of-Pentecost (Acts 2) perspective. Yet he concludes, perhaps unexpectedly, that there is a point to which Tillich's overwhelming pneumatology overshadows the other two Articles that many (even oneness) Pentecostals cannot follow.

The second half of the volume shifts to thematic or more doctrinally focused discussions. Two chapters zero in on the theme of sacramentality. Andreas Nordlander pneumatologizes Tillich's theology of (existential, universal, and ecstatic) participation, which opens up both to a more pneumatologically rich and expansive theology of creation and to a more radically concrete and particular theology of sacramental and spiritual life, while Lisa Stephenson brings Tillich's sacramental spirituality into conversation with representative strands of feminist and pentecostal spirituality toward a mutual enrichment. Other chapters follow this dialogical structure. Tillich's agonistic view of power and ontology of justice can inform while also being extended by pentecostal political theology and praxis, particularly as unfolding on the ground in the developing African context, as Nimi Wariboko delineates. Similarly, Tillich's "religion of the concrete spirit" can inform while also being constructively supplemented by contemporary pentecostal thinking in theology of religions and theology of interreligious or interfaith encounter, as suggested by Tony Richie. Further, Tillich's renowned theology of the demonic, which almost singlehandedly rescued the topic from the oblivion it had fallen into in modern theology, can discipline excessive pentecostal demonological views and, at the same time, be appropriately extended when engaged in dialogue with the broad scope of the pentecostal register, as explored by David Bradnick. And, as Peter Althouse's chapter depicts, Tillich's kairotic eschatology can ground developments in neopentecostal inaugural eschatologies even as the some of the latter's emphases on relational love can enable realization of the Spiritual Presence amid the concrete ambiguities of human existence.

Chapter 14, the last by a pentecostal theologian, is a historically informed analysis of the fortunes of both Tillich and modern Pentecostalism that discerns, in part, where they have failed to fulfill their earlier promise and how, through a prophetic reorientation in conversation with the early Frankfurt school, their potential may be recalibrated. Pamela Holmes's prophetic pentecostal voice is followed by the response of Tillichian scholars Mark Lewis Taylor and John J. Thatamanil to the entire volume. Both chapters represent precisely the kinds of response that the editors of this volume had hoped for, although they are quite different. The former is not only of the sort that takes seriously the pentecostal contributions but, more importantly, one that, inspired by the pentecostal interlocutions, returns to reread, retrieve, and reconsider Tillich's theological—and especially pneumatological—system for the present time. The latter appropriately concludes the volume as it both responds more directly, even apologetically and counterquestioningly, to the chapters as if channeling the spirit of Tillich on the one hand, but also appreciatively notes how the book inspires robust dialogue with the legacy of Tillich and charts innovative paths forward for contemporary Christian theology in global context on the other hand. Thus these final chapters both continue the discussion barely initiated by those preceding and also extend a further invitation to others interested in and working with Tillich's ideas, as well as to other theologians, to join the conversation between pentecostal theologies and liberal theologies.[36]

Notes

1. E.g., Philip Jenkins, *The Next Christendom: The Coming of Global Christianity* (Oxford: Oxford University Press, 2002).

2. See Amos Yong, "Pentecostalism and the Theological Academy," *Theology Today* 64:2 (2007): 244–250.

3. Throughout this volume, Pentecostalism and its cognates will be capitalized only when used as nouns or when they appear as part of proper names; "pentecostal" used as an adjective, however, will remain uncapitalized.

4. Whereas in a prior generation the lines between *conservative* and *liberal* were more hard and fast, and depending on where one was situated, the other side was understood in pejorative terms, today both are recognized as contested domains, if not understood as passé in some respects. I am using these terms descriptively, denoting at least how pentecostal theology and Tillichian theology have been viewed at least historically, fully recognizing that in the present landscape it is irresponsible to apply them to our subjects at hand without qualification. Further, as will be seen from the rest of this introduction and the book as a whole, the conversation between pentecostal theology and

Tillich troubles any inflexible notions of *conservative* or *liberal,* and forges a liminal space between them. For presentations of pentecostal theology that bring forward the conservative aspects of that tradition, see Stanley Horton, ed., *Systematic Theology,* rev. ed. (Springfield, MO: Logion Press, 1995); Henry I. Lederle, *Theology with Spirit: The Future of the Pentecostal and Charismatic Movements in the 21ˢᵗ Century* (Tulsa, OK: Word and Spirit Press, 2010); and David Pafford, *The Last Disciple: A Contemporary Primer on the Theology and Practice of the American Pentecostal Movement* (Eugene, OR: Wipf and Stock, 2011). For a historical perspective on Tillich as a liberal theologian, see Gary J. Dorrien, *The Making of American Liberal Theology: Idealism, Realism, and Modernity, 1900–1950* (Louisville: Westminster John Knox Press, 2003); contemporary reappropriations of liberalism that provide a good sense of the vitality of that tradition include Michael J. Langford, *A Liberal Theology for the Twenty-First Century: A Passion for Reason* (Aldershot, UK: Ashgate, 2001), and Ian C. Bradley, *Grace, Order, Openness and Diversity: Reclaiming Liberal Theology* (London: Continuum, 2010).

5. See Steven J. Land, *Pentecostal Spirituality: A Passion for the Kingdom* (Sheffield: Sheffield Academic Press, 1993).

6. For example, Ronald Knox, *Enthusiasm: A Chapter in the History of Religion* (New York: Oxford University Press, 1950).

7. Frank D. Macchia, "Toward a Theology of the Third Article in a Post-Barthian Era: A Pentecostal Review of Donald Bloesch's Pneumatology," *Journal of Pentecostal Theology* 10:2 (2002): 3–17; see also D. Lyle Dabney, "Otherwise Engaged in the Spirit: A First Theology for the Twenty-first Century," in *The Future of Theology: Essays in Honor of Jürgen Moltmann,* ed. Miroslav Volf, Carmen Krieg, and Thomas Kucharz (Grand Rapids, MI: Eerdmans, 1996), 154–163, and Clark H. Pinnock, *Flame of Love: A Theology of the Holy Spirit* (Downers Grove, IL: InterVarsity Press, 1996).

8. The renaissance in pneumatology has been documented by Veli-Matti Kärkkäinen, *Pneumatology: The Holy Spirit in Ecumenical, International, and Contextual Perspective* (Grand Rapids, MI: Baker Academic, 2002); see also my *Spirit of Love: A Trinitarian Theology of Grace* (Waco, TX: Baylor University Press, 2012).

9. Jean Richard, "The Hidden Community of the Kairos and the Spiritual Community: Toward a New Understanding of the Correlation in the Work of Paul Tillich," in *Paul Tillich's Theological Legacy: Spirit and Community,* ed. Frederick J. Parella, Theologische Bibliothek Töpelmann 73 (Berlin: Walter de Gruyter, 1995), 43–64.

10. See Carl E. Braaten, "Paul Tillich and the Classical Christian Tradition," in Paul Tillich, *Perspectives on 19th and 20th Century Protestant Theology,* ed. Carl E. Braaten (New York: Harper and Row, 1967), xiii–xxxiv, at xxviii.

11. Wayne G. Johnson, *Theological Method in Luther and Tillich: Law-Gospel and Correlation* (Washington, DC: University Press of America, 1981), 44–45; italics orig.

12. John Powell Clayton, *The Concept of Correlation: Paul Tillich and the Possibility of a Mediating Theology,* Theologische Bibliothek Töpelmann 37 (Berlin: Walter de Gruyter, 1980).

13. Clayton, *Concept of Correlation,* 159.

14. Alexander J. McKelway, *The Systematic Theology of Paul Tillich: A Review and Analysis* (Richmond, VA: John Knox Press, 1964).

15. Barth had already clearly said, "Nein!" to the *analogia entis,* so McKelway's own more Barthian commitments come through here; but while Barth also wrote "An Introductory Report" as a foreword to McKelway's book, the latter is to be commended for a very fair exposition and treatment of Tillich's ideas.

16. McKelway, *The Systematic Theology of Paul Tillich,* 98.

17. Ibid., 260.

18. Ibid., 267.

19. Arguably, Hegel himself began with christology, and his system has never been considered wholly acceptable theologically; see my essay, "A Theology of the Third Article? Hegel and the Contemporary Enterprise in First Philosophy and First Theology," in *Semper Reformandum: Studies in Honour of Clark H. Pinnock,* ed. Stanley E. Porter and Anthony R. Cross (Carlisle, UK: Paternoster Press, 2003), 208–231.

20. On this pentecostal emphasis, see the work of Roger Stronstad, especially his *The Charismatic Theology of St. Luke* (Peabody, MA: Hendrickson Publishers, 1984), and *Spirit, Scripture and Theology: A Pentecostal Perspective* (Baguio City, Philippines: Asia Pacific Theological Seminary Press, 1995).

21. For more of this pneumatic hermeneutic, see Veli-Matti Kärkkäinen, *Toward a Pneumatological Theology: Pentecostal and Ecumenical Perspectives on Ecclesiology, Soteriology and Theology of Mission,* ed. Amos Yong (Lanham, MD: University Press of America, 2002), chs. 1–2. My own work has highlighted how pentecostal hermeneutics is more participatory than merely cognitive; see Yong, "Reading Scripture and Nature: Pentecostal Hermeneutics and Their Implications for the Contemporary Evangelical Theology and Science Conversation," *Perspectives on Science and Christian Faith* 53:1 (2011): 1–13, esp. 4–6.

22. Harvey G. Cox, *Fire from Heaven: The Rise of Pentecostal Spirituality and the Reshaping of Religion in the 21st Century* (Reading, MA: Addison-Wesley, 1995).

23. Ibid., 304–317.

24. Ibid., 86 and 285–286.

25. For those interested, Nigerian pentecostal theologian Nimi Wariboko has provided a penetrating reading of Cox on Cox's own terms, albeit with implications for pentecostal self-understanding, in his *"Fire from Heaven:* Pentecostals in the Secular City," *Pneuma: The Journal of the Society for Pentecostal Studies* 33:3 (2011): 391–408.

26. I have developed this argument in my book, *Spirit-Word-Community: Theological Hermeneutics in Trinitarian Perspective* (Burlington, VT: Ashgate, 2002; repr., Eugene, OR: Wipf and Stock, 2006), part 2. Other pentecostal theologians have also begun to seriously consider this methodological lead—e.g., Christopher A. Stephenson, *Types of Pentecostal Theology: Method, System, Spirit,* AAR Academy Series (New York: Oxford University Press, 2012); L. William Oliverio Jr., *Theological Hermeneutics in the Classical Pentecostal Tradition: A Typological Account,* Global Pentecostal and Charismatic Studies 12 (Leiden: Brill, 2012), and Peter D. Neumann, *Pentecostal Experience: An Ecumenical Encounter* (Eugene, OR: Pickwick Publications, 2012); see also Wolfgang Vondey and Martin W. Mittelstadt, ed., *The Theology of Amos Yong and the New Face of Pentecostal Scholarship: Passion for the Spirit,* Global Pentecostal and Charismatic Studies 14 (Leiden: Brill, 2013).

27. This ambiguity is most clearly articulated in John H. Levison, *Filled with the Spirit* (Grand Rapids, MI: Eerdmans, 2009).

28. For example, as propounded by Tillich scholar Terence Thomas, *Paul Tillich and World Religions* (Cardiff, UK: Cardiff Academic Press, 1999).

29. For Spirit-christological reflections, see Frank D. Macchia, *Justified in the Spirit: Creation, Redemption, and the Triune God* (Grand Rapids, MI: Eerdmans, 2010), ch. 6, and Sammy Alfaro, *Divino Compañero: Toward a Hispanic Pentecostal Christology* (Eugene, OR: Pickwick Publications, 2010).

30. See Paul Tillich, *The Protestant Era,* abridged ed., trans. James Luther Adams (n.p.: Phoenix Books, 1957), ch. 11. For some historical perspective on Tillich's Protestant principle, see Lars Christian Heinemann, "The Conception of the Religious Symbol in Tillich's Early Philosophy of Spirit: Guardian against Exclusive Claims about the Absolute," *Bulletin of the North American Paul Tillich Society* 33:4 (2007): 26–35.

31. See Nimi Wariboko, *The Pentecostal Principle: Ethical Methodology in New Spirit* (Grand Rapids, MI: Eerdmans, 2012).

32. As I unpack also in my *In the Days of Caesar: Pentecostalism and Political* (Grand Rapids, MI: Eerdmans, 2010).

33. On this point, see also Wolfgang Vondey, *Beyond Pentecostalism: The Crisis of Global Christianity and the Renewal of the Theological Agenda* (Grand Rapids, MI: Eerdmans, 2010), who argues that pentecostal theological method is critical of the performative categories of traditional Christian theology (in terms of the rational, hermeneutical, doctrinal, ritual, and ecclesiastical dimensions of Christian orthodoxy) and that pentecostal theological method is oriented more toward play than performance—an emphasis that Wariboko connects to in constructing his pentecostal principle.

34. My own *The Spirit Poured Out on All Flesh: Pentecostalism and the Possibility of Global Theology* (Grand Rapids, MI: Baker Academic, 2005) provides one bridge for a pentecostal-Tillichian conversation in regard to these issues.

35. See my "What Spirit/s, Which Publics? The Pneumatologies of Global Pentecostal-Charismatic Christianity," *International Journal of Public Theology* 7 (2013): 241–259.

36. Thanks to Wolfgang Vondey for his comments on an earlier draft.

ONE

Spiritual Power and Spiritual Presence

*The Contemporary Renaissance in Pneumatology in Light
of a Dialogue between Pentecostal Theology and Tillich*

VELI-MATTI KÄRKKÄINEN

First Words: In Search of a New Theology of the Spirit

The American Benedictine pneumatologist Fr. Kilian McDonnell, o.s.b.,
made a critical and formative statement in his acclaimed 1982 state-of-the-
current-pneumatology essay titled "The Determinative Doctrine of the Holy
Spirit." In this same essay, he commends Paul Tillich for his treatment of the
doctrine of the Spirit—one that this current chapter considers pivotal among
late twentieth-century pneumatologies and that merits engagement with pentecostal pneumatology, using the key terms *presence* and *power*. Although McDonnell's 1982 essay, published three decades ago, may be outdated, it remains time-
lessly important. Fr. Kilian laments the limited, secondary role given to the Holy
Spirit both in Catholic and Protestant theology:

> In both Protestantism and Catholicism, the doctrine of the Holy
> Spirit, or pneumatology, has to do mostly with private, not public
> experience. In Protestantism, the interest in pneumatology has been
> largely in pietism where it is a function of interiority and inward-
> ness. In Roman Catholicism, its dominant expression has been in
> books on spirituality or on the charismatic renewal, or when speak-
> ing of the structural elements of the church. In the West, we think
> essentially in Christological categories, with the Holy Spirit as an
> extra, an addendum, a "false" window to give symmetry and balance
> to theological design. We build up our large theological constructs
> in constitutive christological categories, and then, in a second, non-
> constitutive moment, we decorate the already constructed system
> with pneumatological baubles, a little Spirit tinsel.[1]

The main concern for Fr. Kilian in the way pneumatology has been conceived is its lack of connection with the rest of the world and life; in other words,

"how could pneumatology be integral to the theology of history, liberation theology, the theology of hope, political theology, and transcendental anthropology?"[2] With many contemporaries, the Benedictine theologian is searching for a more inclusive, life-affirming approach to the Spirit because "contemporary theology has turned from a theology of the Word to a theology of the World."[3] Thus the title of his more recent landmark work, *The Other Hand of God: The Holy Spirit as the Universal Touch and Goal*,[4] through which he has established his place among leading Catholic theologians of the Spirit. Not surprisingly, Fr. Kilian finds in Paul Tillich's pneumatology an ally in his search for a wider, inclusive, robust account of the Spirit. In stark contrast to Barth (to whom the Benedictine, however, gives credit for an effort to rediscover, particularly in the latter part of his life, the significance of pneumatology),

> Tillich is one of the few Protestant (or Catholic) theologians who has handled the doctrine of the Spirit in its proper section instead of seeing it as part of ecclesiology, as Schleiermacher did, or as part of the doctrine of grace. Tillich attempted to do what Schleiermacher, Hegel, and nineteenth-century liberalism tried to do and never accomplished, that is, close the dangerous gap between culture and religion. His specific intent was to correlate culture, religion, philosophy, and theology.[5]

Indeed, the Catholic pneumatologist praises the Lutheran existentialist: "The role of the Spirit in Tillich's theology is neither the churchy Spirit of ecclesiastical piety, nor the experiential Spirit of pietism, but the universalist Spirit who bridges all the gaps. And that is Tillich's strength."[6] Unfortunately, Fr. Kilian's engagement of Tillich in that programmatic essay is short, toward the end, and functions rather as an invitation for further discussion.[7]

How would Fr. Kilian's call for a new theology of the Spirit relate to emerging pentecostal pneumatologies? In personal conversations—an informal part of my postdoctoral mentoring during a most memorable year-long stay at the Institute for Ecumenical and Cultural Research (St. John's University, Collegeville, Minn.)—he often compared and contrasted Roman Catholic and pentecostal pneumatologies with the terms *presence* and *power*. While Catholics, he maintained, believe in all kinds of powerful manifestations of the Spirit of God (just consider the rich mystical and charismatic spiritual experiences among various religious orders throughout ages), for them the divine *presence,* not only in the sacramental life of the church but in all the world, is the heart of pneumatological belief. For Pentecostals, mere presence, without external and experience-driven manifestations, hardly suffices. It seems to me that this simple template may express well the difference in pneumatological intuitions between not only

Catholics and Pentecostals but more widely, non-Pentecostals and Pentecostals. With that in mind I have selected the topic for my chapter, namely, "Spiritual *Power* and Spiritual *Presence*." With full justification it can be said that if any term faithfully and succinctly describes the Pentecostal experience of the Spirit, it is *power*. With equal justification it can be said—and is routinely noted—that for Tillich, the corresponding expression is (spiritual) *presence*.[8]

The purpose of this chapter is thus to locate Tillich's vision of the Spirit in the wider matrix of evolving pneumatologies of the latter part of the twentieth century and then engage emerging pentecostal pneumatologies. It is hoped that this dialogue may yield some insights into how (what used to be called) "liberal" and "conservative" traditions may jointly enrich each other, collaborate, and continue discerning the ways of the Spirit in the contemporary world.

Tillich's Pneumatology in the Context of the Contemporary Search for a New Theology of the Spirit

In recent years Tillich's aspirations (and McDonnell's hopes) for an inclusive, life-affirming, and robust pneumatology have been met in an unprecedented way in contemporary constructive theology. Just consider the Reformed Jürgen Moltmann's groundbreaking *The Spirit of Life: A Universal Affirmation* (1992), whose agenda is guided by exactly the same kind of directions as Fr. Kilian's:

> In both Protestant and Catholic theology and devotion, there is a tendency to view the Holy Spirit solely as the Spirit of redemption. Its place is in the church, and it gives men and women the assurance of the eternal blessedness of their souls. This redemptive Spirit is cut off both from bodily life and from the life of nature. It makes people turn away from "this world" and hope for a better world beyond. They then seek and experience in the Spirit of Christ a power that is different from the divine energy of life, which according to the Old Testament ideas interpenetrates all the living. The theological textbooks therefore talk about the Holy Spirit in connection with God, faith, the Christian life, the church and prayer, but seldom in connection with the body and nature.[9]

Indeed, one doesn't have to wait until the beginning of the 1990s to see Tillich's dream begin to come true. Tillich's contemporary the Dutch Hendrikus Berkhof attempted a powerful revision of traditional confessional Reformed theology in light of the heritage of classical liberalism and the new challenges of the twentieth-century context. In his 1964 *The Doctrine of the Holy Spirit*, Berkhof envisioned the Spirit as the "vitality" of God, "God's inspiring breath by which he grants life in creation and re-creation."[10] Though strongly modalistic, Berkhof's view of the Spirit is inclusive and universalistic—building on the Reformed tradition stemming from Jean Calvin and Abraham Kuyper, on the one hand, and anticipating the contemporary turn to a holistic doctrine of the Spirit, on the other hand. Rather than focusing on the church, his pneumatology discerned God's acts through the Spirit in history, in creation and preservation, as well as in the human life. Echoing Kuyper,[11] Berkhof concludes that "the Spirit of God also inspires man's culture. The Old Testament connects him with agriculture, architecture, jurisdiction, and politics (Cyrus as God's anointed one!). In general all human wisdom is the gift of God's Spirit. This relation between the Spirit and creation is much neglected in Christian thinking."[12] In other words, "The Spirit is not locked up in the church."[13]

The attempts to release the Spirit from the confines of inner piety and ecclesiastical—sacramental—life without in any way leaving behind these important domains of the Spirit's ministry—abound in current times, including integrating the Spirit into the center of constructive theology and its "method,"[14] christology ("spirit christology"[15]), creation/environment,[16] public life, including sociopolitical liberation and equality,[17] as well as other religions,[18] among others. Without the space in this discussion to go into any further detail concerning this contemporary pneumatological renaissance, let it suffice to acknowledge and hail the dramatically widening domain of the Spirit of God in contemporary theology, in keeping with the hints provided by Tillich.

Tillich's pointers toward an all-encompassing pneumatology are both aided and hindered by his placement of the discussion of the Spirit in his third volume. Tillich's note, as he transitions from volume 2 to volume 3, illustrates the tension: "that the Christ is not the Christ without the church makes the doctrines of the Spirit and of the Kingdom of God integral parts of the christological work." On the one hand, it certainly is a gain to link pneumatology with the kingdom of God rather than (merely) with the church. Notwithstanding the fact that for Tillich, so it seems to me, "kingdom of God" is a more limited category than "history,"[19] this gain opens up a wider horizon for the discussion of the Spirit in the world; God's rule is something "bigger" and "wider" than the church. On the other hand, Tillich's note speaks of the doctrine of the Spirit as a part of christology. While in no way denying the mutual conditioning of the works of the Spirit and Son, in an authentic trinitarian grammar, it is not useful to make the Spirit's work an extension or even fulfillment of Christ's work. It smacks of subordination or, at least, making the Spirit's work the second moment. The Spirit's and Son's works are *mutually* conditioned.

Nevertheless, Tillich forges the link between the Christ and the Spirit and hence points to an emerging spirit christology (ST 3:144–149). While not thematically trinitarian, Tillich is able to go beyond the modalistic pneumatologies of his contemporaries Berkhof and the Anglican Geoffrey Lampe.[20] He rightly argues, on the basis of the synoptic gospels' Spirit-christology, that "it is not the spirit of the man Jesus of Nazareth that makes him the Christ, but that it is the Spiritual Presence, God in him, that possesses and drives his individual spirit" (*ST* 3:146). That said, against the typical tendencies of pietism and, ironically, liberalism, Tillich also reminds us that "the divine Spirit which made Jesus into the Christ is creatively present in the whole history of revelation and salvation before and after his appearance. The event 'Jesus as the Christ' is unique but not isolated" (*ST* 3:147).[21] That he was unable to construct an authentic *trinitarian* spirit christology is part of the bigger problem in his system, which is illustrated by the placement of the short discussion "The Trinitarian Symbols" after even the Spirit (the last section of part 4 in volume 3). At the end of the systematic discussion, not much can be done to make theology authentically trinitarian.

My suspicions of the secondary role given to the Spirit in Tillich's system, as he likes to call it, are strengthened by two other, mutually related considerations, well known among Tillich students. First, going back to the placement of pneumatology in the third volume, it means—as this Lutheran theologian of course himself mentions and makes a theological theme—that the divine Spirit is the "answer" to the questions related to the ambiguities of life, "the conqueror of the ambiguities of life" (*ST* 2:80), or the "unity" of life (as he includes under the term "life" a "'mixture' of essential and existential elements," *ST* 3:12). If so, it means that the "questions" are asked not only by philosophy (following the method of correlation) but also by the doctrine of God (volume 1) and Christ (volume 2). In other words, this means that the Spirit is introduced to the system in the secondary moment. Second, exactly because of the location in volume 3, all the preceding doctrines, from revelation to God to anthropology to christology, are by and large being treated from the *theo-* and *christo*logical point of view. That said, I must hasten to mention that—fortunately—Tillich does not consistently follow his method: against all odds, in the beginning of volume 3 he provides a most robust discussion of "life" that materially deals with key concepts of the doctrine of creation, including evolution and hints at cosmology. But even then, Tillich fails in helping rediscover the primacy of the Spirit alongside the Father and the Son, although his theological program takes significant steps in the right direction.

That said, we must praise the profoundly inclusive, comprehensive, and holistic view of the Spirit and spiritual presence in creation found in part 4 (volume 3). Anticipating important current insights according to which it is reductionist to consider "spirit" as "mind" or "reason"—let alone "ghost"—and rather conceive it as "principle of life" (to use Pannenberg's concept) and, in relation to humanity, instead of "soul" in terms of "unity of power and meaning . . . [and] consciousness . . . awareness, perception, [and] intention" (*ST* 3:21–28 [20]). Tillich also takes for granted the evolutionary creation of creatures, large and small, including humanity.

Having located Tillich among the emerging pneumatologies of the second half of the twentieth century, but before looking at Tillich in relation to Pentecostalism, let me take stock of his pneumatology vis-à-vis a contemporary theological matrix in summary form. Tillich agrees only partially with Fr. Kilian's methodological guide: "The proper study of the Holy Spirit is both the Trinity and the culture."[22] Extending the meaning of the term "culture" to encompass all of life, including the cosmos, Tillich seeks to widen the domain of the Spirit in order to relate it to the whole of life. In that he is a trailblazer. The reasons he is less than successful in that pursuit have been mentioned above. Trinity, on the other hand, as said, is not part of Tillich's pneumatology.[23] Here a corrective has been provided by contemporary pneumatologies that integrate the Spirit fully into the "theological method": doctrine of the Trinity, creation, including humanity, trinitarian spirit christology, church, and eschatology. Some of the current pneumatologies also engage sociopolitical issues, questions of equality, and similar concerns that—had Tillich lived in contemporary times (to ours)—certainly would have loomed large on his agenda. Similarly, the relation of the Spirit to other faiths is basically lacking in Tillich's pneumatology, even though his discussions on religion (volume 3, part 4: III.A.2) and world history (part 5: II.C), among others, would have provided ideal places.[24]

Tillich and Pentecostals on the Spirit

In speaking of pentecostal "pneumatology," one has to make an important distinction between the "original," grassroots-level experience of and intuitions into the power of the Spirit among Pentecostal believers and communities and the more recent academic reflection by Pentecostal scholars.[25] While those in the latter category are not only familiar with developments in contemporary pneumatologies, they also work toward a constructive pentecostal pneumatology in critical dialogue with voices from across the theological and ecumenical spectrum. Throughout the discussion in this section, I indicate whether I am speaking of the grassroots or academic segment of Pentecostalism.

As indicated above, for Pentecostals the main pneumatological category is that of *power*. Accordingly, Tillich's focus on *presence* might not seem to resonate much with charismatic spirituality. Nevertheless, there is, I hypothesize, a deep underlying common *intuition* between Tillich's and Pentecostals' embrace of the "full gospel" vision of the Spirit. Tillich encapsulates the "symbols" in his pneumatological vision in this way:

The three symbols for unambiguous life mutually include each other, but because of the different symbolic material they use, it is preferable to apply them in different directions of meaning: Spiritual Presence for the conquest of the ambiguities of life under the dimension of the spirit, Kingdom of God for the conquest of the ambiguities of life under the dimension of history, and Eternal Life for the conquest of the ambiguities of life beyond history. Yet in all three of them we find a mutual immanence of all. Where there is Spiritual Presence, there is Kingdom of God and Eternal Life. . . . (*ST* 3:109)

If we were only able to get beyond the vast difference in terminology and theological milieu between Tillich and Pentecostalism, we might find the two visions touch each other in their refusal to limit salvation and the Spirit's work merely to the inner spirituality of the believer. Pentecostals often critique mainline Christianity for its limited "spiritualizing" of the gospel. True, for ordinary Pentecostals the Spirit's role in creation or human relationships or universal history—key themes for Tillich—by and large fail to catch the imagination. Materially, however, Pentecostals yearn for the "Spirit who bridges all the gaps." Academically trained Pentecostals have taken up the theoretical task of constructing pentecostal theologies that tap into the riches of the theological storehouses of Tillich and contemporary pneumatologists. The result is a vastly growing reservoir of distinctively pentecostal holistic accounts of the Spirit in the areas of science/creation/environment,[26] social justice and politics,[27] and pneumatological theology of religions.[28]

Pentecostal spirituality resonates well with Tillich's way of linking Christ and Spirit.[29] Indeed, against the assumptions of uninformed outside observers, pneumatology does not necessarily represent the center of pentecostal spirituality.[30] Jesus Christ, rather, is the center, and the Holy Spirit in relation to Christ. At the heart of pentecostal spirituality lies the idea of the "Full Gospel," the template of Jesus Christ in his fivefold role as Savior, Sanctifier, Baptizer with the Spirit, Healer, and Soon-Coming King.[31] What is at the center of pentecostal interest in spirit christology, differently from Tillich, is the expectation of the holistic salvation and healing focused on personal life. It is markedly charismatically loaded.[32]

A question that of course arises sooner or later in the pentecostal engagement is: What is Tillich's account of charismatic miracles and signs? A hasty reading of *Systematic Theology* may suggest a categorically negative opinion: "We rejected miracles in the supranaturalistic sense of the word, and we also rejected the miracle of ecstasy created by the Spiritual Presence when this is understood as inviting the destruction of the structures of the spirit in man (*Systematic Theology*, I, 111–14)" (*ST* 3:114). Indeed, rejection of miracles or "ecstatic" experiences is not meant here when the statement is parsed in the context of Tillich's idio-syncratic theological thesaurus. What Tillich rejects, first, is *supranaturalism,* which "separates God as being, the highest being, from all other beings, along-side and above which he has his existence" and, in doing so, reduces God into the space-time continuum and substance ontology, as well as *naturalism,* which "identifies God with the universe, with its essence or with special powers within it." While the latter comes much closer to Tillich's own intuitions, it fails in that "it denies the infinite distance between the whole of finite things and their infi-nite ground, with the consequence that the term 'God' becomes interchangeable with the term 'universe.'" Instead, he himself opts for a third way, in which God "is the infinite and unconditional power of being," neither alongside things nor even "above" them; he is nearer to them than they are to themselves (*ST* 2:5–10 [6, 7]). The second thing that Tillich rejects, consequently, is the idea that "Ec-stasy . . . destroy[s] the centeredness of the integrated self" (*ST* 3:112), in other words, as mentioned above, "the destruction of the spirit in man." Certainly, there can be found "in the history of religion a large number of reports and de-scriptions which indicate that ecstasy as the work of the Spirit *disrupts* created structure" and thus has "a miraculous character," including bodily effects and changes, let alone those that are psychological (*ST* 3:114–115 [114]). But for Til-lich, by and large, even those should be seen as a means of "supranaturalistic" effects and, insofar as they appear to be such, he wishes to recast them in "de-mythologized" terms (*ST* 3:115). A common misunderstanding of miracles, fol-lowing a supranaturalistic orientation, is to see them as a means of breaking the laws of nature. The biblical and proper theological meaning of miracle rather is a "sign" (*sēmeion*) as it points beyond the reaction of astonishment to its religious meaning. In order to make this significatory aspect more robust, Tillich recom-mends calling miracles "sign-events" (*ST* 1:115).

It is important to note that in keeping with theological tradition, "ecstasy" for Tillich means what it literally says, namely "standing outside of oneself," in other words, being seized by the Spirit but not in a way of negating reason. Rather, "it is the state of mind in which reason is beyond itself," but "in being beyond itself reason does not deny itself" (*ST* 1:112). Without mentioning any specific group but allegedly having Pentecostals and a host of their historical predecessors in mind, Tillich laments that "today the meaning of 'ecstasy' is de-termined largely by those religious groups who claim to have special religious experiences, personal inspirations, extraordinary Spiritual gifts, individual reve-lations, knowledge of esoteric mysteries" (*ST* 1:112). Elsewhere, Tillich—follow-ing his "Protestant principle"—warns against the danger of domesticating the Spirit of God in terms of clericalism or sacramentalism as well as in "secular profanization of contemporary Protestantism which occurs when it replaces ecstasy with doctrinal or moral structure" (*ST* 3:116). That said, however, he is not willing to reject these claims nor deny the possibility of an authentic experience. He is just against "confusing overexcitement with the presence of the divine Spirit" (*ST* 1:112). With that in mind, he refers to Pauline teaching concerning the need for order in the exercise of gifts, the need to avoid self-glorification, and the need to focus on upbuilding of the community (1 Corinthians 12, 14; *ST* 3:117). Furthermore, again following the Protestant principle, he wishes to link the charismatic and other similar ecstatic experiences, as well as any "human words" (as claims to revelation), to the Word of God. He does that, however, in a self-critical manner in relation to his own Lutheran tradition. As is well known, Luther at times claimed that no internal workings of the Spirit can be had without Word and sacraments.[33] Tillich rightly concludes—against both the Spirit-movements, as he calls them, and the Protestant Reformation— that the mediating word is always there; there is no pure "inner word" as it were (*ST* 3:125–128).

Now, with these notes on miracles and signs in mind, we are able to establish the relation of Tillich's view of the workings of the Spirit to pentecostal spirituality. Despite the foundational difference in orientation in terms of focusing on "presence" and "power," respectively, which leads to dramatically different expectations of the effects of the Spirit in Christian life and community, there are hardly deep theological disagreements here. True, grassroots pentecostal spirituality usually operates with what Tillich would call a supranaturalistic and breaking-the-laws-of-nature ethos when it comes to divine interventions—but it does not have to be so to be Pentecostal! Indeed, pentecostal epistemology would be well served by a careful consideration and contextualization of Tillich's point of view. His desire to transcend the grave limitations of both naïve "supranaturalism" and equally naïve, though claiming to be critical, "naturalism"—both of which, as noted above, lead to a highly suspect notion of divine interventions—aligns with pentecostal trajectories. Similarly, Tillich's advice on the need for order, for an other-centered building-up orientation in the exercise of gifts, is also in keeping with pentecostal aims. Tillich would have had much to learn from pentecostal pneumatology as well. Sadly, he fails to discuss topics such as healing and deliverance, which would integrally support his life-embracing view of the Spirit and divine intervention. Furthermore, his spirit christology would have been well served by the Pentecostal Full Gospel template (as much as it is limited in many ways, omitting social and communal aspects of the Spirit's work, a lacuna later picked up by academic Pentecostals).

Again, placing Tillich's and Pentecostals' pneumatologies in a wider perspective, I wonder if—perhaps surprisingly—pentecostal mission and theology of religions could be enriched and corrected by another careful look at the significance of "Spiritual Presence" in the world. What I have in mind are questions such as: What are the connections, if any, between the pentecostal "primal spirituality" and spiritualities of religions, especially those of Asian cultures? It seems to me that pentecostal pneumatology—even when its potential to pursue that question seems to be trapped in a particular fundamentalistic-conservative milieu—has striking similarities with living religions such as Hinduism and Buddhism in their resistance to modernity's reductionistic, over-rationalistic, and at times dualistic worldview. The movement toward a post-/late-modern dynamic worldview, with its willingness to reassess the canons of modernity, has certainly opened up mainline Christian pneumatologies to a more holistic, dynamic reflection on the Spirit. Pentecostalism has that kind of undergirding primal spirituality as a wonderful asset. With those challenges in mind and reflecting on Tillich's way of conceiving the Spiritual Presence in the third volume of his magnum opus, the opening words of Fr. Kilian's above-mentioned essay sound highly appropriate and somewhat disturbing:

> If the Spirit is the finger of God with which divinity touches history, and if the Spirit is the reaching out of the Creator and the Son into the human community, and if the Spirit is our point of entry into the mysterious trinitarian life, then theology must go beyond a trinitarian doctrine in which God is locked up in deity (the phrase is too strong but not without some justification).[34]

Notes

1. Kilian McDonnell, o.s.b., "The Determinative Doctrine of the Holy Spirit," *Theology Today* 39:2 (1982): 142.

2. Ibid., 142; this lacuna is critical as the Benedictine theologian envisions the "repossession of vast areas of culture" as the main goal of pneumatology (143).

3. Ibid., 142.

4. Collegeville, MN: Michael Glazier Books, 2003.

5. McDonnell, "Determinative Doctrine," 155.

6. Ibid.

7. Astonishingly, in his major pneumatological monograph *The Other Hand of God*, Tillich is absent.

8. Hence, the heading in his *Systematic Theology*, volume 3, part II, "The Spiritual Presence," may not be limited to that one aspect of Tillich's pneumatology but can be understood as an umbrella concept, as is of course evident even explicitly in the reoccurring headings throughout his pneumatological discussion (e.g., III.A, B, C, and D).

9. Jürgen Moltmann, *The Spirit of Life: A Universal Affirmation*, trans. Margaret Kohl (Minneapolis: Fortress, 1992), 8.

10. Hendrikus Berkhof, *The Doctrine of the Holy Spirit* (Atlanta: John Knox Press, 1964), 14.

11. For a brief consideration of Kuyper's pneumatology, see Veli-Matti Kärkkäinen, ed., *Holy Spirit and Salvation: The Westminster Collection of Sources of Christian Theology*, general editors John McGuckin, Joseph Wawrykow, Timothy George, and Lois Malcolm (Louisville: Westminster John Knox, 2010), 252–258.

12. Berkhof, *The Doctrine of the Holy Spirit*, 95–96.

13. Ibid., 104.

14. Wolfhart Pannenberg, *Systematic Theology*, trans. Geoffrey W. Bromiley, 3 vols. (Grand Rapids, MI: Eerdmans, 1991, 1994, 1998). While Pannenberg has not produced a separate monograph on pneumatology, his whole theological program is imbued by pneumatology as part of a thoroughgoing trinitarianism.

15. For a current account and constructive proposal, see Veli-Matti Kärkkäinen, *Christ and Reconciliation: A Constructive Christian Theology for the Pluralistic World* (Grand Rapids, MI: Eerdmans, 2012), ch. 8.

16. Joseph Bracken, S. J., *Society and Spirit: A Trinitarian Cosmology* (Selinsgrove, PA: Susquehanna University Press, 1991); Wolfhart Pannenberg, *Toward a Theology of Nature: Essays on Science and Faith*, ed. Ted Peters (Louisville: Westminster John Knox, 1993); J. Moltmann, *Spirit of Life*; Elizabeth A. Johnson, *Women, Earth and Creator Spirit* (New York: Paulist, 1993).

17. Geiko Müller-Fahrenholz, *God's Spirit: Transforming a World in Crisis*, trans. John Cumming (New York: Continuum, 1995); José Gomblin, *The Holy Spirit and Liberation*, trans. Paul Burns (Maryknoll, NY: Orbis, 1989); Elizabeth Johnson, *She Who Is: The Mystery of God in Feminist Theological Discourse* (New York: Crossroad, 1992); Rebecca Button Prichard, *Sensing the Spirit: The Holy Spirit in Feminist Perspective* (St. Louis: Chalice, 1999); and Nancy M. Victorin-Vangerud, *The Raging Hearth: Spirit in the Household of God* (St. Louis: Chalice, 2000).

18. Amos Yong, *Beyond the Impasse: Toward a Pneumatological Theology of Religions* (Grand Rapids, MI: Baker Academic, 2003).

19. I prefer to follow another Lutheran, Pannenberg, for whom, ultimately, under the rule of God belongs everything, including history; see his *Systematic Theology*, volume 3, ch. 14 and passim.

20. In his *God as Spirit*, Lampe drinks from the wells of Classical Liberalism and seeks to set aside the metaphysical questions, since the Spirit he is speaking of, in line with Schleiermacher, is the personal presence of God, first and foremost in Christ and then in his followers. Geoffrey Lampe, *God as Spirit* (Oxford: Clarendon Press, 1977), 11.

21. The link between spirit christology and the whole history of the Spirit in the OT is robustly developed by the Roman Catholic Walter Kasper, *Jesus the Christ*, trans. V. Green (London: Burns and Oates/New York: Paulist Press, 1976).

22. McDonnell, "Determinative Doctrine," 143.

23. That is not to say that Tillich does not "believe" in the Trinity. It is to say that his theology is strongly modalistic and that (for reasons he mentions but into which there is no opportunity to delve here) his theology lacks discussion of the Trinity in any meaningful sense.

24. Just a few days before his death, Tillich is reported to have confessed that had he had an opportunity to rewrite the three-volume *Systematic Theology*, he would have done so widely engaging world religions. This was due to his brief exposure to the forms of Japanese Buddhism at the end of his life as well as the influence from his famed Romanian religious studies colleague Mircea Eliade. Paul Tillich, *The Future of Religions*, ed. Jerald Brauer (New York: Harper and Row, 1966), 91; see also Eliade's comment in his "Paul Tillich and the History of Religions," in ibid., 31.

25. For a brief current report and reflection, see Veli-Matti Kärkkäinen, "'The Spirit Poured Out on All Flesh': Pentecostal Testimonies and Experiences of the Holy Spirit," in "Lord and Life Giver: Spirit Today," *Concilium* 4 (2011): 78–86.

26. See the ambitious research program documented in a growing number of publications: *Science and the Spirit: A Pentecostal Engagement with the Sciences*, ed. Amos Yong and James K. A. Smith (Bloomington: Indiana University Press, 2010); *The Spirit Renews the Face of the Earth: Pentecostal Forays in Science and Theology of Creation*, ed. Amos Yong (Eugene, OR: Pickwick, 2009); Amos Yong, *The Spirit of Creation: Modern Science and Divine Action in the Pentecostal-Charismatic Imagination* (Grand Rapids, MI: Eerdmans, 2011).

27. Eldin Villafañe, *The Liberating Spirit: Toward an Hispanic American Pentecostal Social Ethic* (Grand Rapids, MI: Eerdmans, 1993); Douglas Petersen, *Not by Might Nor by Power: A Pentecostal Theology of Social Concern in Latin America* (Carlisle, UK: Paternoster, 1997); *A Liberating Spirit: Pentecostals and Social Action in North America*, Pentecostals, Peacemaking, and Social Justice Series, ed. Michael Wilkinson and Steven Studebaker (Eugene, OR: Pickwick, 2010); Amos Yong, *In the Days of Caesar: Pentecostalism and Political Theology* (Grand Rapids, MI: Eerdmans, 2010).

28. Amos Yong, *Beyond the Impasse*; Amos Yong, *Discerning the Spirit(s): A Pentecostal-Charismatic Contribution to Christian Theology of Religions* (Sheffield, UK: Sheffield Academic Press, 2000); Tony Richie, "The Wide Reach of the Spirit: A Renewal Theology of Mission and Interreligious Encounter in Dialogue with Yves Congar," ch. 2 in *The Wide Reach of the Spirit: Renewal and Theology of Mission in a Religiously Plural World* (Lexington, KY: Emeth Press, 2011).

29. I wonder if the significant minority of Pentecostals known under the nomenclature Oneness or Jesus-Only Pentecostals would be drawn to Tillich's (somewhat) modalistically oriented spirit christology and find an ally therein.

30. For a fine account of key themes and orientations in pentecostal spirituality, see Russell P. Spittler, "Spirituality, Pentecostal and Charismatic," in *The New International Dictionary of Pentecostal and Charismatic Movements*, ed. Stanley M. Burgess and Eduard M. van der Maas (Grand Rapids, MI: Zondervan, 1992), 1096–1102.

31. The classic study is Donald W. Dayton, *Theological Roots of Pentecostalism* (Grand Rapids, MI: Zondervan, 1987).

32. See the fine study by Sammy Alfaro, *Divino Compañero: Toward a Hispanic Pentecostal Christology*, Princeton Theological Monograph Series (Eugene, OR: Pickwick, 2010), which investigates distinctively Hispanic and Hispanic-American (Mexican-American) resources based on a careful study of both spirituality and some didactic writings by Pentecostals.

33. Classic statements can be found, e.g., in "Schmalcald Articles," part 3, art. 8, pars. 3–12; *The Book of Concord: The Confessions of the Evangelical Lutheran Church,* trans. and ed. Theodore G. Tappert with Jaroslav Pelikan, Robert H. Fischer, and Arthur C. Peipkorn (Philadelphia: Fortress, 1959), 312–313.

34. McDonnell, "Determinative Doctrine," 143.

TWO

Spirit and Nature

Pentecostal Pneumatology in Dialogue with
Tillich's Pneumatological Ontology

WOLFGANG VONDEY

The doctrine of the Spirit is central to both Tillich's theology and Pentecostal experience, despite the fact that little has been written about the pneumatology of either. Tillich did not develop a systematic pneumatological focus until late in life.[1] Pentecostals have just begun to formulate their pneumatological convictions as theological propositions.[2] The present chapter attempts to bring both worlds into dialogue. I argue that Tillich's work forms a bridge for contemporary Pentecostal thought to both Protestant liberalism and German idealism by creating a synthesis of Schelling's philosophy of nature and Schleiermacher's doctrine of the Holy Spirit. The result is a theory of being that posits the Spirit as a central link between the concerns of religion, culture, and morality. My goal is twofold: first, to shed light on the ontological and pneumatological foundations of Tillich's thought, and second, to provide with these elaborations a foundation for a Pentecostal pneumatological ontology. In turn, I am also allowing Pentecostal theology to critically engage Tillich's proposal. In Tillich's framework of the unity of nature and spirit, the formulation of a Pentecostal pneumatology can find its ontological foundation.

The terms "spirit" and "nature" have a long and difficult history. In this chapter, I focus only on the modern history of the terms, beginning with the discussions of German idealism and its impact on Tillich's thought. The German idealists were concerned with the history of nature, not so much of the objects in nature but of nature itself.[3] At the same time, this discussion took place in the contexts of broader concerns about the place of God in the world and the correlation of nature and divine reality.[4] Schelling's philosophy of nature typically occupies a central place in this discussion, while Schleiermacher often remains overlooked despite his affinity to Schelling's work. Tillich, on the other hand, grants both Schelling and Schleiermacher pride of place in his account of the history of Christian thought.[5] This chapter begins therefore with a character-ization of Schelling's philosophy of nature and its impact on Tillich. The next section highlights Schleiermacher's use and transformation of Schelling's position. My concern is to show how the two proposals form the foundation for the concept of "spirit" in Tillich's work and its location within the concrete reality of nature. Schelling's and Schleiermacher's pneumatology have received little attention despite the fact, as I shall argue, that they are indispensable for understanding Tillich's pneumatological proposal and, in turn, for dialogue with Pentecostal pneumatology.

The Unity of Nature and Spirit:
Schelling's Philosophy of Nature

Schelling's widely read *Philosophy of Nature* influenced the romantic period of the early nineteenth century in at least one decisive way: it was rejected precisely on the very premise it sought to establish, namely, that nature and spirit are a single concern. Schelling's attempt to unite the human (or social) sciences and the natural sciences ironically finalized the schism between the two.[6] His goal was to offer a reflection on nature from within the experience of nature, the identity of nature as object and idea, in contrast to the objectifying distancing from nature that dominated the philosophical enterprise of his day.[7] The process to arrive at this goal emerged from his fundamental twofold proposal of the autonomy of nature ("Nature is its own legislator") and the autarchy of nature ("Nature suffices for itself") based on the principle of nature's self-organization.[8] The heart of this principle formed the notion of "spirit."

Schelling's pneumatological principle understands "spirit" less in terms of a force or power within nature (as posited by many contemporary proposals) than in terms of a potency inherent in nature.[9] He speculated about a philosophical method that would unite the realms of nature and spirit.[10] The subtitle of Schelling's work *Bruno* reveals the theological dimensions behind this task as a desire to uncover "The Natural and the Divine Principle of Things."[11] For Schelling, only one principle governed all reality, leading to a philosophy ultimately monistic in its metaphysics. He denied the validity of a fundamental distinction between idea and reality. Instead, he argued that there can be no fundamental opposition in any first principle, but rather a unity or identity of opposites must exist: spirit and nature are but one single principle.[12]

The unity of nature and spirit represents the most characteristic element of Schelling's pneumatology. In principle, neither nature nor spirit is fundamental in the sense of possessing an existence independent of the other. Rather, there exists an indifference or identity of everything that is both real and ideal. Distinctions of phenomena are always related to both nature and spirit, even if in different potencies.[13] Thus no natural body lacks a spiritual dimension, just as spirit does not lack a manifestation in nature. Freedom is the result of the union of nature and spirit and cannot be located in either one exclusively.[14] Schelling rejected the artificial separation of the natural and the spiritual as fundamentally opposite principles of reality. In its place, he understood the history of nature as the journey of spirit from the unconscious productivity of nature to consciousness and eventually to self-consciousness in the human mind.[15] As a result, spirit *is* the organizing principle of the history of nature.

Theologically, Schelling saw in the false separation of nature and spirit also a segregation of the natural and the divine principle of things, ultimately positing God over against nature:

> By opposing nature and the world of freedom in this way, men became accustomed to viewing nature as if it were outside of God, and God as if he were outside of nature. And to the extent to which they banished divine necessity from nature, they subjected nature to the unholy necessity they call "mechanism," and precisely by doing so, they turned the ideal world into the stage for a spectacle of lawless freedom. At the same time, since they had defined nature in terms of inert and passive being, they thought they earned the right to define God (whom they exalted above nature) as pure activity. . . . Yet if you try to tell these people that nature is not extrinsic to God, but has its being within God, they take "nature" to mean the nature they have deprived of life by separating it from God. . . . But neither the natural portion of the world nor the free part are anything independent of the absolute, wherein they are not merely united, but are instead simply undistinguished. . . . Nature, therefore, does not fall outside the providence of the supreme power, the true God, nor does God transcend the realm of nature.[16]

Schelling's reinterpretation of the reality of nature in terms of the divine, and vice versa, is cast elsewhere in the language of trinitarian theology. At the heart of this language stands a pneumatology that interprets the experience of the divine in nature decisively in terms of the Spirit of God.[17] Although Schelling did not further pursue the theological dimensions of this pneumatological proposal, his philosophy suggests that the abandonment of the ultimate distinction of nature and spirit leads to a discovery of the absolute (i.e., God). He followed from the point of union of the supposed opposites the two paths of the natural world and the divine world without separating the two as different modes of inquiry. Schelling thereby offered a unique methodological proposal for the subsequent theological discussion. Schleiermacher found in Schelling's thought the ontological basis for a revision of the concepts of nature and spirit that formed the foundation for a pneumatology thoroughly embedded in the language of the community of faith.

The Spirit in the Church: Schleiermacher's Pneumatology

Schleiermacher essentially adopted Schelling's early philosophy.[18] Both took seriously the concern for the history of nature and rejected the dominant mechanistic concept in favor of a dynamic portrait of the productivity of nature. Nature is neither reducible to the real nor can it be elevated to the pure ideal; the contrast and interpenetration of both are realized in nature as its highest opposition.[19] Hence, Schleiermacher offers the following definition: "The interrelation of all the oppositions encompassed by this highest opposition, seen in material terms, or the interrelation of all material and spiritual being regarded as something material, that is, as something known, is *nature*."[20] Nature and spirit are thus interrelated, as in Schelling. However, Schleiermacher was more directly concerned with the implications this union bears on the understanding of the human being. A philosophy of nature is necessary, although it is in Schleiermacher's perspective unnecessarily restricted to empirical science and not concerned with spiritual knowledge. Since the principle of identity is present within the human being, the union-in-tension of spirit and nature demanded for Schleiermacher a combination of the chief sciences of his day: physics and ethics.[21] This principal union, inherited from Schelling, also forms Tillich's entrance into Schleiermacher's thought.[22]

However, the mutual interpenetration of nature and spirit, seen from the dual perspective of the natural and moral sciences, took Schleiermacher's theology in a different direction. His chief concern was nature only insofar as it is related to human nature and its relationship with the divine. Following Schelling's idea of the development of spirit and nature, Schleiermacher defined human nature as the highest advance of spirit in the material.[23] He followed Schelling's idea of the progressive development of nature, albeit with theological intentions and anthropological (i.e., ethical) focus. The development of nature from inorganic origins to intellectual processes emerges from the mutual interpenetration of nature and spirit.[24] Nonetheless, for Schleiermacher, this interpenetration is not based on an already firmly established system of nature, as for the early Schelling, but is tending toward the full realization of spirit in a process in which everything first has to find its place.[25] The history of nature finds its motivation in the transcendental identity of nature and spirit.[26] The history of the unity of nature and spirit therefore also contains an emphasis on their distinction: while God is found in this unity without any contradictions, the world represents this unity including contradictions.[27] This concept of contradictions became the ground for Tillich's notion of the ambiguity of life. Equally important is Schleiermacher's insistence that the correlation of God and the world is accessible to the human being not in the philosophical, the ethical, or the scientific realm, but in religion; it is the consequence not of human reason but of intuition or feeling.

Schleiermacher's often misunderstood concept of feeling is intimately connected to his philosophy of nature. The correlation of nature and spirit bears witness in human intuition as "the consciousness of being absolutely dependent, or, which is the same thing, of being in relation with God."[28] Nonetheless, this "God-consciousness" remains for Schleiermacher suppressed in the real conditions of life, evidencing the struggle of nature and spirit to come to full communion in the world.[29] The balance between nature and spirit, and thus the completion of the creation of nature in human nature, is for Schleiermacher found only in the incarnation of Christ.[30] Redemption is here integrated in nature as an act of both nature and spirit and as the presupposition for the possibility that Christ's new humanity is mediated to the world.[31] The union of nature and spirit, present in Christ, is mediated to the Christian through the activity of the Holy Spirit.[32] This mediation not only signifies the union of nature and spirit but transforms human life from mere imitation to spontaneous participation in Christ.[33] In Schleiermacher's pneumatology, this attribution and perpetuation of redemption is deeply embedded in ecclesiology.[34] The natural and the supernatural are united in Christ and perpetuated throughout the church by the divine Spirit, who transforms mere intuition into sanctification and the spontaneous impulse of the Christian: "All who are living in the state of sanctification feel an inward impulse to become more and more one in their common co-operative activity and reciprocal influence, and are conscious of this as the common Spirit of the new corporate life found in Christ."[35] Pneumatology marks the connecting point of ontological and theological concerns, formulated from the perspective of the community of faith. The Spirit is the "public spirit"[36] of the church, the principle of the historical realization of the divine presence in the world. These thoughts form the backbone for Tillich's *Systematic Theology* and its identification of God as the ground of being, the mediation of the new being in Jesus as the Christ, and the divine Spirit as the actualization of his pneumatological ontology.

The Great Synthesis: Tillich's Continuation of Classical German Philosophy

Tillich's indebtedness to Schelling and Schleiermacher is well known, and Tillich's own work is often seen as a continuation of classical German philosophy.[37] Tillich himself indicated that his whole identity as a theologian was indebted to the identity of nature and spirit.[38] He valued Schelling as the initiator of a great synthesis between the principle of identity, the participation of the divine in all things, exemplified by Spinoza, and the principle of detachment, the impossibility of participation in the divine, exemplified by Kant.[39] Tillich's own work is an attempt to bring this great synthesis to its conclusion.

Tillich's two doctoral dissertations on Schelling portray the idealist philosopher as a significant link between philosophy and religion.[40] For Tillich, "the nerve of Schelling's development"[41] was the principle of identity of nature and spirit, and consequently, of philosophy and religion. He echoes this principle in his own account of the ontological structure of the cosmos (ST 1.168–171): "Spirit is the unity of the ontological elements and the *telos* of life. Actualized as life, being-itself is fulfilled as spirit. The word *telos* expresses the relation of life and spirit more precisely than the word "aim" or "goal." It expresses the inner directedness of life toward spirit, the urge of life to become spirit, to fulfill itself as spirit."[42]

For Tillich, Schelling offered motives for a new synthesis of spirit and nature that found further development in Schleiermacher's emphasis that there exists an awareness of this *telos* in the human being.[43] While he regrets Schleiermacher's use of the term "feeling" and its frequent misinterpretation as a purely psychological function, Tillich nonetheless adopts Schleiermacher's idea and reinterprets the "feeling of absolute dependence" ontologically as "the impact of the universe upon us in the depth of our being" that could also be described theologically as the "intuition of the universe, and . . . an awareness of the divine immediately."[44] Schleiermacher's emphasis on teleological dependence becomes in Tillich's thought "a dependence which has moral character, which includes freedom and excludes a pantheistic and deterministic interpretation of the experience of the unconditional" (ST 1.42).

The wedding of Schelling's principle of identity and Schleiermacher's feeling of absolute dependence emerge in Tillich's ontology as the well-known emphasis on the ultimate concern, or "that which determines our being or not-being" (ST 1.14).[45] Tillich urges the importance for theology to address existential questions of human reality, that is, to find an analytical pattern for the interpretation of human existence that accounts for God as the ground of all being. Schelling and Schleiermacher direct him to the important synthesis of spirit and nature, the significance of the human being, the importance of human history, and the role of the community. These elements constitute the framework for the culmination of Tillich's systematic theology (ST 3). However, this framework is less concerned with a philosophy of nature, although it includes the natural world in its organic and inorganic dimensions.[46] Neither is Tillich directed to pneumatology proper, if by that is meant the classical discussion on the essence and person of the Holy Spirit.[47] Rather, he understands "spirit" initially as the

union of power and meaning, a synthesis of the ontological elements of life with
each other and with the transcendent (*ST* 1.156–157, 180, 249–251). In this union,
the spirit is the "all-embracing function in which all elements of the structure
of being participate" (*ST* 1.250). Tillich's primary concern is the comprehensi-
bility of the identity of nature and spirit, that is, the implications this identity
has for human existence.

> There is no spirit without nature, just as there is no nature without
> spirit. In the spirit, nature comes to itself, and spirit is nothing other
> than this coming-to-itself of nature. . . . This union of spirit and na-
> ture arrives in the human being not at a separation, but nonetheless
> at a break. The human being is broken nature. Nature asks for itself,
> demands something from itself. By so doing nature accomplishes
> what succeeded nowhere else in nature. nature finds itself. . . . Na-
> ture had to lose itself in the human being in order to find itself. And
> this losing-itself and finding-itself-again is what we call spirit. . . ."[48]

The identity of nature and spirit defines for Tillich the extent of existential
concerns. Tillich can be described as a theologian of being only insofar as this
title takes account of Tillich's theology of spirit.[49] From Schelling, Tillich develops the insight of the fundamental unity of God and world: in spirit, nature
comes to itself. From Schleiermacher, Tillich develops the idea that history is
the process in which this reconciliation of spirit and nature is actualized in the
community of faith through religion, morality, and culture. Within this existentialist framework, Tillich's notion of "ultimate concern" emphasizes the reconciliation of God and nature in the activity of the divine Spirit. It is Tillich's
pneumatological ontology that unites nature and spirit and reconciles a theology
of nature with the idea of God by portraying God as both immanent and transcendent in the Spirit. This foundational aspect of Tillich's work, comprising the
largest section of his systematic theology, is also the least examined.[50] In the concluding section of this chapter, I intend to shed light on this thought in dialogue
with Pentecostalism and its experiential pneumatology that is rapidly gathering
theological momentum.

Tillich's Pneumatological Ontology:
A Dialogue with Pentecostalism

Modern-day Pentecostalism shares with Tillich a concern for the ultimate,
an emphasis on the Spirit, and a focus on concrete existence. However, Pentecostals lack a thorough theological formulation of any of these emphases. On
a popular level, the ultimate concern is typically framed by the goal of salvation; the emphasis on the Spirit is an emphasis on empowerment, sanctifica-

tion, and mission; and pentecostal existentialism centers on the affections and the charismatic life. Pentecostalism does not offer an independent ontological system, although it is inherent in the pneumatological persuasions of Pentacostals. Tillich's pneumatological ontology can assist Pentecostals in the formulation of their own perspective. On the other hand, Pentecostals also do not possess a developed theology of nature and tend to a basic dualism between the divine and the natural realm that Tillich sharply rejects as "supranaturalism."[51] At the very least, Pentecostals struggle to maintain the balance between a metaphysical supernaturalism, which accounts for the miraculous, the divine, and the demonic, and a methodological naturalism, the pragmatic stance of the modern scientific worldview that explains the world in exclusively natural terms.[52] Tillich directs Pentecostals to develop their pneumatology more explicitly in an ontological framework.[53]

According to Tillich's insistence on the identity of spirit and nature, both realms are interwoven in the struggle for the self-actualization of life. Three basic functions characterize the multidimensional unity of life: self-integration, self-creativity, and self-transcendence (*ST* 3.30–110).[54] Each function represents a core element of Tillich's pneumatological ontology and testifies to his indebtedness to Schelling and Schleiermacher. Self-integration in the dimension of the spirit is morality, or the constitution of the personal self. In this dimension, the "the realm of the spirit comes into being. Morality is the constitutive function of spirit . . . an act in which life integrates itself in the dimension of spirit" (*ST* 3.38). Self-creativity under the dimension of spirit is culture, or the creation of linguistic, technical, cognitive, aesthetic, personal, and communal acts of life (*ST* 3.57–68). Self-transcendence is not an empirical function of the spirit but an inherent function in the self-integration and self-creativity of life that tend toward the transcendent (*ST* 3.87). The self-transcendence of life under the dimension of spirit is religion, or "the essential unity of religion with morality and culture" (*ST* 3.96). This unity of functions is necessary for Tillich in order to address the ambiguities of life, essential and existential elements caught in the tension of created goodness and estrangement present in all realms of life.

The three basic functions are ultimately functions of the dimension of nature and spirit that tend toward their transcendent union. Tillich's religious symbol for this pneumatological quest is the Spirit of God, or "Spiritual Presence." "The symbol 'Spiritual Presence' uses the dimension of spirit, the bearer of which is man, but in order to be present in the human spirit, the Divine Spirit must be present in all the dimensions which are actual in man, and this means, the universe" (*ST* 3.108). Tillich's pneumatological starting point allows him not only to embrace the synthesis of nature and spirit but to create a pneumatological ontology that is directed toward the divine Spirit without falling into the error of pantheism. The latter presented a problem for Tillich, not so much because it upheld God as "the ground and unity of everything" (which the divine referent of the synthesis allows) but because it suggested a principle of identity in which "God is everything"[55] (which equates the divine referent with the synthesis). The relationship between Spirit and spirit thus forms the heart of Tillich's pneumatology. He rejects a descending pneumatology, in which the Spirit of God can be compelled to enter the realm of spirit, in favor of an ascending or ecstatic pneumatology, in which "the spirit, a dimension of finite life . . . , goes out of itself under the impact of the divine Spirit."[56] In this ecstatic process, the divine Spirit creates unambiguous, transformed life within the structures given by the union of nature and spirit.

Pentecostalism is no stranger to ecstasy, but it has failed to make the ecstatic a defining moment for a pneumatological ontology. Instead, from an existentialist perspective, Pentecostals are more likely to equate the ecstatic with the charismatic dimension of life. This hermeneutic is based on a descending pneumatology strongly influenced by a reading of Luke–Acts that favors the imagery of the "outpouring" of the divine Spirit from above, the "falling" of the "latter rain," or more prominently, the "baptism" of the Spirit.[57] More recent Pentecostal theology is at pains to expand the boundaries of Spirit baptism but continues to avoid existential questions and ontological categories.[58] Spirit christology has proven fruitful for the expansion of a more existentialist reading of Luke–Acts, yet few Pentecostals have worked out a consistent theology of creation based on this pneumatological ontology.[59] As a result, most Pentecostals maintain the subject-object distinction that Tillich endeavored to overcome.

In contrast, Tillich's emphasis on the Spiritual Presence within the finite identity of nature and spirit makes the physical, biological, and psychological dimensions of life cooperative dimensions with the divine (ST 3.111–161). He describes these ecstatic manifestations of the divine Spirit as "sacramental" acts, understood in the broadest sense as "everything in which the Spiritual Presence has been experienced" (ST 3.120–121). Pentecostals are divided over the use of sacramental categories, despite arguments for the fundamental significance of linking sacramental and ontological concerns.[60] Tillich's broad use of the term, however, is liberating: while the sacramental acts through which the Spirit is manifested must be recognizable as experiences of the revelation of Christ, "within these limits the Spiritual Community is free to appropriate all symbols which are adequate and which possess symbolic power. . . . However, the decisive question is whether they possess and are able to preserve their power of mediating the Spiritual Presence" (ST 3.123–124). Tillich's theology directs Pentecostals not only to the "liberty in the Spirit" but also to the importance of "judging the Spirit." Echoing Schelling, freedom and constraint, or "destiny" in Tillich's words, are the result of the union of nature and spirit. Between these two poles, the Spiritual Presence is actualized in the Spiritual Community.

Tillich's emphasis on the church as Spiritual Community finds no counterpart among Pentecostals, who have yet to develop a genuine Pentecostal ecclesiology. The manifestation of the divine Spirit in history through the unity of religion, culture, and morality represents a starting point for Pentecostal ecclesiology that is both pneumatological and ontological. At the same time, Tillich's account of the Spiritual Presence lacks the charismatic component central to the Pentecostal experience. His insistence on "word" and "sacrament" as "the two modes of communication in relation to the Spiritual Presence" (*ST* 3.120) leaves Pentecostals with a paradox—namely, the fact that they participate in the identity of nature and spirit, on the one hand, and that they are "empowered" (to use Pentecostal language) to transcend that identity. In Tillich's thought, "word" and "sacrament" are media of participation in the divine Spirit, but the union is one of faith and love, not charismatic endowment. At this point, Tillich abandons the realm of nature and spirit and locates the spiritual union in the transcendent to which the human spirit must ecstatically move (*ST* 3.129–130). Pentecostals would admonish Tillich that at his own admission the transcendent union must remain grounded in the finite union of nature and spirit. How exactly the Spiritual Presence is manifested pneumatologically and ontologically as faith and love in the church remains vague from a Pentecostal perspective. In Tillich's emphasis on the concrete manifestation of the Spiritual Presence in Jesus Christ and the church, the charismatic dimension is absent as a defining moment of the new ontological reality. Despite Tillich's emphasis that "the Spirit transforms actually in the dimension of the spirit" (*ST* 3.277), the charismata are not included as fruits of that transformation.

The Charismatic Life: A Pentecostal Response to Tillich

For Pentecostals, the charismata are gifts of the Spirit. In Schelling's terms, spiritual gifts can be seen as a concrete manifestation of the union of nature and spirit. Charismatic experiences reject the artificial separation of the natural and the spiritual as fundamentally opposite principles of reality. At the same time, Pentecostals follow Schleiermacher's hesitance to collapse spirit completely into nature. The difficulty of the charismatic life shows that the union of nature and spirit as such remains ambiguous. These ambiguities are brought to light by the Holy Spirit. For Pentecostals, the charismata are the gifts of the Holy Spirit to the union of nature and spirit. Charismatic manifestations dismantle the false distinction of "natural" and "supernatural."[61] In turn, Pentecostals disqualify pantheism by upholding that charismatic manifestations are "simply a more obvious sign of the interpenetration of the divine and the orders of creation"[62] without collapsing them into a single reality. As gifts of the Spirit, the charismata require both the union of nature and spirit and the Spiritual Presence of the divine.

The connotation of charismata as gifts of the Spirit emphasizes the inability of finite creation to create the Spiritual Presence; it signifies, in traditional terms, the dependence of nature on grace. This dependence is the primary "intuition of the universe." It is the original idea of what some Pentecostals have called the pneumatological imagination.[63] This imagination is dependent upon the charismatic dimension of life. Simply put, the reception of charismata is subsequent to the outpouring of the Holy Spirit. At the same time, this descending order is complemented by an ascending pneumatology which acknowledges that the reception and exercise of spiritual gifts transforms and elevates the bearer of the Spirit. The pentecostal terminology of being "filled" with the Spirit reflects this perspective. For Pentecostals, spiritual gifts can be cultivated and developed by the individual and the church.[64] The exercise of the charismata, in Tillich's terms, confronts the ambiguities of life from within the unity of nature and spirit driving toward the transcendent. In Pentecostals' terms, the charismata are the participation in the Spirit of the coming kingdom of God.[65] With this argument, we have arrived at the closest point of contact between Tillich and Pentecostalism.

Pentecostals are inadvertently following Tillich's pneumatological quest. Both quests are framed by a passion for the coming kingdom of God. While for Tillich eschatology forms the conclusion, Pentecostals possess a more causative or realized eschatology at the beginning of their theology.[66] Nonetheless, for both, the inbreaking of the kingdom demands a discernment of spirit. Tillich's emphasis on discernment amid the conflict between the Spiritual Presence and the presence of the demonic finds its concrete counterpart in the Pentecostal experience of spiritual warfare.

Spiritual warfare is a manifestation of the charismatic dimension of the struggle against the demonic.[67] In Tillich's language, it is a function of the churches in relation to the Spiritual Presence (ST 3.182–216). For Pentecostals, the charismatic dimension must be added to the constitutive, expansive, constructive, cognitive, communal, personal, and relating functions of the Holy Spirit. The demonic is the most concrete manifestation of the opposite of the divine Spirit. Pentecostal demonology is of course more radical than Tillich's, that is, more personified and apparent than hidden in the structures of life.[68] More than Tillich's general ontological identification of the demonic in history,[69] Pentecostals envision the demonic as a radically embodied manifestation of evil. The confrontation of the charismatic and the demonic constitute a central feature of pentecostal worldview and cosmology that is missing from Tillich's pneumatological ontology. This confrontation represents the most concrete manifestation of the uneasy union of nature and spirit and its struggle toward the divine. Here, the union is most intimate and volatile. The demonic is the most concrete starting point for the development of a pneumatological ontology that is genuinely Pentecostal while remaining indebted to Tillich and his expansion of Schleiermacher and Schelling. The global expansion of Pentecostalism and the accompanying ecumenical dissemination of the charismatic life underscore the importance of this dimension. In Pentecostalism, Tillich's idea of the great synthesis finds its most radical conclusion.

Notes

1. See Andrew O'Neill, *Tillich: A Guide for the Perplexed* (London: T and T Clark, 2008), 93.

2. See Wolfgang Vondey, *Pentecostalism: A Guide for the Perplexed* (New York: Continuum, 2012), chap. 7.

3. See F. W. J. Schelling, *System des transzendentalen Idealismus,* in *Gesammelte Werke,* vol. 3 (Stuttgart: J. G. Cotta, 1858), 588.

4. See Ueli Hasler, *Beherrschte Natur: Die Anpassung der Theologie an die bürgerliche Naturauffassung im 19. Jahrhundert* (Frankfurt: Peter Lang, 1982), 41–44.

5. Paul Tillich, *A History of Christian Thought: From Its Judaic and Hellenistic Origins to Existentialism,* ed. Carl E. Braaten (New York: Simon and Schuster, 1967), 386–410; Tillich, "Schelling und die Anfänge des Existentialistischen Protestes," in *Gesammelte Werke,* vol. 4, *Philosophie und Schicksal,* ed. Renate Albrecht (Stuttgart: Evangelisches Verlagswerk, 1959), 133–144.

6. See Marie-Luise Heuser-Keßler, *Die Produktivität der Natur: Schellings Naturphilosophie und das neue Paradigma der Selbstorganisation in den Naturwissenschaften* (Berlin: Duncker & Humblot, 1986), 13–28.

7. F. W. J. Schelling, *Ideas for a Philosophy of Nature as Introduction to the Study of this Science,* trans. Errol E. Harris and Peter Heath, 2nd ed. (Cambridge: Cambridge University Press, 1988), 9–42.

8. See F. W. J. Schelling, *First Outline of a System of the Philosophy of Nature,* trans. Keith R. Peterson (Albany, NY: SUNY Press, 2004), 13, 17. Emphasis original.

9. See Heuser-Keßler, *Die Produktivität der Natur,* 50–51. See Schelling, *Ideas for a Philosophy of Nature,* 49–50.

10. Schelling, *First Outline of a System of the Philosophy of Nature,* 13–19.

11. F. W. J. Schelling, *Bruno, or On the Natural and the Divine Principle of Things,* trans. Michael G. Vater (Albany, NY: SUNY Press, 1984).

12. Ibid., 3–7.

13. Ibid., 53–54.

14. Schelling, *Philosophical Investigations into the Essence of Human Freedom,* trans. Jeff Love and Johannes Schmidt (New York: SUNY, 2006), 1–77.

15. See Heuser-Keßler, *Die Produktivität der Natur,* 95–110.

16. Schelling, *Bruno*, 202–203; F. W. J. Schelling, *Gesammelte Werke*, vol. 4, 306–307.

17. Schelling, *Bruno*, 152; Schelling, *Gesammelte Werke*, vol. 4, 252.

18. See Herman Süskind, *Der Einfluss Schellings auf die Entwicklung von Schleiermachers System* (Tübingen: J. C. B. Mohr, 1909), 57–98.

19. Friedrich Schleiermacher, *Lectures on Philosophical Ethics*, "Introduction" (1816/17), trans. Louise Adey Huish, ed. Robert B. Louden (Cambridge: Cambridge University Press, 2002), 147 (no. 46).

20. Ibid., no. 47.

21. Ibid., no. 61. See Gustav Mann, *Das Verhältnis der Schleiermacher'schen Dialektik zur Schelling'schen Philosophie* (Stuttgart: Stuttgarter Vereins-buchdruckerei, 1914), 38–57.

22. See Tillich, *History of Christian Thought*, 391–392.

23. Friedrich Schleiermacher, "Doctrine of Goods" (1816/17), in Louden, *Lectures on Philosophical Ethics*, 168 (no. 1).

24. Friedrich Schleiermacher, "Über den Unterschied zwischen Naturgesetz und Sittengesetz," in *Kritische Gesamtausgabe*, vol. 11, *Akademievorträge*, ed. Martin Rössler and Lars Emersleben (Berlin: Walter de Gruyter, 2002), 431–451.

25. See Hasler, *Beherrschte Natur*, 86.

26. Friedrich Schleiermacher, *Dialectic, or, The Art of Doing Philosophy: A Study Edition of the 1811 Notes*, trans. Terrence N. Tice (Atlanta: Scholars Press, 1996), 37–41.

27. See Hasler, *Beherrschte Natur*, 110.

28. Friedrich Schleiermacher, *The Christian Faith*, ed. H. R. Mackintosh and J. S. Stewart (Edinburgh: T and T Clark, 1928), 12.

29. Ibid., 476.

30. Ibid., 365–369.

31. Schleiermacher, *The Christian Faith*, 724.

32. See Kevin W. Hector, "The Mediation of Christ's Normative Spirit: A Constructive Reading of Schleiermacher's Pneumatology," *Modern Theology* 24:1 (2008): 1–22.

33. Schleiermacher, *The Christian Faith*, 377–385.

34. See Wilfried Brandt, *Der Heilige Geist und die Kirche bei Schleiermacher* (Stuttgart: Zwingli Verlag, 1968).

35. Schleiermacher, *The Christian Faith*, 560.

36. Brandt, *Der Heilige Geist*, 33.

37. See Christian Danz, "Tillich's Philosophy," in *The Cambridge Companion to Paul Tillich*, ed. Russel Re Manning (Cambridge: Cambridge University Press, 2009), 173–188.

38. Paul Tillich, *Gesammelte Werke*, vol. 12, *Begegnungen: Paul Tillich über sich selbst und andere*, ed. Renate Albrecht (Stuttgart: Evangelisches Verlagswerk, 1972), 49–50.

39. See Tillich, *History of Christian Thought*, 370–371.

40. Paul Tillich, *The Construction of the History of Religion in Schelling's Positive Philosophy: Its Presuppositions and Principles*, trans. Victor Nuovo (Lewisburg, PA: Bucknell University Press, 1974); Tillich, *Mysticism and Guilt-Consciousness in Schelling's Philosophical Development*, trans. Victor Nuovo (Lewisburg, PA: Bucknell University Press, 1974).

41. Tillich, *Mysticism and Guilt-Consciousness*, 23.

42. Ibid., 249.

43. Tillich, *A History of Christian Thought,* 448.

44. Ibid., 392.

45. See Michael F. Drummy, *Being and Earth: Paul Tillich's Theology of Nature* (Lanham, MD: University Press of America, 2000), 13–58.

46. See Drummy, *Being and Earth,* 77.

47. See Frederick J. Parrella, "Tillich's Theology of the Concrete Spirit," in Manning, *Cambridge Companion,* 74–90.

48. Paul Tillich, "Natur und Geist im Protestantismus," in *Gesammelte Werke,* vol. 13, *Impressionen und Reflexionen,* ed. Renate Albrecht (Stuttgart: Evangelisches Verlagswerk, 1972), 101. My translation.

49. Langdon Gilkey, *Gilkey on Tillich* (New York: Crossroad, 1990), 164.

50. See Parrella, "Tillich's Theology of the Concrete Spirit," 74.

51. See Oswald Bayer, "Tillich as a Systematic Theologian," in *The Cambridge Companion to Paul Tillich,* ed. Russell Re Manning (Cambridge: Cambridge University Press, 2009), 18–36 (31).

52. See James K. A. Smith, "Is There Room for Surprise in the Natural World? Naturalism, the Supernatural, and Pentecostal Spirituality," in *Science and the Spirit: A Pentecostal Engagement with the Sciences,* ed. James K. A. Smith and Amos Yong (Bloomington: Indiana University Press, 2010), 34–49.

53. See, for example, Amos Yong, *The Spirit of Creation: Modern Science and Divine Action in the Pentecostal-Charismatic Imagination* (Grand Rapids, MI: Eerdmans, 2010).

54. See Parrella, "Tillich's Theology of the Concrete Spirit," 76–79.

55. Paul Tillich, *Perspectives on 19th and 20th Century Protestant Theology,* ed. Carl E. Braaten (New York: Harper and Row, 1967), 95.

56. Ibid., 112.

57. See Koo Don Yun, *Baptism in the Holy Spirit: An Ecumenical Theology of Spirit Baptism* (Lanham, MD: University Press of America, 2003), 23–44.

58. See Frank D. Macchia, *Baptized in the Spirit: A Global Pentecostal Theology* (Grand Rapids, MI: Zondervan, 2006), 61–88.

59. See Amos Yong, *The Spirit Poured Out on All Flesh: Pentecostalism and the Possibility of Global Theology* (Grand Rapids, MI: Baker Academic, 2005), 83–91, 267–302.

60. See Wolfgang Vondey and Chris W. Green, "Between This and That: Reality and Sacramentality in the Pentecostal Worldview," *Journal of Pentecostal Theology* 19:2 (2010): 243–264.

61. See Walter J. Hollenweger, "*Creator Spiritus:* The Challenge of Pentecostal Experience to Pentecostal Theology," *Theology* 81:1 (1978): 32–40.

62. Yong, *The Spirit Poured Out,* 295.

63. Ibid., 27–30. See Wolfgang Vondey, *Beyond Pentecostalism: The Crisis of Global Christianity and the Renewal of the Theological Agenda* (Grand Rapids, MI: Eerdmans, 2010), 16–46.

64. See Harvey Cox, *Fire from Heaven: The Rise of Pentecostal Spirituality and the Reshaping of Religion in the 21st Century* (Cambridge, MA: Harvard University Press, 1995), 99–110.

65. See Steven Jack Land, *Pentecostal Spirituality: A Passion for the Kingdom* (Sheffield: Sheffield Academic Press, 1993), 49–116.

66. See Vondey, *Beyond Pentecostalism*, 26–34.

67. See Wolfgang Vondey, *Pentecostalism: A Guide for the Perplexed* (London: Bloomsbury, 2013), 29–47.

68. See chapter 12 in this volume on the intersection of Tillichian and Pentecostal demonologies.

69. See Paul Tillich, "Das Dämonische: Ein Beitrag zur Sinnbedeutung der Geschichte," in *Gesammelte Werke*, vol. 6, *Der Widerstreit von Raum und Zeit,* ed. Renate Albrecht (Stuttgart: Evangelisches Verlagswerk, 1959), 42–71.

THREE

To the Ground of Being and Beyond

Toward a Pentecostal Engagement with Ontology

RHYS KUZMIČ

The ground between pentecostal theology and Paul Tillich does not, at first glance, appear to share even the same tectonic plate. Can liberal Protestant theology offer anything to the burgeoning development and dynamism of pentecostal theology? Or, put differently, can the new wine of pentecostal theology be poured into the old wineskins of theological liberalism?[1] These questions are no less pressing in regard to the doctrine of God. Early pentecostal theology in this area largely focused on the split between oneness Pentecostals and the trinitarian doctrine of God taken over from evangelicals and fundamentalists. Only recently has interest arisen in developing distinctive pentecostal notions of God that contribute to wider theological areas of scholarship. Even so, engaging Paul Tillich as an interlocutor in the doctrine of God may seem a perilous task. The other chapters in this volume focus attention largely on the third volume of Tillich's systematics, which, arguably, offers much more in the way of dialogue via the concept of Spiritual Presence than the philosophically laden concept of the ground of being in volume 1. But if pentecostals can only draw from Tillich's pneumatology in the course of their dialogue, an opportunity will be missed to engage in the philosophical theology[2] (and, by extension, ontology) that volume 3 presupposes. As Tillich himself notes, his system is circular, which means that the later volumes depend on their antecedents, while also deepening their insights (*ST* 2.5). Thus, a much stronger case for Tillich's benefit as an interlocutor for pentecostals can be made if he can contribute not only to pneumatology, but to the doctrine of God (with its underlying ontology) as well.

Before directly engaging Tillich's doctrine of God, let us step back and take a broader view of the purpose behind his systematics and what some of his philosophical assumptions/influences are. As this foray into Tillich's philosophical theology deepens, I propose bringing into the discussion the work of Jean-Luc Marion as an aid for a pentecostal appropriation of Tillich's doctrine of God.[3] We will conclude with a proposal, albeit brief, for pentecostal ontology in constructing a doctrine of God.[4] To the first part of the discussion we now turn.

Tillich's "Ground of Being" and Pentecostals:
Theology *and* Ontology?

The main goal of Tillich's systematics is apologetic: to serve as an aid in answering questions (*ST* 1.viii). His endeavor seeks to respond to the questions that plague modern existence, such as finding meaning and courage in the face of despair (*ST* 2.12).[5] In fact, for Tillich existence itself, given its disruptive nature,[6] implies certain questions that pave the way for theological answers based on the method of correlation, which is a decidedly "philosophical task" (*ST* 1.63). Briefly put, systematic theology employs the method of correlation in addressing the questions that arise from the core of human existence, i.e., existential questions (*ST* 1.62). In this method, theology both formulates the questions and provides the answers; but such answers will remain meaningless unless they speak to the human situation and address the ultimate concern of humanity, or "that which determines our being or non-being" (*ST* 1.14). In the course of this endeavor theology relies heavily on philosophy—or, as Tillich states, "The systematic theologian must be a philosopher in critical understanding" (*ST* 1.21). Both theology and philosophy are constrained by and oriented toward the question of being (*Seinsfrage*),[7] although they diverge in how they approach this *leitmotiv* (*ST* 1.22–28). As he puts it in *Theology of Culture*, the dual absolutes of *Deus* (for religion) and *esse* (for philosophy) are connected in the simple statement "God *is*."[8] Once these "absolutes" are combined, the specter of being has been raised (although not in the Derridean sense of hauntology), rendering ontology inseparable from theology.[9] For Tillich the apologetic task of theology, which seeks to make the Christian message relevant to the contemporary situation, strives to connect theology and philosophy, existential questions and theological answers, the concepts of "God" and "being." In this way, "apologetics presupposes common ground" (*ST* 1.6). This move, McKelway avers, leads inexorably to an anthropological *anknüpfungspünkt* for Tillich.[10] But what common ground does this move have with pentecostal theology?

While admittedly pentecostal apologetic theology has taken a very different path than that which Tillich traverses, the goals of relevance and legitimacy are certainly shared. Furthermore, pentecostalism also shares a similar anthropological starting point in the foundational role the experience of the Spirit plays in the development of its theology.[11] Although this label of an anthropological starting point is often taken pejoratively, Amos Yong understands theology as both derivative from and regulatory of experience.[12] In a sense, pentecostal theology maintains its relevancy by starting from the experience of the Spirit. Pentecostal theology, through its various stages, has sought legitimacy, both from defending the practice of glossolalia in early writings[13] to recent works that seek to demonstrate pentecostal theology's ecumenical relevance to the wider theological dialogue.[14] Similarly, Tillich strives to make systematic theology relevant precisely by taking seriously that which ultimately concerns humanity. In starting from the experience of meaninglessness and the existential threat of nonbeing, Tillich endeavors to connect his theology to one of the cultural contexts of his day, namely existentialism. While our present scope does not permit a detailed treatment of how Tillich conceives of experience in relation to systematic theology,[15] it is noteworthy that Tillich considers experience not a source for theology, but rather its medium. Because it functions in this way, any revelation to an individual (presumably via the Spirit) does not (note the Barthian language that follows here, emphasis mine) come *from* the individual herself, but rather comes *against* her and *to* her (*ST* 1.46). Thus the individual's experience is not the source of theology, unless she is one with the divine Spirit. This insight appears largely consistent with pentecostal theology and its use of experience as a starting point.[16] The major divergence between the two is Tillich's robust philosophical underpinning compared with pentecostal theology's historical reticence to engage the discipline of philosophy meaningfully.[17] As this gulf narrows, dialogue between both sides via a foray into philosophical theology appears viable and salutary. To this we now turn.

Following Heidegger, Tillich's basic assumption is that the problem of being is the fundamental issue theology (and philosophy) must wrestle with. If so, God stands as the answer to this question (*ST* 1.162). Being is defined here as "the whole of human reality, the structure, the meaning, and the aim of existence" (*ST* 1.14).[18] But this human reality finds itself threatened by the possibility of nonbeing; this is the problem of finitude (*ST* 1.187–189). For Tillich, the only adequate answer to the threat of nonbeing or finitude is God (*ST* 1.211). Importantly, this move that gives God/Being ontological priority over finitude/nonbeing constitutes an act of faith or courage, Tillich admits.[19] The concept of God that Tillich fleshes out in the final section of volume 1 is philosophical to the core. First, he notes that as God serves as the placeholder for what ultimately concerns humanity, a tension arises from the concrete situation explicit in the *experience* of concern (humans can only be concerned about something that encounters them concretely). On the other hand, the *concept* of ultimate concern is not concrete, but universal. It transcends every concrete experience, while still serving as their representation. This conflict between abstract and concrete, universal and particular, is endemic to every doctrine of God, Tillich asserts (*ST* 1.211). Pentecostals are certainly sympathetic with this tension, as they seek to hold together both the immanence and the transcendence of God.

Tillich does identify more personal elements of the divine, particularly in his treatment of polytheism. For example, Tillich acknowledges that one can only be ultimately concerned about that which meets her in a "person-to-person relation-ship" (ST 1.223). Humans cannot be ultimately concerned about something that is less than personal, yet if such concern is indeed ultimate, its object must also be suprapersonal. In this regard Tillich gives a very sympathetic reading of the mythological gods, whether they are animal, transhuman, or celestial in nature. The point for pentecostal theology, however, is that the personal nature of the divine is being upheld in Tillich's concept; there is a dialectical tension present between God as personal and suprapersonal that Tillich is willing to accept.[20]

With that in view, Tillich moves on to unite the concept of God with "be-ing-itself" or "the ground of being." This move is critically important in that Til-lich is responding to the problem of being in philosophy, seen as most pressing in light of Heidegger's *Being and Time*. If God is treated as another being among others, including created beings, then she becomes immanentized on the same plane as human finitude (ST 1.235).[21] Given how Tillich has elevated the con-cept and problem of being above every other, the only viable option for him is to equate God with being-itself; otherwise, God would become subordinate to being. Therefore, the gap between being-itself and beings is the same as that between the finite and the infinite, but it is equally true for Tillich that "every-thing finite participates in being-itself and in its infinity" (ST 1.237). This partic-ipatory ontology attempts to hold finite and infinite together in such a way that beings participate in being-itself in a finite way, even while they are "infinitely transcended by their creative ground" (ST 1.237).

When Tillich then explicates the meaning of God as living, person, and spirit, he makes reference to the symbolic function of religious language.[22] Sym-bols are directed to the infinite, yet are produced by the finite. Furthermore, un-like a sign that points to its referent, "every true symbol participates in the re-ality which it symbolizes" (ST 1.242). God as living is not a pure philosophical absolute like being-itself. Because in God there is no distinction between actu-ality and potentiality. God is not living in the same manner as created beings, but lives as the one who functions as the ground of life (ST 1.242). Similarly, God is understood as person, but not as an individual or self; rather, God is personal in "an absolute and unconditional participation in everything" (ST 1.244). As such, God functions as "the ground of everything personal," but is not *a* person (ST 1.245).[23] Lastly, as spirit, God is understood as ultimately unifying power and meaning. Life is understood as spirit in holding together the dual aspects of body and soul, while transcending them. Spirit serves as "the all-embracing function in which all elements of the structure of being participate" (ST 1.250). This view of human life thus serves as a window into the divine life. Interestingly, Tillich claims that theology must start with the underlying assertion that God is Spirit before moving on to any basic trinitarian statements (ST 1.250).

With this quick tour of select elements of Tillich's doctrine of God in view, the striking dissimilarity in tone and treatment with pentecostal theology must be admitted at the outset. The notions set forth in Tillich's philosophical theology do not appear easily amenable to pentecostal sensibilities. Perhaps most problematic from a pentecostal perspective is Tillich's use of theological language depicting God as living, personal, and spirit. For Tillich in *ST* 1 these depictions are understood purely as symbols; the only literal statement one can attribute to the divine is that of being-itself (*ST* 1.239). This distinction was not adequately clarified by Tillich in his writings, which both speak of the equation of the divine with being itself as literal (as noted above) and as possessing "symbolic power."[24] Literal statements refer to ontology, while symbolic statements belong to the domain of theology. In bringing together the statement "God is being" (*Deus est esse*), these two categories/levels of discourse can become easily confused.[25] The difficulty in regard to personal language for the divine is that if such terminology only functions on the symbolic level, it fails to address the ontological problem of being (which would require a literal statement). Under this view, theology then offers a (symbolic) response that falls short of humanity's ultimate concern (being itself). It is also questionable whether depicting God as personal in a purely symbolic sense can address the existential problems that adhere to the decidedly personal aspect of human existence. But there may be a way out of this impasse. Pentecostals can take up Tillich's claim that the "Spirit is always personal" for Protestant thinking (*ST* 3.116) by pushing for a constitutive understanding of divine personhood beyond the symbolic. This stance falls closer in line with the Tillichian depiction of prayer as transcending the subject/object structure so that "Spirit speaks to Spirit" (*ST* 3.192). Prayer for Tillich is not a matter of communing with a divine being, but of dialogue with and in the Spirit. This occurs when "God prays to himself through us" (*ST* 3.120). Taking divine personhood as in some way constitutive for ontology (God as dialectically personal and suprapersonal) by means of the Spirit can help bring consistency to Tillich's project and may offer Pentecostals a promising entrée into ontology.

But if Pentecostals follow Tillich down the path of ontology, how can they avoid the impersonal overtones of the philosophical tradition without making God one being among others? There are no easy answers to this dilemma. One of the problems is that when philosophy employs the concept of being, it also carries with it the unspoken need to provide a ground for all created beings.[26] Just as created beings need a ground for their being (being-itself, or *esse ipsum*, to use Tillich's terminology in *ST* 1.230), God would need a ground for her being as well.[27] Tillich elects to identify completely God with the ground of being or being-itself, which overcomes the philosophical problem of making God one being among others, but fails to address the theological problem of conceptualizing

God in no less than personal terms. While Tillich provides openings in this latter regard (as noted above), pentecostal theologians may struggle with appropriating his concept of the ground of being in their respective doctrines of God. One way forward lies in accepting the philosophical concept of being but attempting to elucidate and highlight its more personal elements. However, below I want to suggest a turn to phenomenology *à la* the work of Jean-Luc Marion in order to address the philosophical issues that underlie ontology and to pave the way for a theology that conceptualizes God in no less than personal terms.[28] Here I assume the affinity of pentecostal theology with Tillich's notion of God as including personal elements, yet also remaining suprapersonal; however, pentecostal theology will take both elements as ontologically constitutive of the divine, following the Tillichian insights on prayer noted above.

With the above analysis of Tillich in view, I want to highlight four areas of potential interaction/collaboration between Tillich's doctrine of God and pentecostal theology. First, the apologetic nature and experiential starting point for theology are essential for both. Pentecostal theology may wish to probe its apologetic task in dialogue with the method of correlation (rightly understood as rendering the existential questions and theological answers as interdependent), which Tillich claims is based on religious commitment (*ST* 2.15), or what we might deem faith.[29] Second, the Tillichian understanding of God as suprapersonal (*überpersönlich*), which he argues is not tantamount to impersonal (*ST* 2.12), opens up pentecostal doctrines of God to a dialectical concept of the divine that goes beyond what is exclusively personal. Third, Pentecostals can press Tillich toward consistency in taking divine personhood not merely symbolically, but as ontologically constitutive as well. Fourth, in view of the necessary ontological distinction between God and all other beings, Tillich accentuates the need to develop a philosophical ontology that can serve as a basis for systematic theology. In light of this final point, for assistance in this task we turn to a French thinker steeped in the tradition of phenomenology flowing from Husserl all the way through Heidegger.

Beyond the Ground of Being *à la* Marion: Whither Ontology?

The writings of Jean-Luc Marion have generated considerable discussion and interest, provoking critical comments from philosophers and theologians alike.[30] In Marion the line between theology and philosophy at times appears blurred, and this is especially true of the work that primarily concerns us here, *God Without Being*.[31] Just as Tillich responded to Heidegger in constructing his doctrine of God, Marion reacts to this towering figure as well; but instead of adopting the Heideggerian primacy of Being, Marion seeks "to bring out the absolute freedom of God with regard to all determinations, including, first of all, the basic condition that renders all other conditions possible and even necessary . . . the fact of Being" (*GWB* xx). Freeing God from the confines of Being places theology within its proper domain, which is faith (*GWB* 68). For this reason Marion turns to revelation in order to surpass the conceptual idol of Being, based as it is in the inescapable circle of ontological difference (between Being and beings). In contrast to Tillich, who accepts this concept of ontological difference *simpliciter,* Marion seeks to do justice to Heidegger's critique of onto-theology precisely by staying true to the divine God before whom humans pray and fall to their knees in worship.[32] For although biblical revelation does not heed the categories of ontological difference, it nevertheless has something to say about "being, nonbeing, and beingness" (*GWB* 86). In Romans 4:17, when God calls nonbeings as beings (*kalountos ta mē onta hōs onta*), the divine call takes no consideration of fundamental ontological difference according to Marion. What follows here is not the destruction of ontological difference, but the divine indifference to this ontic distinction. This posture of indifference marks God and the divine call as "extrinsic" to ontological difference and thus outside the domain of being (*GWB* 88). The point then is not that ontological difference is nonexistent, but that it does not define the God revealed in scripture.

Another biblical passage, that of the parable of the prodigal son, is instructive as Marion makes a further exegetical move away from identifying God and being. Luke employs the term *ousia* to refer to the disposable goods of the father requested by the son (Luke 15:11). In Marion's reading, the son is not asking simply for a share of something he does not already enjoy (the son already partakes in all the father has), but instead the son seeks to possess the *ousia* or goods himself. The son desires the *ousia* without the gift (*GWB* 97) and this marks an important transition for Marion away from being to the gift.[33] In biblical revelation "Being/being is given according to the gift. *The gift delivers Being/being"* and, in the process, frees being from Being, from the whole circle of ontological difference (*GWB* 101; italics orig.). But the gift does not simply give on its own; it has its origin in a giver.[34] *Agape* is what gives being, and *agape* is identified with God (*GWB* 102–106). It is through revelation that the theologian escapes the dilemma of ontological difference. Gschwandtner aptly summarizes the argument and its outcome here: "By invalidating and undoing philosophical categories and by opening onto another plane, the insight of revelation is able to lead beyond the confining philosophical categories and free the divine from its restrictive definitions."[35] Although Marion's language in this passage may appear hostile to philosophy,[36] I contend that this only applies to a particular segment of philosophical discourse: metaphysics. Metaphysics, for Marion, is largely interchangeable with onto-theology in that "God" becomes identified with the being that grounds the metaphysical system.[37] The enemy is not philosophy per se, but a particular philosophical concept of God that only biblical revelation can over-come. In revelation the quotation marks of "God" are left behind in order to re-veal Godself "without condition, antecedent, or genealogy" (*GWB* 70). It should also be noted that Marion's use of revelation is largely analogous to his under-standing and application of phenomenology in *Being Given*. Just as biblical reve-lation does not destroy ontological difference in *God Without Being*, Marion's phenomenology of givenness developed in *Being Given* seeks to pass "beyond metaphysics" and thus leave it to itself.[38]

Appropriating Marion: Ontology without *Ontos*

By accepting Marion's philosophical assist, pentecostal theology can seek to construct a doctrine of God that is no less philosophically robust than Til-lich's, without remaining inscribed within the discourse of being. Arguably, this move is more in line with Heidegger's approach than with Tillich's doctrine of God in that it removes the conceptual preconditions for understanding and describing the divine.[39] However, pentecostal theology does not have to leave Tillich completely behind at this point. Constructing an ontology consistent with pentecostal theology may serve as one of the more salutary contributions of Tillich's thought. But how should this enterprise proceed without becoming entangled in the language of being, as even the very term 'ontology' finds itself? In light of the foregoing discussion, I submit that a pentecostal ontology should, at minimum, satisfy the following concerns: 1) the language used to articulate its ontology must be consistent with and central to pentecostal thought;[40] 2) the ontology must not repristinate the same category of being simply within a new term; 3) the ontology should be consistent with current understandings of the sciences, especially in regard to divine action; and 4) the ontological language employed should open up more robust personal yet nonetheless transpersonal depictions of God than Tillich's theology is often thought to have done.[41]

Although I can only briefly sketch a response here, I suggest pentecostal theology continue to develop the concept of Spirit as the basic ontological cate-gory. Substituting the placeholder *being* with that of *Spirit/spirit* does not *tout court* solve the numerous problems referred to above, but it may point a promis-ing way forward for pentecostal thought. For example, Philip Clayton has traced some of the positive implications in the move away from a substance ontology to that of the subject, which opens up exciting new vistas for an ontology of the Spirit.[42] Following Clayton's lead and in dialogue with his advocacy of emer-gence,[43] Amos Yong has begun to develop a pneumatological cosmology, with concomitant implications for ontology.[44] Similarly, James K. A. Smith has ex-plored a participatory pentecostal ontology that views nature as en-spirited to various degrees or intensities.[45] Evidently, pentecostal theology is already moving in this ontological direction and as it does so, I suggest it do away with the conceptual idol of being in philosophy that ineluctably narrows the contours of understanding present in revelation as well as in pentecostal experience. The concept of Spirit attested to within Christian scripture is polyvalent enough to include both personal and suprapersonal elements as both *ruach* and *pneuma* can denote personal interaction and infilling as well as impersonal *wind* or even the more ambiguous *breath*.

Returning to Tillich, if spirit, understood as personal (*ST* 3.116), is also a dimension of life, and if it, as the unity of all ontological elements furthermore serves as "the most embracing, direct, and unrestricted symbol for the divine life" (*ST* 1.249), then developing a Spirit ontology appears fully consistent with Tillich's project.[46] Moving away from a substance ontology, Tillich asserts that Spirit "is not a mysterious substance; it is not a part of God. It is God himself . . . as present in communities and personalities, grasping them, inspiring them, and transforming them."[47] It follows that there must be a personal element in Spirit that is not based on a substance ontology,[48] which makes Tillich a fitting dialogue partner in this task. Pentecostal theology should be encouraged to appropriate Tillich in developing a Spirit ontology, which would maintain pneumatology at the forefront of its doctrine(s) of God. In line with Marion, I submit that such an ontology ought to seek to avoid the pitfalls of being and the onto-theological nexus of concepts that inevitably limit the available categories for conceiving and experiencing the divine. As Tillich's depiction of prayer elucidates, it is only by means of the Spirit that the ontological divide between subject and object is overcome.

Notes

1. "Liberal" and "liberalism" are here enunciated with a concurrent wink, playfully calling into question the rigid dichotomy between liberal and conservative thought that this volume as a whole seeks to address within its own limited scope.

2. Here I follow Philip Clayton's definition of philosophical theology as "systematic theological proposals developed with an eye to breadth, coherence and underlying conceptual structures, particularly as these structures have been developed within the philosophical traditions," in his "In Whom We Have Our Being: Philosophical Resources for the Doctrine of the Spirit," in *Advents of the Spirit: An Introduction to the Current Study of Pneumatology*, ed. Bradford E. Hinze and D. Lyle Dabney, Marquette Studies in Theology 30 (Milwaukee: Marquette University Press, 2001), 179.

3. For, as Tillich notes, "Theology must apply a phenomenological approach to all its basic concepts" (*ST* 1.106).

4. It must be acknowledged that the very language of "doctrine of God" is fraught with difficulties and inconsistencies from the outset. For one, theologians use the phrase both for describing God in the abstract (read: as a philosophical or theological concept)

as well as for the first article of the creed in trinitarian terms. In addition, the "doctrine of God" can also refer to the triune God (with or without the adjective). For example, Tillich's doctrine of God in volume 1 takes the abstract and more philosophically robust notion of God as its primary placeholder. In contrast, when Veli-Matti Kärkkäinen titles his volume *The Doctrine of God* in his series of global introductions, he is speaking primarily of what "is called Father" in trinitarian dogma. See *The Doctrine of God: A Global Introduction* (Grand Rapids, MI: Baker Academic, 2004), 7. While there is significant overlap between theological treatments of Kärkkäinen's use of the phrase and specifically focused trinitarian discussions, this is not necessarily true of the philosophical concept used by Tillich in relation to either of the other two notions.

5. See especially Paul Tillich, *The Courage to Be* (New Haven: Yale University Press, 1952), 186, where the theistic notion of God as being must be transcended in order to overcome doubt and meaninglessness. Tillich employs the concept of "the God above God" in order to transcend the God of theism, which functions as an apologetic to those disillusioned with classical or traditional theism. For Pentecostals who may be suspicious of the language of transcending the God of theism, it is important to note that Tillich is referring to concepts here rather than to simply displacing God understood as personal. The concept of God that objectifies the divine into a being must be transcended so that both personal and transpersonal elements are held together, according to Tillich (187).

6. See David Kelsey, *The Fabric of Paul Tillich's Theology* (New Haven: Yale University Press, 1967), 4.

7. Tillich's understanding of being here is indebted to Heidegger's work, which elevated the concept of being to the forefront of philosophical and theological discussion. See, for example, Adrian Thatcher, *The Ontology of Paul Tillich* (Oxford: Oxford University Press, 1978), 2–5, for this point as well as for Heidegger's influence on Tillich.

8. Paul Tillich, *Theology of Culture,* ed. Robert C. Kimball (New York: Oxford University Press, 1959), 12.

9. In fact, Tillich avers that ontology logically "precedes every other cognitive approach to reality." See his *Love, Power and Justice: Ontological Analyses and Ethical Applications* (London: Oxford University Press, 1954), 20.

10. Alexander J. McKelway, *The Systematic Theology of Paul Tillich: A Review and Analysis* (Richmond: John Knox Press, 1964), 38.

11. Frank Macchia recalls the pivotal role of this experience for him personally in *Baptized in the Spirit: A Global Pentecostal Theology* (Grand Rapids, MI: Zondervan, 2006), 13–14. He later notes, "I am always called back to my early commitment to Christ and experience of Spirit baptism when I think of those memories that nourish me as a theologian" (18). Or, as Simeon Zahl states, "That Pentecostal theology puts 'experience' of God . . . at the heart of its message and practice is beyond dispute"; see his *Pneumatology and Theology of the Cross in the Preaching of Christoph Friedrich Blumhardt: The Holy Spirit Between Wittenburg and Azusa Street* (New York: T and T Clark, 2010), 159.

12. Amos Yong, *The Spirit Poured Out on All Flesh: Pentecostalism and the Possibility of Global Theology* (Grand Rapids, MI: Baker Academic, 2005), 32.

13. Donald W. Dayton, *Theological Roots of Pentecostalism* (Grand Rapids, MI: Francis Asbury, 1987), 15.

14. See, for example, Macchia, *Baptized in the Spirit,* as well as his *Justified in the Spirit: Creation, Redemption, and the Triune God* (Grand Rapids, MI: Eerdmans, 2010).

15. See *Systematic Theology* 1, 40–46 for his understanding.

16. It also coheres well with pentecostal theologies that highlight the ongoing nature of revelation by the Spirit.

17. This state of affairs appears to be shifting in recent scholarship. Cf. the work of James K. A. Smith, esp. *Thinking in Tongues: Pentecostal Contributions to Christian Philosophy* (Grand Rapids, MI: Eerdmans, 2010).

18. Following Heidegger, Tillich does not simply equate being with human existence; being extends to all of reality and (for Tillich at least) ultimately to God. This passage draws the human being (Heidegger's *Dasein*) into sharp focus as the being who can inquire into the overarching structure of Being and who finds herself threatened by nonbeing. In *Love, Power and Justice* being is more broadly identified as the "power of being," which extends to everything that exists (37). Tillich also uses being to refer to "ultimate reality," which translates *Sein* in the title of his *Biblical Religion and the Search for Ultimate Reality* (Chicago: University of Chicago Press, 1955), 12–13.

19. Tillich, *Love, Power and Justice, 39.*

20. Tillich understands the dialectical method, largely in Hegelian terms, to reflect reality in moving through various stages of affirmation, negation, and transcendence. Dialectical realism, Tillich claims, seeks "to show that the concrete is present in the depth of the ultimate" (*ST* 1.235). Cf. Hegel's *Phenomenology of Spirit,* trans. A. V. Miller (Oxford: Oxford University Press, 1977), esp. the renowned "Preface." Furthermore, Tillich's dialectical approach tends to emphasize the suprapersonal over the personal and additionally, as Nimi Wariboko notes, precedence of the ontological over the cosmological, form over dynamics, and reason over experience. See Wariboko, *The Pentecostal Principle: Ethical Methodology in New Spirit* (Grand Rapids, MI: Eerdmans, 2011), 65.

21. The feminine pronoun is, of course, not Tillich's, but my own preferred designation.

22. For an insightful critique of Tillich's theory of language see Philip Clayton, *The Problem of God in Modern Thought* (Grand Rapids, MI: Eerdmans, 2000), 470f.

23. Tillich notes that in classical theology *person* is never applied to God as a trinitarian whole, but only to the divine hypostases (*ST* 1.245).

24. See Tillich, *The Protestant Era,* abridged ed., trans. James Luther Adams (Chicago: University of Chicago Press, 1957), 63–64. For further discussion see Thatcher, *The Ontology of Paul Tillich,* 33–40.

25. See Clayton, *The Problem of God,* 470.

26. On this nexus of being and ground in both philosophy and theology, see Martin Heidegger, *Identity and Difference,* trans. Joan Stambauch (New York: Harper and Row, 1969), which includes his essay "The Onto-Theo-Logical Constitution of Metaphysics." Heidegger states, "Inasmuch as Being becomes present as the Being of beings, as the difference, as perduration, the separateness and mutual relatedness of grounding and

of accounting for endures, Being grounds beings, and beings, as what *is* most of all, account for Being" (69).

27. Schelling depicts well the rather tenuous relationship that ensues between God and ground in his *Philosophical Investigations into the Essence of Human Freedom,* trans. Jeff Love and Johannes Schmidt (Albany: State University of New York, 2006), 27–28, where God has the ground in herself, although the ground does not exist before God. As Clayton notes in *The Problem of God,* 479, for Schelling these two aspects are intertwined, but not identical, leading to a dipolar concept of God.

28. I share the sentiment with Merold Westphal, where he speaks analogously about the necessity of overcoming metaphysics for Christian faith: "The right kind of phenomenology may well provide a partial but significant overcoming of metaphysics and . . . a robust theology will always be needed to complete the task." See Westphal, "The Importance of Overcoming Metaphysics for the Life of Faith," *Modern Theology* 23:2 (April 2007), 271.

29. Tillich depicts faith as "the state of mind in which we are grasped by the power of something unconditional which manifests itself to us as the ground and judge of our existence," in *The Protestant Era,* 163.

30. See Graham Ward, "The Theological Project of Jean-Luc Marion," in *Post-Secular Philosophy: Between Philosophy and Theology,* ed. Philip Blond (London: Routledge, 1998), 229–239; John D. Caputo, "God Is Wholly Other—Almost: *Différance* and the Hyperbolic Alterity of God," in *The Otherness of God,* ed. Orrin F. Summerell (Charlottesville: University Press of Virginia, 1998), 190–205; Dominique Janicaud, et al., *Phenomenology and the "Theological Turn": The French Debate* (New York: Fordham University Press, 2000); and the various contributions in *Counter-Experiences: Reading Jean-Luc Marion,* ed. Kevin Hart (Notre Dame: University of Notre Dame Press, 2007).

31. In text references are to Jean-Luc Marion, *God Without Being,* trans. Thomas A. Carlson (Chicago: University of Chicago Press, 1991), hereafter cited as *GWB.* In his preface to the English edition, Marion acknowledges that the stand he takes here is both philosophical and theological (xx). Nevertheless, debate remains concerning whether Marion is doing theology or, as David Tracy avers, "a phenomenology of theological language in the Dionysian tradition" (in Tracy's "Jean-Luc Marion: Phenomenology, Hermeneutics, Theology," in Hart, ed., *Counter-Experiences,* 60).

32. See Heidegger, *Identity and Difference,* 72.

33. For his later and more mature phenomenological analysis of the gift and givenness see Jean-Luc Marion, *Being Given: Toward a Phenomenology of Givenness,* trans. Jeffrey L. Kosky (Stanford: Stanford University Press, 2002).

34. Considerable debate has emerged on the gift; see John D. Caputo and Michael J. Scanlon, eds., *God, the Gift, and Postmodernism* (Bloomington: Indiana University Press, 1999).

35. Christina Gschwandtner, *Reading Jean-Luc Marion: Exceeding Metaphysics* (Bloomington: Indiana University Press, 2007), 57.

36. Gschwandtner, *Reading Jean-Luc Marion,* 57–58.

37. For more on onto-theology and its current misunderstandings see Merold Westphal, *Overcoming Onto-theology: Toward a Postmodern Christian Faith* (New York: Fordham

University Press, 2001), 2–8. Elsewhere Westphal encapsulates the term as occurring "when philosophy allows God to become a theme of its discourse on its terms and in the service of its project." See his "Onto-theology, Metanarrative, Perspectivism, and the Gospel," in Myron B. Penner, ed., *Christianity and the Postmodern Turn: Six Views* (Grand Rapids, MI: Brazos: 2005), 144.

38. Marion, *Being Given,* 4–5. In contradistinction, John Milbank argues that only theology can overcome metaphysics. See Milbank, *The Word Made Strange: Theology, Language, Culture* (Oxford: Blackwell, 1997), 36–52.

39. On the difference between Tillich and Heidegger on the God of Christian faith, cf. McKelway, *The Systematic Theology of Paul Tillich,* 27.

40. My sense is that many Pentecostals think of some aspect of pneumatology such as spirit baptism as occupying such a center. See Frank Macchia's attempt in *Baptized in the Spirit.*

41. While I am not unsympathetic to the project of emphasizing Tillich's dialectical suprapersonal/personal depiction of the divine in order to make it more palatable for pentecostal theology, I wish to highlight another possible route in this essay.

42. Clayton, "In Whom We Have Our Being," 181–182.

43. See Philip Clayton, *Mind and Emergence: From Quantum to Consciousness* (Oxford: Oxford University Press, 2006).

44. See Amos Yong, *The Spirit of Creation: Modern Science and Divine Action in the Pentecostal-Charismatic Imagination* (Grand Rapids, MI: Eerdmans, 2010), chap. 6, esp. 207–25.

45. See James K. A. Smith, *Thinking in Tongues: Pentecostal Contributions to Christian Philosophy* (Grand Rapids, MI: Eerdmans, 2010), 86–105.

46. For the Tillichian relation between spirit and Spirit that justifies this leap see *ST* 3.111–116. Also cf. John Charles Cooper, *The "Spiritual Presence" in the Theology of Paul Tillich: Tillich's Use of St. Paul* (Macon, GA: Mercer University Press, 1997), 67.

47. Paul Tillich, *The Eternal Now* (London: SCM Press, 1963), 55.

48. The rejection of a substance ontology also brings Trinitarian Pentecostals closer to Oneness Pentecostals. See Wolfgang Vondey, *Beyond Pentecostalism: The Crisis of Global Christianity and the Renewal of the Theological Agenda* (Grand Rapids, MI: Eerdmans, 2010), 95–96.

FOUR

God as Being and Trinity

Pentecostal-Tillichian Interrogations

STEVEN M. STUDEBAKER

Tillich's Trinitarian Theology

For Pentecostals accustomed to warm experiences of the Holy Spirit and a personal relationship with Jesus Christ, Tillich's description of God is not particularly fetching. According to Tillich, God is "being-itself" (*ST* 1:235). Expanding on this idea he says, "God as being itself is the ground of the ontological structure of being without being subject to the structure himself" (*ST* 1:239). In other words, God is the structure and power that determines all being. Thinking of God as the power or source of things that have being is straightforward, but what about God as the *structure* of being? The structure of being is central to Tillich's view of God and leads directly to Tillich's trinitarian theology.

Trinitarian Principles

The foundation of Tillich's trinitarian theology begins with the trinitarian principles and not the Christian doctrine of the Trinity. The trinitarian principles express the dynamic and dialectical nature of being. God, as being-itself, is a dialectical structure and process. In this respect, Tillich refers to God as living. Tillich clarifies that "if we call God the 'living God' . . . we assert that he is the eternal process in which separation is posited and is overcome by reunion" (*ST* 1:242). The polarities in this dialectical process are 'power' and 'meaning,' which are the basic ontological elements. Power is the raw and unrestricted freedom to be. Meaning provides the form and structure for power. Tillich uses the category of 'spirit' to unite these two polarities. Spirit is the actualization of power and meaning. God is spirit, and thus also the living God, because the poles of power and meaning are fully actualized in God. The three-step structure or dialectical movement within the nature of being is what Tillich calls the trinitarian principles (*ST* 1:250–251).

The first principle is the ground of being, the ineffable source of all that is. Tillich identifies this principle as the "basis of Godhead, that which makes

God God" (*ST* 1:250). The first principle corresponds to the ontological element of power. Though it is the source of being, it requires its opposite, the ontological element of meaning or structure. He refers to the second principle as *logos*. Without logos, power is chaotic. Logos provides the structure for the creative manifestation of power. The third principle, the Spirit, is the "actualization" of the first two principles (*ST* 1:251).

By themselves the first two principles are nothing. Power without form is chaos and an abyss. Structure without the power of being yields nothing. As the actualization of the ground/power of the first principle and the meaning of the second principle, Spirit concretely expresses or actualizes the specific ways that absolute potentiality is conceived in the second principle. The second principle is not a concrete actualization of potentiality, but is rather specific conceptualizations of potentiality. God, as Spirit and life, "gives actuality to that which is potential in the divine ground and 'outspoken' in the divine *logos*" (*ST* 1:251).

Consequently, pneumatology features prominently in Tillich's vision of God. Indeed, the most basic and comprehensive statement about God is pneumatological. "God *is* spirit. This is the most embracing, direct, and unrestricted symbol for the divine life," according to Tillich (*ST* 1:249). At the same time, the statement that God is spirit is unavoidably trinitarian. God, as being-itself, has a trinitarian structure, and all being participates in the trinitarian structure of God's being.[1] As Nimi Wariboko elucidates, the Christian doctrine of the Trinity symbolically affirms "the living God in whom the ultimate and the concrete are united."[2] The Christian doctrine of the Trinity also arises from the Christian understanding of Jesus Christ. The trinitarian principles, however, are more basic and are present in all meaningful discussion of God. Since the affirmation of God as spirit or as life comprehends the trinitarian structure of God, it follows that at the more basic level of trinitarian principles theology begins with pneumatology (more on this point in the section on Tillich and pentecostal trinitarian theology).

Trinitarian Doctrine

Tillich's work on the Trinity shared common cause with other notable trinitarian theologians of the twentieth century, such as Karl Rahner and Karl Barth. Like Rahner, Tillich believed that the theological traditions relegated the doctrine of the Trinity to functional irrelevance and intellectual inanity. The doctrine ceased to serve as a symbol that opened up the meaning and nature of life.[3] Tillich, in contrast, believed that the Christian doctrine of the Trinity is a symbolic expression of the dialectical nature of life (*ST* 3:284). The doctrine of the Trinity states in religious symbols the dialectical nature of the life process. More specifically, Tillich states, "the doctrine of the trinity is the fullest expression of man's relation to God."[4] The Father, the Son, and the Holy Spirit are terms that denote finite things—a father, a son, and a holy spirit. As names, they give the trinitarian principles (the elements and dynamic process of being) concrete expression. For example, the name *Father* communicates something of the first divine principle—unrestrained being. But at the same time, the term is finite; it does not convey exhaustively who and what the Father is. Though not comprehensive, the revelatory nature of the term derives directly from its concreteness and finitude.

The doctrine of the Trinity does not describe God per se. God is not three divine persons, though God is not less than personal (*ST* 1:244–245). Indeed, Tillich explicitly rejects such an idea as nonsense (*ST* 1:56, 3:284–285). The doctrine of the Trinity is not the belief in the mathematical riddle of three is one and one is three. On the contrary, the Trinity "describes in dialectical terms the inner movement of the divine life as an eternal separation from itself and return to itself" (*ST* 1:56). The dialectical process of life, "going out from itself and returning to itself," implies the number three and, hence, the Trinity (*ST* 3:293). Initially, the dialectical process of life appears binitarian—ineffable power over and against structure and form (logos) separating and uniting. But that is not the case. Spirit, or the divine life, is the actualization of the two poles. A dialectical movement achieves synthesis, which incorporates and transcends the polar realities.

Tillich's doctrine of the Trinity is also christological. The Christian doctrine of the Trinity emerges from christological claims (*ST* 3:285). Tillich describes his understanding of Jesus Christ in terms of Spirit christology. The divine Spirit or Spiritual Presence finds its highest historical actualization in the life of Jesus Christ. The Spirit here, however, is not the Holy Spirit of orthodox trinitarian theology. The divine Spirit is the manifestation of God that enables Jesus' spirit to live fully in the "transcendent union of unambiguous life" (*ST* 3:146).[5] Thus, the Christ that is the bearer of revelation and salvation is not the historical Jesus per se, but the manifestation of the Spiritual Presence or divine Spirit in him. Christian faith, therefore, is not in the historical man, Jesus, but in the reception and participation of the divine Spirit that made Jesus the Christ (*ST* 3:147). Jesus, the historical man, became the Christ through his participation and union with the divine Spirit "under the conditions of existential estrangement" (*ST* 2:122). In other words, through God's Spirit Jesus embodied the New Being or the Spiritual Presence (the essential nature of human being) in the concrete circumstances of his life. As the embodiment of the New Being, Jesus attained the full expression of his potentialities in relation to the infinite ground of being, or God.[6] Jesus' unity with God does not mean escape from the travails of life, but quite the opposite. Jesus experiences the darkest depths of finite life, the nadir of which is his death on the cross, but throughout them remains in unbroken unity with God (*ST* 2:134 and, for a fuller elaboration, *ST* 3:121–138). Consequently, Jesus is the Christ.

The problem with Tillich's view is that, on a superficial read, it sounds rather similar to traditional ways of talking about Jesus and salvation. His description of the Spirit reproducing in the believer the life of Jesus Christ sounds like the standard doctrines of union with Christ and sanctification. Tillich's terms, however, do not carry the conventional meanings. The Christ manifest in Jesus is not the second person of the Trinity (i.e., the Son), but a quality of spiritual life— a life in which the dialectical equilibrium has been achieved in response to the manifestation of God's Spirit. Tillich sees Jesus as the "keystone" or the highest expression of the manifestation of the divine Spirit. Jesus Christ is the benchmark, though not the exclusive instance, of the presence of the divine spirit (the Spiritual Presence) (*ST* 3:147). In this respect, Tillich affirms a high christology, but not in the sense of a definitive incarnation of the second person of the Trinity. Furthermore, God's Spirit is not the third person of the Trinity, the Holy Spirit, but the manifestation of the integrated life of the ground of being to human consciousness.

Though Jesus serves as the paragon of what it means to live an integrated life on earth (e.g., the integration of power and meaning, nonbeing and being), Jesus is not an incarnation of a divine person. Jesus was a finite and historical revelation of God as the ground of being, but cannot be directly identified with the Logos (*ST* 3:290). Tillich's point is not to diminish Jesus as a revelation of God, but to recognize that the Logos cannot be restricted to any one historical manifestation. In orthodox trinitarian theology and christology, however, Jesus is the incarnation of a divine person, the eternal Son. Jesus is the union of the Son with the human nature of Jesus. Moreover, Jesus is not merely an expression of the Logos, but the definitive incarnation of the divine Son. Christ does not exhaustively reveal the eternal Son, but the person revealed in Christ corresponds to the personal identity of the eternal Son.

Tillich and Traditional Trinitarian Theology

Here I want to consider points of similarity and tension between Tillich's dialectical-existential trinitarian theology and traditional Western trinitarianism. His view of God bears structural similarities with Western trinitarian theology. Moreover, his understanding of the Spirit and the nature of the divine persons have elements of continuity and yet discontinuity; hence, tension characterizes their relationship on these points.

Correspondences

First, the structure and conceptual movements in Tillich's trinitarian theology correspond with those in traditional Western trinitarian theology. Tillich's notion that the first principle is the transcendent and ultimate origin of being is similar to the doctrine that the Father is unbegotten and ultimately the source of the procession of the Son and Holy Spirit and, by extension, of created beings. Second, his view of the second principle as a self-objectification of the first one matches the understanding of the Son as the Word of the Father. Western trinitarianism usually relied on the psychological analogy to describe the procession of the Son, according to which the Son subsists as an intellectual objectification of the unbegotten and ineffable Father. The procession of the Son is the Father's act of self-communication that introduces diversity into the divine life.[7] Tillich's third principle has two parallels. On the one hand, Tillich's theory that the third principle is the actualization of the logos/second principle is similar to the traditional idea that the forms contained in the eternal Logos are instantiated in creation through the activity of the Spirit. On the other hand, the unifying role of the Spirit in Tillich resonates with the Augustinian theology of the Holy Spirit as mutual love, which constitutes the communion of the Father and the Son.[8] Finally, Tillich's trinitarian movements in God seem to be real moments in the being of God. They are enduring characteristics of the living God. Although these moments are not the divine persons of traditional trinitarianism, they are not merely logical points in a dialectical process. They are movements with abiding ontological reality.

Tensions

Notwithstanding these significant similarities, is the traditional doctrine of the Trinity compatible with Tillich's dialectical Trinity? Adrian Thatcher thinks not. Thatcher maintains that Tillich "has fallen into the error of *confusing the triadic structure of dialectical thinking with the triadic structure of Trinitarian thinking.*"[9] Tillich's Trinity requires the dialectical polarities of nonbeing and being, abyss and structure, which have no parallels in traditional trinitarianism. For instance, the Father is unbegotten and ineffable, but is neither nonbeing nor in tension with the ordered nature of the Son and the Spirit. Indeed, the Son is not the dialectical counterpart of the Father, but the image of the Father. Thus, key elements of the dialectical nature of life and being do not correspond to the identity of the divine persons in traditional trinitarianism. Thatcher also rejects the idea that one of the divine persons is "the unity of the other two."[10] This point highlights not only the tension between Tillichian and traditional trinitarianism, but also a central ambiguity in Western trinitarianism.

First, both Tillich and the doctrine of the Trinity take the Spirit as a source of unity. Western trinitarian theology portrays the Son as the objectification of the unbegotten Father. The Holy Spirit is usually portrayed as *their* mutual love. The Holy Spirit is, therefore, their unifying action.[11] In this respect Thatcher has overlooked a major feature of Western trinitarianism. But is Tillich's and the Western view of divine unity in the Spirit the same?

For Tillich, the Spirit is not a third something in the divine life, but the unification of the first two. In other words, Tillich's unity in the Spirit is not a third subsistence, as is the Holy Spirit of trinitarian doctrine; it is the synthesis of the first two elements of being. The Spirit is the end product or fusion of the dialectical movement from the abyss of being (the Father) and the form and structure of being (the Son or Logos). The Spirit is the union of the dialectical elements of beings.[12] Tillich's Trinity is trinitarian and not binitarian. But dialectical movements within the nature of being and not subsistences of the divine nature make it trinitarian. Traditional trinitarianism seems to posit something more about the divine persons. It maintains that they are subsistences of the divine nature and not only movements in the structure of being. The result is that you have three subsistent realities that define the Trinity and not Tillich's dialectical-trinitarian process within the nature of being. Tillich's reduction of the Christian doctrine of the Trinity to one, even if the clearest, way of understanding the dialectical or trinitarian nature of the "living God" is inconsistent with traditional trinitarian theology. The latter considers the Father, the Son, and the Holy Spirit the irreducible datum of God's being and not merely a symbol for a more fundamental dialectical and trinitarian ontology.

Second, the identity of the Holy Spirit as the mutual love or bond of union of the Father and the Son is ambiguous. Thatcher's point that the doctrine of the Trinity does not treat one divine person as the unity of the other two is partially correct. Strictly speaking, the divine persons are equal subsistences of the divine nature. Functionally, the Holy Spirit as the mutual love of the Father and the Son is the act of the Father and the Son. The Spirit is not an agent. The Spirit is an instrumental function of the Father and the Son. The Spirit goes forth as the love that establishes the union of the Father and the Son. This unity is a third subsistent reality in the divine nature, and, in this respect seems more tangibly distinct than Tillich's Spirit of unity. Nevertheless, the Holy Spirit's identity as a divine person is unclear in Western trinitarianism. The Spirit is the mutual act of the Father and the Son and is not, like the Father and the Son, a distinct agent within the triune life. The latent ambiguity over the identity and status of the Holy Spirit in Western trinitarianism is the reason that Tillich could so easily reinterpret it in the less personal categories of a dialectical Trinity.

Tillich and Pentecostal Trinitarian Theology

At this point I want to return to the question raised in the introduction: what can Tillich's and pentecostal trinitarian theology possibly share in common? The obvious barrier to Tillich's appropriation by Pentecostals is the genre of his thought. His theology trades on the tradition of German dialectical philosophy and existentialism. Its forms of thought are pedestrian neither to most Pentecostals nor to most contemporary theologians, for that matter. Nevertheless, I propose three areas where Tillich's theology shares affinities with and contributes to pentecostal trinitarian theology. The first is the role of the experience of the Spirit of God in the task of theology. The second is the central place of pneumatology in theology. The third is a comparison of Tillich's trinitarian understanding with the views of oneness and trinitarian Pentecostals.

Theology and the Place of Experience

Tillich's rationale for the ability of finite symbols and human experience to serve as the vehicle of revelation resonates with a pentecostal approach to theology. Tillich's question is: How can something within finite reality communicate something about infinite reality? His answer is, this is possible because "that which is infinite is being-itself and because everything participates in being-itself" (*ST* 1:239). The participation of finite being in infinite being is the basis for the *analogia entis* (analogy of being) and, as Tillich argues, "our only justification for speaking at all about God" (*ST* 1:240, 242).

Tillich's insight is a sound one and reflects the same logic as Rahner's trinitarian dictum, which is as much a principle of divine revelation as one of trinitarian theology. Rahner's principle is: the "economic" Trinity is the "immanent" Trinity and vice versa.[13] It means that what God does in the history of redemption and revelation is who God is in the eternal Trinity. Rahner's principle is crucial for the Christian doctrine of revelation. Without the correspondence between God's economic activities and immanent being, knowledge of God is impossible.

How does the above relate to Tillich's idea that finite symbols and human experience can communicate truth about God because they participate in the infinite ground of being? The key is the notion of participation. For Tillich, since finite things exist only because they participate in the infinite, they can communicate something true, though in a limited way, about the infinite. John P. Dourley notes that "with this theological methodology Tillich seeks to establish in human experience itself, and especially in man as driven to questioning his humanity, a latent basis in life itself which asks for the fullness of Christian revelation and which is in some real sense the precondition of its being received humanly."[14] For

Rahner, redemptive history reveals the Trinity for the same reason. Redemptive history is the product of the self-communication of God to the world. Put in Tillichian terms, redemptive history is the world's participation in the life of the triune God. Note here that I am not arguing that Tillich and Rahner understood God in the same way. I think for Rahner, the Christian doctrine of the Trinity was the most basic concept for understanding God and not the discursive symbol of a more fundamental notion of God, as it was for Tillich. Nevertheless, they both believed that God's activity in creation reveals what God is like. The consequence for Tillich's theological method is that theology begins with and explicates the experience of God in human life.

Pentecostals have intuitively or at least implicitly embraced this aspect of Tillich's theological method. Based on their experience of baptism in the Holy Spirit, Pentecostals developed the doctrine of Spirit baptism. They assumed that their experience of the Spirit bore a theological yield. Historically, they articulated this doctrine in terms of theological categories inherited from their Reformed and Wesleyan-Holiness predecessors.[15] The problem lies not in the assumption that experience of God is fruitful for theology, but in the categories of its articulation. The theological categories of the Reformed and Holiness traditions are ill suited to express the theology implicit in the pentecostal experience of the Holy Spirit. I maintain that the pentecostal experience of the Spirit reveals not only something about the nature of Christian redemption, but about God too. Thus, like Tillich, I affirm that finite participation in God becomes the vehicle for a theological understanding of God. Speaking on the Spiritual Presence and the Presence of God, Tillich affirms that symbolic (doctrinal) expressions of God derive from God's presence in religious experience and traditions (*ST* 3:283). Yet, theology is not merely discourse on religious psychology. Theological expressions, though shaped by religious experience, Tillich maintains, have a *"fundamentum in re,"* a foundation in reality (*ST* 3:283). The notion that religion projects ideas of God is correct, but by itself the theory overlooks the fact that "the realm against which the divine images are projected is not itself a projection. It is the experienced ultimacy of being and meaning. It is the realm of ultimate concern" (*ST* 1:212). Jean Richard notes that God as ultimate concern "is not a purely objective reality; He/She is essentially connected with our human experience. But neither is He/She purely subjective, that is, a pure expression of human desire, a pure illusion."[16] In other words, the foundation of theology is participation in and experience of God. If pentecostal experience is the experience of God, then it has ramifications for theology. But where do we draw the boundary of experience and participation in the Spirit? Is all pentecostal experience an experience of the Spirit? If all life participates in the ground of being, then are all realms of life equal sources for insight into the nature of God? These

questions raise the concern of criteria for discerning the Spirit. I think the revelation of God in Christ and the Spirit of Pentecost are ultimate, though not exclusive, criteria. In other words, when theology turns to discern the ways pentecostal experience or the rest of creation participate in the divine life, Christ and
the Spirit of Pentecost are the benchmarks for adjudication.[17]

What are its implications for the Trinity? The centrality of the Spirit in
pentecostal experience coheres with the role of the Spirit in the biblical drama
of redemption. In fact, the outpouring of the Spirit of Pentecost is the capstone
of God's redemptive work. Because human experience of God is a participation
in the life of God, the Spirit's role in redemption, as the Spirit of Pentecost, reveals the Spirit's trinitarian identity. As the Spirit of Pentecost, the Holy Spirit
consummates and constitutes God's redemptive work. Consequently, the Spirit
is the divine person who fulfills God's triune identity (in Rahnerian terms, the
economic activity reveals immanent identity). The Spirit fulfills the tri-unity
of God not only as the third subsistent person, but also as one who consummates
the trinitarian God and as such plays a role in the identity formation of the Son
and the Father.[18]

Tillich and Starting with the Spirit

Tillich maintained that the trinitarian principles are the foundation or the
"presuppositions" for the Christian doctrine of the Trinity (*ST* 1:251). Moreover,
he states that at the level of the Christian doctrine of the Trinity, theology begins
with Christology, but at the more fundamental level of the trinitarian principles,
theology begins with the Spirit. Tillich's turn to pneumatology sounds promising for Pentecostals, but is it? The answer is "no," and "yes."

First, the Spirit Tillich has in mind at the level of trinitarian principles is not
the Holy Spirit of Pentecost. Spirit is the unity of the ontological elements and
the *telos* of life. *Spirit* in this context means the fulfillment of the nature of life;
that is, Spirit is the actualization of the dialectical polarities of power and meaning. Spirit, then, is "the inclusive symbol for the divine life" (*ST* 1:250). Spirit is
inclusive because it stands for the union or actualization of the ontological elements of power and meaning. Tillich's fundamental view of God does begin
with a pneumatological category. It is so far removed, however, from the way
Pentecostals understand pneumatology that its utility for pentecostal theology
is unclear. Trinitarian Pentecostals fall within the orthodox trinitarian tradition.
Accordingly, they believe the Spirit is a subsistence of the divine nature. Spirit in
Tillich is not a subsistence of the divine nature, but the culminating movement
of a dialectical process.

Second, and despite the distance of Tillich's philosophical theology from
pentecostal theology, his pneumatological starting point indicates the way to-

ward a pentecostal approach to the Trinity.[19] The outpouring of the Spirit is a culminating and hence eschatological work of the Holy Spirit. The outpouring of the Spirit of Pentecost fulfills the work of redemption. The implication for trinitarian theology is that the Spirit fulfills the triune life of God, just as Spirit completes the dialectical process of being in Tillich's thought. The Spirit plays a constituting role in the identities and the fellowship of the triune God.

Tillichian, Oneness, and Pentecostal Trinitarianism

An early schism among Pentecostals over the Trinity occasioned the most significant instance of pentecostal reflection on the doctrine. The controversy began in April of 1913 at a camp meeting in Arroyo Seco (near Los Angeles). The disagreement was over a new understanding of the nature of and formula for water baptism. Based on Acts 2:38, a group of Pentecostals, later to be known as oneness Pentecostals, began baptizing in the name of the Lord Jesus Christ rather than in the trinitarian pattern of Matthew 28:19. By 1916 the oneness insistence on baptism and rebaptism in the name of Jesus and its nontraditional trinitarianism led the Assemblies of God (a trinitarian pentecostal denomination) to include a clear trinitarian confession in its Statement of Fundamental Truths and, thereby, to exclude Jesus Name ministers and congregations.[20] Though the flashpoint was a dispute over the proper baptismal formula, the root of the controversy was rival trinitarian theologies.

Oneness Pentecostalism rejects Nicene trinitarianism. Oneness theology affirms that the terms Father, Son, and Holy Spirit are titles that Scripture uses to indicate the different roles of the one God in salvation history. Trinitarian language, therefore, applies only to the distinct redemptive roles of the one God and not to eternal distinctions or persons within the one God. The critical point is that the titles of Father, Son, and Holy Spirit are not names of divine persons. God has one personal identity. Consequently, the one God has one name, the Name of Jesus. According to Nicene trinitarian theology, oneness Pentecostalism is a form of economic modalism, which sees God as one eternal being without internal distinction of persons. Though ultimately beyond human conception, the name of the Father, the Son, and the Holy Spirit refer to eternal distinctions, persons, in God. For their part, oneness Pentecostals see Nicene theology as a corruption of monotheism that implies either polytheism or subordinationism.[21]

Tillich also rejected the traditional understanding of divine persons and emphasized the Spirit as the unity of the elements of being. This view seems to suggest compatibility with the oneness pentecostal understanding of God. But is that the case?

Although oneness Pentecostalism reflects a trinitarian structure, this structure is limited to the manifestation of God in creation and redemption. The names of the divine persons do not refer to any distinctions within the being of God. In other words, Oneness recognizes the trinitarian structure or *moments* not as something essential to God, but rather as historical episodes of divine activity and revelation.[22] Tillich's trinitarian moments, however, are not merely modes of God's relation to creation. In language that sounds similar to the traditional Christian notion of an eternal and triune differentiation within God, Tillich affirms that "the living God is always the trinitarian God, even before Christology is possible, before the Christ has appeared."[23] Tillich did reject the idea that Father, Son, and Holy Spirit are "persons." He believed the doctrine of the Trinity symbolically expresses the dialectical process of being. But just as important, he believed the dialectical process that characterizes being is enduring. God, as being-itself, is always a dialectical dynamic and, thus, is trinitarian. Tillich's trinitarian moments, therefore, share more in common with trinitarian than oneness Pentecostalism.

This chapter brings the trinitarian thought of Paul Tillich into conversation with pentecostal trinitarian theology. Though in many respects inhabiting incommensurable thought-worlds, they nevertheless share significant points of correspondence. The procession of the Son, which introduces relational diversity, and the procession of the Spirit, which unites the Father and the Son, have close parallels with the dialectical movements of Tillich's Trinity. His conviction that theology begins at the nexus of God's Spirit and human experience dovetails with pentecostal instincts on the role of the experience of the Holy Spirit in theology. Tillich's dialectical view of the nature of the "living God" also aligns more closely with trinitarian Pentecostalism than with oneness Pentecostalism. Yet, the convergences should not be overplayed. Tillich's trinitarian structure of being is not equivalent with the traditional understanding of the triune God. Traditional trinitarianism, and I *think* pentecostal trinitarian theology, affirms that the Trinity of the Father, the Son, and the Holy Spirit is the irreducible divine reality and not the epiphenomenal symbolic expression of the dialectical nature of being.

Notes

1. John P. Dourley, *Paul Tillich and Bonaventure: An Evaluation of Tillich's Claim to Stand in the Augustinian-Franciscan Tradition* (Leiden: Brill, 1975), 184; and Pan-Chiu Lai, *Towards a Trinitarian Theology of Religions: A Study of Paul Tillich's Thought*, Studies in Philosophical Theology (Kampen, NL: Kok Pharos, 1994), 148.

2. Nimi Wariboko, *God and Money: A Theology of Money in a Globalizing World* (Lanham, MD: Lexington, 2008), 22. Wariboko leverages Tillich's trinitarian thought to develop a theological and trinitarian critique of the inequities of the current global monetary system (based on the monarchial currencies of the dollar, euro, and yen) and a proposal for a socially just single global currency.

3. Maarten De Jong, "Trinity or not Trinity: That is the Question," in *Trinität und/ oder Quaternität: Tillichs Neuerschließung der trinitarischem Problematik/Trinity and/or Quaternity: Tillich's Reopening of the Trinitarian Problem,* ed. Werner Schüßler and Erdmann Sturm, Tillich Studien 10 (Munster: LIT, 2004), 222–223.

4. Paul Tillich, *A History of Christian Thought: From Its Judaic and Hellenistic Origins to Existentialism,* ed. Carl E. Braaten (New York: Touchstone, 1968), 408.

5. For a helpful discussion of Tillich's theory of Spiritual Presence and its relation to his Christology, see John Charles Cooper, *The "Spiritual Presence" in the Theology of Paul Tillich: Tillich's Use of St. Paul* (Macon, GA: Mercer University Press 1997), 64–67 and 85–88.

6. For an informative discussion of the way Jesus became the Christ and the way it relates to human life, see Nimi Wariboko, *The Principle of Excellence: A Framework for Social Ethics* (Lanham, MD: Lexington, 2009), 8–10, 89–91, and especially 97–111.

7. The idea that in the Logos all created forms are contained is also part of Tillich's and the Western tradition of trinitarian theology.

8. Russell R. Manning draws similar correlations in "The Trinitarian Background to Tillich's Theology of Culture," in Schüßler and Sturm, eds., *Trinität und/oder Quaternität* (Munster: LIT, 2004), 9.

9. Adrian Thatcher, *The Ontology of Paul Tillich* (New York: Oxford University Press, 1978), 91 (emphasis original).

10. Thatcher, *Ontology of Paul Tillich,* 92.

11. I realize that in the last half of the twentieth century the Augustinian mutual love model has come under severe criticism. During Tillich's time, however, to describe it as the dominant form of Western trinitarianism is fair. Moreover, the basic concept of the mutual love model, the Holy Spirit as the source of union between the divine persons, remains popular in contemporary theology.

12. For a similar interpretation of Tillich's relationship to Western pneumatology, see Manning, "Trinitarian Background to Tillich's Theology of Culture," 9.

13. Karl Rahner, *The Trinity,* trans. Joseph Donceel (1970; reprint, New York: Crossroad, 1998), 22.

14. John P. Dourley, "Trinitarian Models and Human Integration: Jung and Tillich Compared," in *Carl Gustav Jung: Critical Assessments,* vol. 4, *Implications and Inspirations,* ed. Renos K. Papadopoulos (New York: Routledge, 1992), 203.

15. For the Reformed and Holiness roots of Pentecostalism and how they shaped the pentecostal theology of Spirit baptism, see Donald W. Dayton, *Theological Roots of Pentecostalism* (Grand Rapids, MI: Francis Asbury Press, 1987).

16. Jean Richard, "The Trinity As Object and As Structure of Religious Experience," in Schüßler and Sturm, eds., *Trinität und/oder Quaternität,* (Munster: LIT, 2004), 22.

17. Amos Yong has done more than any other pentecostal scholar to develop pneumatological criteria for theology, see *Discerning the Spirit(s): A Pentecostal-Charismatic Contribution to Christian Theology of Religions* (Sheffield, UK: Sheffield, 2000).

18. I develop this argument at length in *From Pentecost to the Triune God: A Pentecostal Trinitarian Theology,* Pentecostal Manifestos Series (Grand Rapids, MI: Eerdmans, 2012).

19. Amos Yong develops an approach to theological hermeneutics on the basis of pneumatology and trinitarian theology; see Yong, *Spirit-Word-Community: Theological Hermeneutics in Trinitarian Perspective* (Burlington, VT: Ashgate, 2002). Frank D. Macchia also uses the Trinity as a basis to illuminate the meaning of Spirit baptism; see Macchia, *Baptized in the Spirit: A Global Pentecostal Theology* (Grand Rapids, MI: Zondervan, 2006). Also see my *From Pentecost to the Triune God* (ch. 1 and 2), which proposes a pentecostal trinitarian theology on the basis of the Spirit of Pentecost.

20. For the history and theology of oneness Pentecostalism, see David A. Reed, *"In Jesus' Name": The History and Beliefs of Oneness Pentecostals* (Blandford Forum, UK: Deo, 2008).

21. For oneness understanding of God, see "Oneness-Trinitarian Pentecostal Final Report, 2002–2007," *Pneuma: The Journal of the Society for Pentecostal Studies* 30 (2008): 208–224 and Reed, *"In Jesus' Name,"* 265–273.

22. Oneness theology is consistent with Rahner's maxim, but in a qualified way. Oneness theology sees the manifestations of God as Father, Son, and Spirit as revelatory. In this sense, the economic Trinity is the immanent Trinity. The revelation, however, is not of divine persons, but of the person of God and God's redemption revealed supremely in Jesus Christ.

23. Tillich, *History of Christian Thought,* 408.

FIVE

Tillich's Picture of Jesus as the Christ

Toward a Theology of the Spirit's Saving Presence

TERRY L. CROSS

Few Christian theologians have been as engaged with art as has Paul Tillich. Since his days as a chaplain in the trenches of World War I where he held onto small pictures of classical paintings so as to relieve the tension of war, Tillich found something transcendent about art.[1] It is no surprise then that in an attempt to sketch a christology for the twentieth century, Tillich used the image of an expressionist portrait to illustrate the biblical record of the New Being in Jesus as the Christ. Underlying his use of expressionism is a rich understanding of the relation between faith and history, along with expressionism's influence on christology, soteriology, and pneumatology. It is this complex interweaving of these elements that this chapter will examine.

Tillich underscores the relation of these various doctrines in several key statements. He says, "But Christology is not complete without pneumatology (the doctrine of the Spirit), because 'the Christ is the Spirit' and the actualization of the New Being in history is the work of the Spirit" (*ST* 3.285). Moreover, christology and soteriology belong together: "Christology is a function of soteriology" (*ST* 2.150). Jesus as the Christ saves humans from their old being by bringing to them the New Being. How does this salvation occur? Tillich describes it succinctly: where there is revelation, there is salvation (*ST* 2.166). The Spirit does not reveal to humans "information about divine things," but rather "the ecstatic manifestation of the Ground of Being in events, persons and things. Such manifestations have shaking, transforming, and healing power" (*ST* 2.166–167; cf. 3.115). The Spirit helps us recognize the power of New Being in the biblical picture of the Christ, thereby creating faith in us.

It is Tillich's creative weaving of these three aspects—christology, soteriology, and pneumatology—within the expressionist picture of Jesus as the Christ that becomes fertile ground for our own theological understanding of salvation. In this chapter we will examine Tillich's understanding of the portrait of Jesus and the role that history plays in his christology. While critiquing his approach throughout the chapter, we will conclude with a constructive consideration that correlates Tillich's doctrinal proposals with a pentecostal viewpoint in order to address the issue of the certainty of faith.

The Portrait of Jesus as the Christ and the Historical Jesus

Tillich's Expressionist Portrait

One of the most creative yet ambiguous images that Tillich provides for understanding his christology is that of a picture. Frequently, he speaks of the "biblical picture of Jesus as the Christ."[2] Tillich believes that all of the New Testament is unified in its claim that Jesus of Nazareth is now the Christ of God. Yet this picture of the Christ does not come to us through a photograph—as those searching for the "historical Jesus" behind the biblical picture might desire (ST 2.115). Neither does this picture of the Christ come to us through some idealized painting that projects the most profoundly religious minds of the first century CE; instead, Tillich proposes that the biblical picture of the Christ is more like an "expressionist portrait," explaining that painter of this genre of art tries to "enter into the deepest levels of the person with whom he deals" (ST 2.116). There is a "profound participation" in the "reality" of what he/she is painting as well as its intended meaning for the observer (ST 2.116). Expressionist artists in the early 1900s broke from the naturalists and impressionists of the 1800s by emphasizing participation from the inside (Mitteilung von innen) as the essential worth of a picture (Bildwürdige). In order to achieve this internal perspective and power, they needed new, more abstract forms of art that no longer related to reality as a frame of reference (Bezugssystem zur Wirklichkeit), but performed as a matter of analysis with the world on the level of an intensive human participation (intensiven menschlichen Beteilung)—of an increasing feeling of the I (eines gesteigerten Ichgefühls).[3]

Such "expressionism" has a long history in the story of art.[4] It also stands on the other side as an alternative to the naturalistic or idealistic styles of art.[5] Thus, when speaking of the "real picture" (Realbild) of Jesus as the Christ in the Gospel records, Tillich means this expressionistic style of painting. The Gospels do not offer us a photograph or even a movie of the life of Jesus; such naturalism or realism would presume that we could get behind the faith of the witnesses and discover the real historical life of Jesus—something that modern history recognizes as quite impossible.[6] Affected by the power of the New Being that the disciples witnessed in the life of Jesus of Nazareth, they "painted" their experiences of this power in which they participated. Their expressionist portrait may distort the reality of the subject in one way in order to emphasize other features of that same reality.[7] The result is they give us a picture that allows us to have "personal participation in his being," that is, in the New Being (ST 2.116).

The Origin of Tillich's Biblical Picture—Jumping the Ugly Ditch

Tillich's use of the concept of the biblical picture of Jesus as the Christ was not of his own making. In response to historical criticism of the 1800s and the dead end of its research into finding the historical Jesus, two well-known German professors attempted to anchor the Christian faith on something other than history. Martin Kähler (Halle) and Wilhelm Herrmann (Marburg) used the idea of the biblical picture (*Bild*) of Jesus in order to sidestep the problems created by modern historical research. The classic challenge came from Gottfried Lessing in 1777: "If no historical truth can be demonstrated, then nothing can be demonstrated by means of historical truths. That is: accidental truths of history can never become the proof of necessary truths of reason . . . That, then, is the ugly, broad ditch (*der garstige breite Graben*) which I cannot get across, however often and however earnestly I have tried to make the leap."[8] It was this "ugly ditch" of history that Herrmann, Kähler, and Tillich tried to bypass through their appeal to the power of the spiritual inner life of Jesus as the Christ. While Herrmann and Kähler engaged this historical problem with slightly different approaches, their "picture" motif and approaches to history were passed along to Tillich.

Wilhelm Herrmann began his writing about the "inner life of Jesus" in the 1880s with his book, *The Communion of the Christian with God.*[9] This book was so popular that it underwent seven editions in German. While Tillich did not have Herrmann as a teacher, he could not have missed the powerful impact that Herrmann's theology had on the German academy and populace.[10] For Herrmann, faith in Jesus the Christ cannot rely on historical judgment since "however certain it may appear," it can attain nothing more than "probability."[11] Therefore, faith must bypass critical-historical study of Jesus. In tones highly reflected in Tillich's own christology, Herrmann states, "It is a fatal error to attempt to establish the basis of faith by means of historical investigation."[12] Nonetheless, there is the "historical fact [*geschichtliche Tatsache*] of the Person of Jesus" that provides an objective ground (*Grund*) for our faith.[13]

How did Herrmann achieve this certainty for faith? His argument was that the inner life of Jesus was so powerful that it not only left an impression on his original disciples but also congealed in their testimonies about the Christ. The power of Jesus' personality rushes forward like a current in a stream throughout history into the present. When we are asked to step into this stream, we are connected immediately with its power and purpose. In this way, we sidestep the "ugly ditch" of historical incertitude and are able to believe with certainty that Jesus is the Christ because of the power of his personality and its impact upon the original witnesses—as well as on us. History cannot give faith its certainty. Only the influence of this picture (*Bild*) of Jesus can establish the certitude of faith.[14]

In 1896, Martin Kähler entered the discussion with a similar attempt to by-pass the problems of historical research.[15] Kähler was Tillich's professor at the University of Halle. Kähler's view of the "biblical Christ" had profound and last-ing influence on him. Writing a foreword to the English translation of Kähler's book in 1964, Tillich stated that "one emphasis in Kähler's answer is decisive for our present situation, namely, the necessity to make the certainty of faith inde-pendent of the unavoidable incertitudes of historical research."[16] Indeed, some quotes from Kähler's book could easily be mistaken for Tillich's own.

Kähler argued that the Gospel records prior to the last week of Jesus' life have some connection to our faith, but not as a history of Jesus. The purpose of these records is "not so much *what* happened as *who* acted and *how*."[17] The Gos-pels transmit to us a character sketch (*Charakterbild*)[18] of Jesus, not so that we can demand "faith in facts," but so that we can profess "faith in the person whom we know from the facts."[19] Like Herrmann, Kähler seems to acknowledge the need for some type of "fact" on which faith is based, but it cannot be the facts of history. "For historical facts which first have to be established by science can-not *as such* become experiences of faith. Therefore, Christian faith and a history of Jesus repel each other like oil and water."[20]

What, then, brings us to certainty in our salvation? Kähler speaks with amazing similarity to Herrmann: it is the drawing power of the Savior (*die an-ziehende Macht des Heilandes*) that is offered in the biblical picture of the Christ.[21] For Christians, then, this picture is reliable not because it has been "torturously extracted by the modern methods of historical research," but rather because Christians find themselves "being 'overpowered' [*überwältigt*] by Christ as he encounters us in the picture the Bible paints of him."[22] It is this biblical picture of Christ that confronts humans with a decision—an "Either/Or."[23] Such a pic-ture is not "a poetic idealization [*idealisierende Dichtung*] originating in the hu-man mind"; it is instead the reality of Christ himself that has "left its ineffacea-ble impress upon this picture."[24] The end result is that we believe in Christ only because Christ himself evokes such faith in us from the reality of his presence in the picture of the Gospel record.[25] By means of the Spirit of God, humans ob-serve the reality of Jesus within the picture of the biblical Christ and are moved to faith in him.[26]

One is struck by the linguistic and conceptual similarity between Herrmann and Kähler, yet even more so by their similarity with Tillich's own words and concepts. Wrapped up in Tillich's brief reference to the biblical picture of Christ is the portrayal previously established by Herrmann and Kähler. There is power in the biblical picture of Christ because there is a reality of the inner life of Jesus (or New Being) that shines through the portrait. The details of the por-trait of Jesus are less important because faith does not need a biography, a Life of Jesus, or a historical account of the Savior's life on earth. What faith needs instead is an encounter with the same Christ who was portrayed by the first witnesses. With such approaches, Herrmann, Kähler, and Tillich believe that they can sidestep the ditch of history.

For Tillich, the biblical picture of Jesus as the Christ shows us three dimensions in the biblical records: historical, legendary, and mythical (*ST* 2.151). It is the final aspect—the mythical—that gives rise to the symbolic, which is the element that holds universal significance for Jesus as the Christ; the historical and legendary elements of the biblical records are only to be used "in a corroborative sense" (*ST* 2.152). Therefore, the accuracy of historical details about Jesus is not essential for faith.

What do we see today when we look at the biblical record—this expressionist portrait—of Jesus as the Christ? How is the picture crafted? Unlike those who quest for the historical Jesus, Tillich sees no historical certainty *behind* the portraiture. Indeed, one can never know any aspect of the historical Jesus from such an expressionist portrait. Tillich states, "No special trait of this picture can be verified with certainty. But it can be definitely asserted that through this picture the New Being has power to transform those who are transformed by it" (*ST* 2.114). The vicissitudes of historical research and the uncertainty that results can never reach a satisfying conclusion about Jesus of Nazareth. At best there can only be degrees of probability (*ST* 2.104). Only through a *soteriological* experience produced by the Spirit is the certainty of faith satisfied, not through some *historical* or even *speculative* conjecture. The power of this picture of the New Being to transform human lives that observe it brings about the assurance of its accuracy and reality. In other words, the proof is in the experience!

Against those who try to distort this picture by seeing a "God walking on earth" (*ST* 2.133), Tillich states that this finite, human element must be emphasized in our theological reading of the portrait over against a "hidden omnipotence, omniscience, omnipresence, and eternity" (*ST* 2.132).[27] Thus for Tillich, the incarnation cannot mean the eternal Son of God *became human,* but rather that "a divine being, either the heavenly man, or the pre-existent Christ, or the divine *Logos,* appears in the shape of a physical man or of a man in the flesh."[28] It is this that establishes the paradox of the incarnation: "Not God becomes man, but a divine being who represents God and is able to reveal him in his fullness, manifests himself in a form of existence which is in radical contradiction to his divine, spiritual and heavenly form."[29]

So what important *details* for faith belong to this portraiture? Only one: the reality of the New Being, "who conquers existential estrangement and thereby makes faith possible" (*ST* 2.114). Tillich has been clear that the attempt to isolate the factual element from the symbolic element in the portrait of Jesus as the

Christ is "not a primary interest of faith" (ST 2.154). "Faith itself is the immediate (not mediated by conclusions) evidence of the New Being within and under
the conditions of existence" (ST 2.114). Faith is a creation of the Spirit within humans, not the intellectual conclusion that arises from historical research of the
question of Jesus of Nazareth. Therefore, Christians have a *direct* and *immediate
certainty* that cannot be erased by the questions of historical uncertainty. "No historical criticism can question the immediate awareness of those who find themselves transformed into the state of faith" (ST 2.114). Given these parameters,
faith can only "guarantee" the reality of the New Being behind and within the
portrait; it "does not guarantee his name to be Jesus of Nazareth . . . He might
have had another name" (ST 2.114), as absurd as such a thing might sound. And
so, have we jumped the ditch or fallen in?

Facts and Faith—a Bridge for the Ditch?

For Tillich, we can only possess the picture that portrays Jesus *as the Christ*
and never a "hypothetical description of what may lie behind the biblical picture" (ST 2.115). Therefore, the Jesus of history can never be known apart from
his reception by the early believers. Tillich calls this twofold dimension to the
"event" of Christianity the "historical fact" (Jesus of Nazareth) and the "reception of this fact by those who received him as the Christ" (ST 2.98, 97). It is important to note that like Herrmann and Kähler, Tillich insists on some *factual
dimension* to this biblical picture. "If the factual element in the Christian event
were denied, the foundation of Christianity would be denied" (ST 2.107). He asserts that there must be *a personal life* in which the New Being must overcome
existential estrangement within time and space. "This is the reason that Christian theology must insist on the actual fact to which the name Jesus of Nazareth refers" (ST 2.98). If there were no personal (historical?) life within space and
time, then there could be no power of New Being that would overcome the conditions of existence.

Bruce McCormack offers a keen insight into Tillich's factual dimension
of Jesus as the Christ. He notes: "All Tillich really needs is that there be *a* personal life of some kind behind the transforming event by which that faith was
awakened and then expressed in the biblical symbols."[30] It did not have to be Jesus
of Nazareth—it could have been someone else. It just had to be *someone* under the
conditions of existence. Since the "fact" of Jesus is not based on historical argument but on participation in the power of the New Being that exudes from the
portrait of Jesus as the Christ, the Christian faith stands secure with its experiential guarantee rising above the probabilities of historical judgment.

Yet Tillich seems to want *something* historical in his picture of Christ—even
if it cannot be securely established through historical research. If Jesus as the

Christ is ahistorical in the sense that he is cut off from everything before the year 1 and after the year 30, then the contemporary Christian of today is removed from "direct connection with the New Being in Christ"; in such a case, the contemporary Christian "is asked to jump over the millennia to the years '1 through 30' and to subject himself to the event upon which Christianity is based. But this jump is an illusion, because the very fact that he is a Christian and that he calls Jesus the Christ is based on the continuity through history of the power of the New Being" (*ST* 2.136). And so Tillich attempts to build a bridge over Lessing's "ugly ditch" of history by claiming the longevity and duration of the power of the New Being in Jesus the Christ. But is this truly a bridge or merely a pirouette on the same island of subjectivity where Tillich started? While one may applaud and even follow this attempt to bridge the ditch, does it not simply dig another ditch around observing believers so that they are left stranded on something like an island surrounded by a deep moat, yet without connection to the mainland of historical reality?

In her essay titled "Tillich's Christology," Anne Marie Reijnen responds to this very proposal with these words: "Tillich's position is questionable." Reijnen then offers the reason this position is so disturbing to some of Tillich's critics: it combines the "principle of the historical 'unknowability' in matters of faith and the importance of the concrete 'picture.'"[31] In other words, if we are experiencing the power of the New Being through the portrait of the man Jesus, should we not ask for a reliable (historical?) picture of Jesus the Christ from the biblical records? If the resurrection did not occur as a historical event, on what basis (other than our experience) can we affirm the certainty of our faith? I would ask whether it is reasonable to hold (as Tillich attempts) to some *factual* dimension of the portrait without also having some *historical* dimension to it. It seems Tillich ends up in the strange position of not needing the historical Jesus while at the same time desperately wanting *the fact* of the historical Jesus![32]

But more questions arise for me here: What is this facticity that is needed by all three theologians—this "something historical" to give shape, edge, and contour to the portrait? If this is not *historical* fact, then what type of fact is it? Unless the expressionist painting devolves quickly into some morass of subjective judgment (that is, the painting may have no connection with reality, but it does move me in my own sphere of reality), surely Tillich needs *something* historical to secure faith.

To be sure, Tillich thinks this is not the case. He asserts the need for "fact" to be the basis behind the faith-response of the believing observer. However, Tillich neither can nor wishes to sketch that "fact" in the realm of historical reality (thereby subjecting it to the vagaries of research). Yet, how can the impact of a portrait of the power of New Being be enough to create faith? Does not the *fact* of Jesus' life, death, burial, and resurrection have anything to do with over-coming estrangement in *our* history—our own lives, deaths, burials, and, yes, resurrections? If this portrayal of New Being in Jesus the Christ is not in some way a realistic portrait of what happened to this particular human under the existential reality of first-century history, then how can it bring forth any message of faith and hope for our present reality under the conditions of our existence? Perhaps Tillich has inherited from Herrmann and Kähler not only their theme of the picture of Jesus but also their own faith's need for historical fact as a ground of faith.

Hence, rather than simply an expressionist portrait of Jesus as the Christ, does not this require some *realistic dimensions*—something sketched by the biblical witnesses that records not only their response to Jesus as the Christ, but also the reality of the God-human who made such an impression on them in the historical events of the lives they shared in Palestine? And if so, have we not returned to the problem of faith and history—and Lessing's ditch? If faith does not rely on history for its certitude, then on what does it rely?

The Certainty of the Spirit:
Pentecostal–Tillichian Correlations

How might we genuinely hurdle over the ditch of history without mistakenly twirling ourselves around in some form of myopic subjectivity? I submit that one answer to this question exists in a response that Herrmann, Kähler, and Tillich offered, albeit in muted tones—namely, the Holy Spirit. We jump over the ugly, broad ditch of history and its concomitant contingencies because *we are grasped by the Spiritual Presence of God and carried to a real encounter with the Risen and Crucified One.* Tillich's christology gives priority to the pneumatological encounter that fosters an experience of the New Being in the Christ, but it fails to make any connection of the Spirit with the reliability of that christic history. It is the Spiritual Presence in that event-encounter creating faith and spawning an inner certainty of the reality of the possibility of the New Being of the unambiguous life. We humans have been "grasped by the Spiritual Presence" before we have encountered Jesus the Christ as a "historical event"; the same Spirit who made Christ the expression of New Being also prepares and encounters us in New Being—the "transcendent union of unambiguous life" (*ST* 3.146).

So why isn't this sufficient for me? Tillich's modernism speaks louder than this voice of the Spirit. Downplaying any hermeneutic of literalism in reading miracles of the biblical record throughout his *Systematic Theology,* Tillich nonetheless wants to establish his entire theological enterprise on a *transcendent, invisible power of the Spirit*—something that will never meet the criteria of empirical evidence for moderns! Why is he so willing to reinterpret the record through symbols in order to achieve—in the end—the miraculous, supernatural transcendent power? Why is he so allergic to anything historical in connection with Jesus the Christ? We will never be able to satisfy the modernist agenda in historical research, but there should be something historically reliable in the witnesses of Jesus of Nazareth—even Tillich wants to admit that.

In the end, Tillich seems to be a nineteenth-century German Protestant theologian who surrendered to modernity's charge that the history of Jesus was overlaid with a mystical fog to such a degree that now we cannot penetrate its original reality. Does faith rely on history and historical research? In one sense, Tillich (and others) was right: faith cannot rest entirely on the uncertainty and variableness of historical investigation. Yet in another sense the ambivalence here toward the need for some historical "fact" in Herrmann, Kähler, and Tillich leads us to believe that their critics are right: faith must rest—even if lightly—on something that actually happened in human history. The biblical materials claim to be unique testimonies in the history of humankind. They offer witness to God dwelling among us—something that not everyone who walked with Jesus could see. If there were no historical basis on which this faith could be founded, then how is this "picture" able to transform anyone living in history here and now?

It is here that I believe some aspects of pentecostal theology may assist Tillich and all of us in jumping the ditch. Pentecostals have long testified that the assurance of their faith has been pressed into their hearts by the Spirit. This begins at conversion: "Jesus is presented to the person through the scriptural testimony by the Holy Spirit. It is the Spirit who moves upon the person to receive Christ."[33] Grasping us and jumping the millennia, the Spirit re-presents Jesus Christ to us, assuring us that the "facts" as stated in the biblical record are truthful "expressions" of the portrait of Jesus the Christ. The Spirit who creates the Christ in the incarnation is the same Spirit who creates faith in us now—a faith based on the fact that God became a person in human history with all that entails.[34] The Spirit assures us that the picture of Jesus is reliable as the necessary component of a historical basis for our belief. It is the Spirit who brings this certainty of faith to our hearts.

To be sure, Pentecostals have a certainty of faith that rides the stream of history flowing from Jesus of Nazareth. Unlike Tillich, however, for Pentecostals this reality is based not only on the fact of the *continuity* of the New Being throughout history, but also on the historical fact of Jesus of Nazareth *and* God becoming a human in this historical Jesus. Tillich's is an argument for the facticity of the New Being based on its history of effect; ours is an argument for the historical reliability and facticity of Jesus of Nazareth being God in the flesh based on the Spirit's *re-presentation* of this biblical truth and its confirmation in our hearts.

In one segment on the Spiritual Presence, Tillich presents a potential aid for his own approach to the work of the Spirit within humans. He provides the interplay between the "inner word" of the Spirit and an external, established Word (ST 3.126). He wants to suggest that the Reformation idea of the relation and meaning of the "established" Word and Sacrament is not something to which God's Spirit may be bound, since "God is not bound to any of his manifestations" (ST 3.125). Those who follow "Spirit-movements" tend to eliminate the need for any mediation. As Frederick Parrella suggests, "While Tillich rejects the unmediated presence of the Spirit to spirit, as well as the concept of the 'inner word,' he emphasizes that 'God is not bound to any of his manifestations' (ST 3.124–126)."[35]

What is Tillich doing here? He seems to be taking away precisely what he could be using. He is allowing for some kind of "revelatory event" by the Spirit to provide an "immediate certainty of reunion with God," while not allowing for wordless mediations by this same Spirit (ST 3.127–128). It is this "inner word" that could be helpful to Tillich at this point. Pentecostals who have experienced the presence of the Spirit through such nonrational experiences as speaking in tongues or as groaning in the Spirit will find it odd that Tillich denies any wordless mediation to the Spirit. Why do I believe in the reliability of the history of Jesus as offered in the Gospels? It is not due to some word-filled, historically laden research that convinces me of its veracity; it is a wordless communication within my being that finds assurance by the Spirit for the truthfulness of the biblical records.[36] This helps me jump the ditch!

Christianity is like "the breathing-in of another air" (ST 3.236). There is something strange and exhilarating in the air of the Spirit! Christology, soteriology, and pneumatology belong together because Spiritual Presence integrates them in our lives. The certitude of our faith in Jesus as the Christ cannot be based on the contingencies of historical research, but still needs to relate to the historical happenings within time and space of our human history. Perhaps instead of an expressionist portrait, the biblical picture is one that combines the styles of naturalism (realism), impressionism, and expressionism. There needs to be enough historical *reality* in the portrait that believers understand this painting as reflecting events in human history; there needs to be enough force in the portrait to leave observers with an *impression* of God in Jesus Christ; and finally, there needs to be enough witness to the reality as experienced in the lives of the painters to impact observers with the sense that such paintings are an *expression* of God's presence upon the lives of painters.

Yet such a portrait is not enough—it is not *living or life-giving.* Only the Spirit of God can grasp the painters and observers in order to impact them with the powerful presence of New Being. While Tillich headed in the right direction by considering the Spirit as the source of power to make Lessing's leap, the depth and breadth of modernity's ugly ditch was too extensive for him to overcome. Today, history's ditch seems less expansive and demanding—yet there it is nonetheless! Only the Spirit of God can grasp us within the conditions of our existence in the twenty-first century and transport us over the ditch, bringing us face-to-face with the only one who can overcome our estrangement. The Spirit introduces us to Jesus Christ through the portrait offered by the first witnesses to his power and presence. Our inner certainty of faith rests on the Spirit's testimony to us; our inner certainty that the testimony of the first witnesses is based on reliable history also depends on the Spirit's inner testimony to us. In this way, christology, soteriology, and pneumatology are inseparably joined.

Notes

1. As cited in Russell Re Manning, "Tillich's Theology of Art," *The Cambridge Companion to Paul Tillich*, ed. Russell Re Manning (Cambridge: Cambridge University Press, 2009), 155.

2. For the phrase "the biblical picture of Jesus as the Christ," see *ST* 2.114–115, 126, 135.

3. These terms are from Paul Vogt, *Expressionismus: Deutsche Malerei zwischen 1905 und 1920* (Cologne: DuMont Buchverlag, 1992), 6. The translation is mine.

4. While one might argue that expressionism of a sort has always existed in art (that is, the subjective crafting of the painting of a subject according to the affect experienced by the painter and how she/he interprets that effect), the direct group of artists to whom Tillich refers are the Post-Impressionists, mainly in Germany from about 1905 to 1920. Hints of it may already be seen in Van Gogh, in Gauguin, and especially in Edvard Munch's *The Scream* (1893). Expressionism features a distortion of "reality" for the benefit of emotional effect on the observer. It is less concerned about the physical reality that can be found underlying the final portrait and more about the expressed meaning for the artist. Hence, distorted shapes and exaggerated colors abound in this style, delivering a potent impression on observers that frequently enhances a feeling of *Angst*. In this way, expressionism is an intensely personal form of artwork that reacted to individualism from positivism as well as naturalism. An excellent example that illustrates Tillich's point here might be the portrait by Georges Rouault called *Head of Christ* (1905). It provides "savage slashing strokes of the brush" that indicate the artist's "rage and compassion." One can easily see the head of Christ in this portrait—there is enough of the subject on the expressionist portrait to reveal this—but the eyes and face and brush-strokes draw the viewer powerfully into the image. The end result is a bold impression on the observer that can be described only with the word "power." See H. W. Janson, *History of Art,* 4th ed., rev. and expanded by Anthony F. Janson (Englewood Cliffs, NJ: Prentice-Hall, 1991), 712–713.

5. While is not precisely stated in this way in the English version of Tillich's *Systematic Theology,* this idea is so stated in the later German translation. See Tillich, *Systematische Theologie: Band II,* trans. Renate Albrecht and Gertraut Stöber (Stuttgart: Evangelisches Verlagswerk, 1958), 126–127.

6. It is interesting that the German edition adds the word *"Film"* after *"Photographie,"* whereas the English version parenthetically describes a possible corroboration by a "phonograph" or even a "psychograph," but not "film." See Tillich, *ST* 2.115; *Systematische Theologie,* 2.126.

7. As one representative of expressionism (Paul Klee) has described this style, it emphasizes the tragic relational split between the ego and the world. Because of this, art no longer was about reproducing again the visible world, but rather was about making it visible to the observers (as quoted in Paul Vogt, *Expressionismus,* 6). I find this expressionist approach to the Gospels quite profound and provocative.

8. Gottfried E. Lessing, "Über der Beweis des Geistes und der Kraft," in *Gesammelte Werke,* ed. Paul Rilla (Berlin: Aufbau-Verlag, 1956), 8:12, 14; English translation: "On the Proof of the Power of the Spirit and of Power," in *Lessing's Theological Writings,* ed. and trans. Henry Chadwick (Stanford: Stanford University Press, 1956), 53, 55.

9. Wilhelm Herrmann, *Der Verkehr des Christen mit Gott, in Anschluss an Luther Dargestellt,* Vierte Auflage, 4th ed. (Stuttgart: J. G. Cotta'sche Buchhandlung Nachfolger, 1903); English translation: *The Communion of the Christian with God, Described on the Basis of Luther's Statements,* ed. Robert T. Voeckl, trans. J. Sandys Stanyon and R. W. Stewart (Philadelphia: Fortress Press, 1971).

10. Tillich mentions Herrmann's approach as better than previous ones in relation to his work with Jesus, but he finds it failing due to the fact that no one can get back to the psychological interior of Jesus. Tillich asserts that we can never achieve certitude about the characteristics of Jesus' inner being because these "are always questionable and especially so in the case of Jesus" (*ST* 2.124).

11. Herrmann, *Communion,* 72. Tillich says precisely the same thing (*ST* 2.104).

12. Herrmann, *Communion,* 76.

13. Ibid., 102; *Verkehr,* 83. Here and in some of what follows I will either cite or include the original German text reference with the English translation when I highlight a word in German that has significance for the author's point but may not be as clearly delineated in English or may have other translation possibilities. This double referencing will lead the reader to the context of the original and the translation itself.

14. Herrmann, *Communion,* 78; *Verkehr,* 62.

15. Martin Kähler, *Der sogenannte historische Jesus und der geschichtliche, biblische Christus,* hrg. E. Wolf, Theologische Bücherei: Neudrucke und Berichte aus dem 20. Jahrhundert, Band 2, Systematische Theologie (München: Chr. Kaiser Verlag, 1953; orig. ed., 1896); English translation, *The So-Called Historical Jesus and the Historic Biblical Christ,* trans. Carl E. Braaten (Philadelphia: Fortress Press, 1964).

16. Paul Tillich, "Foreword," in *The So-Called Historical Jesus,* x.

17. Kähler, *The So-called Historical Jesus,* 81; emphasis his.

18. Kähler, *Der sogennante,* 60.

19. Kähler, *The So-called Historical Jesus,* 81.

20. Ibid., 74; emphasis his. Compare his statements in his later lecture in the same book: "Thus, we possess no historical documents concerning those specific events in which God's revelation took place—if at all—in the form of historical facts" (126).

21. Ibid., 76 (*Der sogenannte,* 54).

22. Kähler, *The So-called Historical Jesus,* 73, 77.

23. Ibid., 77, *Der sogenannte,* 55.

24. Ibid., 79 (*Der sogenannte,* 58).

25. Ibid., 87.

26. Ibid., 97.

27. In other places in volume 2, Tillich cites a "monophysitic tendency" in church history that leans toward removing the humanity of Jesus the Christ and replacing it with a thoroughly divine nature. See *ST* 1.127–128, 141, 145–146.

28. Paul Tillich, "A Reinterpretation of the Doctrine of the Incarnation," *Church Quarterly Review* 147: 294 (January–March, 1949): 136.

29. Ibid., 137. Tillich says similar things in *ST* 2.94–95, 133f., which is about eight years after the appearance of this article on the incarnation in 1949.

30. Bruce McCormack, "Why Should Theology be Christocentric? Christology and Metaphysics in Paul Tillich and Karl Barth," *Wesleyan Theological Journal* 45:1 (2010): 42–80; here, 60.

31. Anne Marie Reijnen, "Tillich's Christology," in *Cambridge Companion to Paul Tillich,* 70.

32. Compare the criticisms of Heywood Thomas and George Tavard as well as the overall critique of H. D. McDonald, as found in H. D. McDonald, "The Symbolic Christology of Paul Tillich," *Vox Evangelica* 18 (1988): 75–88, here 85. Also, Michael Palmer has said it very well in this regard: "If, following Tillich, the quest for an historical Jesus behind the Christological meaning of his being is truly irrelevant to theology, how can it be then maintained that the New Testament portrait of that man is not a fiction?" (as quoted in Reijnen, "Tillich's Christology," 70).

33. Steven J. Land, *Pentecostal Spirituality: A Passion for the Kingdom* (Sheffield: Sheffield Academic Press, 1993), 133.

34. Unlike Tillich, I view the incarnation as God becoming a human being under the conditions of finitude. I do not view the incarnation as a mere "appearance" of God, as if he were flesh, but rather that God became flesh and lived among us.

35. Frederick J. Parrella, "Tillich's Theology of the Concrete Spirit," in *Cambridge Companion to Paul Tillich,* 81.

36. I find John Calvin's "inner testimony of the Spirit," which he uses to establish the authority of Scripture and certainty of faith within believers, to be parallel to what I have described for the inner work of the Spirit in Pentecostals. See John Calvin, *Institutes of the Christian Religion,* 2 vols., trans. Ford Lewis Battles, ed. John T. McNeill (Philadelphia: Westminster Press, 1960), 78–79; sec.1.7.4.

SIX

Spiritual Presence

The Role of Pneumatology in Paul Tillich's Theology

FRANK D. MACCHIA

The pentecostal movement accents the work of the Holy Spirit. Although there is a sharp focus on Jesus Christ as the one who saves, heals, imparts the Spirit, and is coming again, the emphasis is on the fact that he is doing all of this now as a living presence in the power of the Spirit and as the one through whom the life of the Spirit is imparted. One does not have to read very far in the early literature of the movement to discover that the overwhelming attention is paid to how the human vessel is taken up into the presence and power of the Spirit in becoming a living channel of the Spirit in the world, as well as the signs or consequences that one might expect to witness as a result. Spirit baptism, broadly conceived as our participation in the eschatological self-impartation of God, is arguably the movement's chief accent.[1] As a theologian influenced by this pneumatological accent, I have had as one of my interests the question of how theological reflection on the first two Articles of the Creed might be viewed afresh from the Third Article. It is from this interest that I approach the theology of Paul Tillich, a person I have always admired as a theologian of the Spirit. My interest in reading him for this chapter is precisely on the role of the Spirit in Tillich's theological system.

Theology from the Third Article

Tillich's theology was arguably done with a priority granted the Holy Spirit. He wrote that the spiritual movements of the modern era (such as pietism) that impacted Schleiermacher had "essentially" influenced him as well (*ST* 3.126). In another context, he noted that, though he was intellectually indebted to Schelling, he regarded Schleiermacher as his spiritual father.[2] Hence, one is not surprised to find that Tillich's theology is implicitly pneumatological from the start, since he insists that doctrinal symbols must be discussed only in the light of the actual participation of faith in the ultimate reality to which the symbols point (*ST* 3.285). Tillich's entire emphasis on the language of faith as symbolic is pneumatological in that taking this language literally strips it of its power to function dynamically and transformatively as a vehicle of Spiritual Presence in grasping and overcoming ambiguous life. In considering doctrinal symbols, one thus takes into consideration the dynamics of faith as they relate to the concrete challenges of finite and estranged existence.

Is Tillich's theology in this light vulnerable to Barth's christological criticism of Schleiermacher's theology as centered on the human subject before God rather than on the divine self-disclosure as the ground and possibility of faith? Tillich is sympathetic with this criticism (*ST* 3.285), since his goal is to accent the revelatory situation symbolized for us and open to understanding through the participation of faith. But he charges that Barth's point of departure in trinitarian dogma appears as authoritarian pronouncements dropped down from heaven, "the heaven of an unmediated ecclesiastical authority" (*ST* 3.285). Tillich takes sides with Schleiermacher in maintaining that revelatory symbols arise from the participation of faith in the Spiritual Presence: "Schleiermacher is right when he derives these symbols from the different ways in which faith is related to its divine cause" (*ST* 3.285). Tillich, for example, claims in this light: "We speak of Spirit only because we have spirit; so, we speak of creation only because creative power is given to us" (*ST* 3.31). In another context, he writes that the doctrine of atonement as victory over estrangement makes sense only in the experience of New Being as a transformative and healing power: "Without the experience of the conquest of existential estrangement, the Christus Victor symbol could never have arisen" (*ST* 2.171). Tillich does not deny that there is "objective" validity to such doctrines; he only maintains that they arose and carry meaning in the context of a transformative and powerful participation in Spiritual Presence by faith. Doctrinal symbols like the Holy Spirit, creation, atonement, the Trinity, and salvation make sense from the vantage point of the participation of faith in the revelatory symbols. The fact that the symbols are "broken" means that they are finite and never to be taken as literal or as identifiable with the transcendent reality that takes hold of us in them. They are broken in order to facilitate an encounter with the Spirit.

The Spirit and the First Article

More specifically, Tillich's theology from the Third Article means that the Spirit is arguably the dominant and most encompassing way that Tillich talks about God. Such seems to be the case explicitly in the second two volumes of the *Systematic Theology* (which cover christology and pneumatology respectively). These volumes center on the chief revelatory event in which Christ is the central focus and the major impetus for the rise of the trinitarian dogma (*ST* 2.139). However, Tillich's system does grant the Spirit priority, even with regard to christology. David Kelsey thus wrote justifiably that it becomes "unmistakably clear in the last two parts of Tillich's theology that 'Spirit' is indeed his central theological term."[3]

The priority granted the Spirit may even be implied in the first volume of the *Systematic Theology* as well. Tillich wrote that "Spirit" is the "most embracing, direct, and unrestricted symbol for the divine life" (*ST* 3.249). Kelsey goes so far as to maintain that God for Tillich "is simply identified with the 'divine Spirit'" and that within his understanding of the Trinity "the Spirit has a certain priority to the other two persons."[4] Tillich's understanding of all three trinitarian symbols, God as creative power, saving love, and ecstatic transformation, have a pneumatological quality (*ST* 3.283). We think of the Spirit when we think of power, love, and transformation. Kelsey writes that in referring to God as creator (ground of being, responding to finitude), Christ (responding to estrangement), and Spirit (responding to ambiguity of life), Tillich actually maintains throughout that Spirit or Spiritual Presence "is the most embracing symbol for God, the symbol that embraces all three of these aspects together."[5] In describing Tertullian's doctrine of the Logos in God, Tillich remarks that the Logos as the "inner word" in God is "characteristic of spiritual existence." He concludes: "If we say God is Spirit, we must also say he is trinitarian; he has the word within himself and has the unity with his self-objectivation."[6] The implication is that Spirit functions as the most encompassing symbol of God's own self-objectivation, even ecstatic self-transcendence, into which all of creation is drawn. When Tillich's friend Nels F. S. Ferré found a tension in Tillich's thought between his more abstract philosophical ways of referring to God, such as the Ground of Being, and his preference developed after the first volume of the *Systematic Theology* for the dynamic concept of *Spirit*, he discussed with Tillich the possibility of reworking the entire *Systematic Theology* with Spirit language as the primary means for referring to God, and he found Tillich agreeing "that this could and should be done."[7] One might say that Tillich's system reaches for such a development. Tillich's system implies the development of the First Article of the Creed from the vantage point of God as the universal Spirit. Tillich could very well have started with the universal Spirit and then worked from there to God's decisive and ultimate manifestation in the Christ and then to a dynamic understanding of the Ground of Being, Articles 1 and 2 understood from the vantage point of Article 3.

Actually, one may argue that Tillich reaches for such a methodological move, using the Third Article of the Creed to avoid abstractions in the first two Articles and to understand them in the context of God's participation in creation and creation in God. Interestingly, he defends his use of the term "Being" for God by stating that this term, "the emptiest of all concepts when taken as an abstraction, becomes the most meaningful of all concepts when it is understood as the power of being in everything that has being" (*ST* 2.11). Tillich elaborates that "the experience of God as the 'living God' and not as dead identity is a work of the Spiritual Presence" (*ST* 3.286). In fact, Tillich's fundamental theological quest from the time he was a doctoral student was to respond to Kant's vision of the human being as faced with a moral imperative but to view this Kantian challenge from the vantage point of our captivity to the estrangement and ambiguities of finite existence. Tillich's crucial problem thus lay in how to understand our capacity to find unity with our ideal essence while caught in the throes of finitude and estrangement. He was not willing to view the rescue of humanity from finitude and the grip of moral failure as possible through a pantheism that simply identified the human spirit as the Infinite. Such a flight from finite existence does not take seriously enough the conditions of estrangement that hold finite humanity in their grip. Neither did he resort to a supernatural dualism that has the Spirit encounter us from a location separate from the human spirit. That would be to take less than seriously God's infinity by objectifying God as also a finite being standing over against the finite creature. Tillich's eventual solution was to conceive of God as the Spiritual *Presence* that may be described as the "depth" from which the human spirit is driven out of itself without losing itself: "Spiritual Presence is the dimension of depth" (*ST* 3.113). This experience is dialectically described as both distinct from and in unity with the self-transcending human spirit. God is the powerful and transformative "depth" or ground of being from which the human spirit is grasped and to which it strives in its drive for self-actualization and self-transcendence, including the fragmentary or ambiguous fulfillment of the moral imperative.[8] For Tillich, viewed from the vantage point of Spiritual Presence, Being is experienced as power, namely, that infinite depth from which one reaches for an infinite horizon, only to discover that both depth and horizon are indistinguishable as subject and object are transcended in a moment of self-transcending ecstasy.

The Spirit and the Second Article

God as source and sustainer of life is described above as "the power of being in *everything* that has being" (*ST* 2.11, emphasis mine), implying a universal pneumatology that is vital to all being and life. New Being is thus integral to being. Indeed, Tillich notes that "to some degree all men participate in the healing power of New Being. Otherwise, they would have no being" (*ST* 2.11). This construal of the First Article in the light of the Third will have radical implications for Tillich's understanding of the Second Article, namely, christology, the central, decisive, and ultimate actualization of New Being on the stage of history. In the light of the Third Article, Jesus as the Christ becomes the embodiment of the *universal Spirit* at the essence of "healing and saving power through the New Being" everywhere and at all times (*ST* 2.167). Jesus as the Christ is thus not the only means by which New Being grasps and heals humanity—obviously not, since this is to some degree a universal experience. Neither is he the only manifestation of the New Being or the Spiritual Presence in the world or in history (*ST* 2.144). However, he is everywhere to be viewed as "the *decisive* embodiment of the New Being for historical mankind" (*ST* 2.144, emphasis mine). He is the decisive and "ultimate" manifestation of New Being (*ST* 3.147). For Tillich, "Christ is the one who brings the new eon" (*ST* 2.118). He manifests universal Spiritual Presence in a way that represents its central actualization in history for all times and places. In the original experience of Jesus as the risen Christ he was inseparably united among the earliest Christians with the New Being so that participation in him became participation in New Being: "In an ecstatic experience, the concrete picture of Jesus of Nazareth became indissolubly united with the New Being. He is present wherever the New Being is present" (*ST* 2.157). The symbol of the incarnation arose as meaningful in the church from the fact that this unison between New Being and Jesus as the Christ was viewed as eternal (*ST* 2.149). We thus know Christ precisely as the eternal Spirit: "In this way, the concrete individual life of the man Jesus of Nazareth is raised above transitoriness into the eternal Presence of God as Spirit" (*ST* 2.157). The result is that the Christ thus becomes the enduring criterion for all spiritual experience: "Every new manifestation of the Spiritual Presence stands under the criterion of his manifestation in Jesus as the Christ" (*ST* 2.148).

This point about the universal significance of Jesus as the one who actualizes New Being in history helps Tillich to distinguish his christology from adoptionism. For Tillich there is in the Christ an uninterrupted unity between God and humanity that sets him apart as unique (*ST* 2.149). Participation in the Spiritual Presence or the New Being *is* participation in the Christ. A universal pneumatology implies a universal christology. The key for Tillich's pneumatological christology is Christ as the central event that makes possible God's decisive participation in existential estrangement and suffering and the focal point for our participation in the Spiritual Presence or New Being. Tillich thus sees the unity with our essence through being grasped by Spiritual Presence to be an experience that grants a real (though fragmentary and ambiguous) experience of overcoming estrangement and ambiguity in wholeness and self-transcendence. Tillich thus distinguishes his christology from Schleiermacher's precisely here: namely, Schleiermacher's view of Christ as the *Urbild* (essential humanity) is abstract, merely representing the "idealistic transcendence of true humanity over human existence," while Tillich wishes to add that in Christ the union with true human essence (*Urbild*) through union with the New Being is actualized in existence through dynamic participation. He maintains that for Schleiermacher "*Urbild* remains removed above existence," but for him "the New Being participates in existence and conquers it" (*ST* 2.150). For Tillich, "the participation of him who is also the *Urbild* ('essential man') is decisive" (*ST* 2.150). Tillich's pneumatological christology stresses participation in New Being or Spiritual Presence by Christ and (to a degree) by us.

The Christ is for Tillich the "word" in that he is the final manifestation of God to humanity, and "the word is the bearer of spiritual life" (*ST* 2.121). If "Christology is a function of soteriology" (*ST* 2.150) for Tillich, christology is arguably also a function of pneumatology. The incarnation is thus not a literal metamorphosis of God (or God's Son) into flesh (for Tillich, a pagan idea) but is rather symbolic of God's "total manifestation in a personal life" (*ST* 2.149). The abstract two-nature christology of Chalcedon is symbolic of a deeper participation of creative and transformative New Being in the estrangement and ambiguities of life in a way that overcomes them (*ST* 2.146–147). Tillich's pneumatological christology is participationist: Christ participates in finite estrangement so as to conquer it as the manifestation in history of the Spiritual Presence and to provide the revelatory situation from which we also participate in this Spiritual Presence (e.g., *ST* 2.146–147, 150). Tillich's pneumatological "participationist" christology may be described as functional and not substantialist (Tillich defines his christology as "dynamic-relational" [*ST* 2.148]), and it is functional in a way that navigates its way in between identification and dualism. The Spirit is not to be identified with the spirit of Jesus, but neither is the Spirit something separate from Jesus. The Spirit is the power of New Being that drives the spirit of Jesus from its ultimate depth toward self-transcendence and self-sacrificial love in a way that conquers the distortions of finite existence and provides the focus for our participation in the Spiritual Presence (*ST* 2.143–146). In Christ we powerfully grasp "participation through the divine participation, accepting it and being transformed by it" (*ST* 2.176).

More specifically, Tillich ends up with a pneumatological understanding of the atonement. Christ on the cross is not an objective "substitute" for humanity but rather the means by which he "participates" in our estrangement and we participate in his New Being (*ST* 2.173). According to Tillich, we should not say that such participation is only possible through Christ's atonement; it is rather that the atonement centrally, decisively, and ultimately manifests or actualizes the Spirit's universal participation in humanity and humanity in the Spirit. Jesus is not the only but is "the decisive embodiment of the New Being for historical mankind" (*ST* 2.144). Jesus is the central and decisive manifestation of divine-human participation because "divine Spirit was present in Jesus as the Christ without distortion. In him the New Being appeared as the criterion of all spiritual experiences in past and future" (*ST* 2.144). "Every new manifestation of the Spiritual Presence stands under the criterion of his manifestation in Jesus as the Christ" (*ST* 2.148).

Tillich's Pneumatological View of Faith

Tillich's viewing theology from the lens of the Third Article of the Creed means that faith is primarily viewed as a pneumatological rather than an anthropological possibility. Tillich views faith also from the vantage point of participation in the universal Spirit, meaning that everyone who implicitly expresses ultimate concern in a direction consistent with the appearance of New Being in Christ reveals a being grasped by the Spiritual Presence (*ST* 2.131). In a Christian context, faith is explicitly understood as a gift of the divine Spirit: "Faith, justifying faith, is not a human act, although it happens in man; faith is the work of the divine Spirit, the power which creates the New Being, in Christ, in individuals, in the church" (*ST* 2.178). Here is where Tillich connects once more with Schleiermacher's legacy. This legacy was arguably to confront the Enlightenment myth of human autonomy with a focus on absolute dependence on God's Spirit for our awareness of and participation in the divine. Schleiermacher famously argued in his little book *On Religion: Speeches to Its Cultured Despisers* that the religious *a priori* is not a human faculty like the intellect or Kant's moral will but is rather an openness to (or, he would later say, absolute dependence upon) the Infinite as disclosed to us in faith.[9] In Tillich's *Dynamics of Faith*, which can be read as a contemporary response to Schleiermacher's *On Religion*, Tillich rightly notes that Schleiermacher's notion of faith as *Gefühl* (feeling) is not emotion as a mere psychological capacity but is "unconditional dependence, a phrase related to what we have called ultimate concern."[10] Tillich's understanding of Schleiermacher's *Gefühl* as unconditional dependence implies an anthropology oriented toward God in a way that is fundamentally determined by God. Whatever human potential exists for this dependence, it is actualized only by divine power; otherwise the ultimate basis for its actualization would be conditional upon our autonomous cooperation and would not be unconditional dependence. Following Schleiermacher, faith for Tillich is by nature ultimate concern, oriented to and determined by the ultimate. Faith must be a gift by the Spirit, for "there is no finite way of reaching the infinite."[11] Religion is fundamentally explained not through an anthropological *a priori* but rather, implicitly, through a pneumatological one: "The divine Spirit takes hold of a personal life through the creation of faith" (*ST* 3.222).

Of course, faith for Tillich does involve passionate emotions; "but emotion does not produce faith."[12] Faith cannot be confused with emotional outbursts or feelings of rapture, though it can involve such things. Faith for Tillich also includes a cognitive component, but only "as an inseparable element in a total act of acceptance and surrender."[13] If one reduces faith to a cognitive act, faith would be confused with mere belief.[14] It would lose its quality as a living reality. Similarly, faith involves the will, but "faith is not a creation of the will."[15] To reduce faith to an act of the will is to confuse it with a mere act of obedience to a moral imperative.[16] As a Lutheran, Tillich was keenly aware of how devastating a reduction of faith to moral obedience can be. He thus sought to view ambiguous finite existence as taken up in the Spiritual Presence, which confirms the unconditional nature of the moral imperative as it relates to respecting persons, but also provides the means by which one may live by the Spirit in grace (ST 3.45). "The Spirit elevates the person into the transcendent unity of the divine life" and in so doing "it reunites the estranged existence of the person with his essence" (ST 3.272). And this reunion "is just what the moral law commands and what makes the moral imperative unconditionally valid" (ST 3.272). In sum, faith assumes "being grasped and changed by Spiritual Presence," without which faith is degraded "into a belief, an intellectual act produced by will and emotion" (ST 3.222). Human capacities cannot ultimately account for the reality of faith. In other words, the philosophical effort to understand how the Infinite rescues us from the finite drove Tillich intellectually to Schelling, but his spiritual quest was shaped by Schleiermacher's "pietistic" theology of the Third Article.

By defining faith pneumatologically, Tillich enriches a Protestant heritage that had impoverished spirituality by tending to define faith as a mental assent rather than as a yielding to the Spirit. He wrote that it was a "pitfall" in Protestant theology when Melanchthon placed the reception of the Spirit after the act of faith. Through this, "faith became an intellectual work of man, made possible without participation in the New Being" (ST 2.178). Faith as an intellectual capacity is impossible in part because of the pneumatological nature of revelation (ST 2.166–167). The Spiritual Presence grants not abstract meaning but rather "meaning-bearing power which grasps the human spirit in ecstatic experience" (ST 3.115). He held this view of faith as participation in Christ decades before it became popular through the Finnish interpretation of Luther.[17]

Tillich thus defines love as integral to the faith that receives justification rather than as a mere moral command, as the Reformers tended to see it in distinction from justifying faith. He wrote that "faith is the state of being grasped by the transcendent unity of unambiguous life—it embodies love as the state of being taken into that transcendent unity" (ST 3.131). The quality of our love, however, is not the basis of justification. In justification, "we surrender our goodness to God" and affirm unambiguous life in the midst of the ambiguity and estrangement of finite existence (ST 3.224). Justifying faith as a transformative reality also locates justification within regeneration and healing as the more encompassing soteriological reality. Tillich is adamant in maintaining that "faith means being grasped by a power that is greater than we are, a power that shakes us and turns us, and transforms us and heals us."[18] Indeed, "there is no faith (but only belief) without the Spirit's grasping the personal center of him who is in the state of faith, and this is a mystical experience, an experience of the presence of the infinite in the finite"; for this reason, Tillich maintains that one should follow the pietists in placing regeneration (defined as a transformative participation in New Being) before justification (ST 3.242). Tillich is clear that justification is, first, by the healing power of grace, before it is ever by faith understood as our participation in this healing. It is justification by grace before it is through faith (ST 2.179). Justification is thus the overcoming of ambiguous finite existence in the acceptance of unambiguous life through the Spirit. In this acceptance of unambiguous life in the midst of ambiguity (wholeness in the midst of estrangement) one feels the "in spite of," about which Luther wrote, but in a way that is not detached from life.

Humans caught up in the Spiritual Presence by faith can grasp unambiguous life only fragmentarily and ambiguously. Consistent with pentecostal piety, Tillich uses Paul's "groanings too deep for words" in Romans 8:26 as the point of departure for making his case that faith is an acceptance of the unity or wholeness of life in the midst of finite estrangement. This groaning implies for Tillich that we reflect within our awareness of the divine the priority of the Spiritual Presence in the finite participation in the Infinite. "Man is the mirror in which the relation of everything finite to the infinite becomes conscious" (ST 3.87). Following Schleiermacher, Tillich assumes that the point of contact with God is pneumatologically and not anthropologically enabled. Empirical investigation can only fathom finite interdependencies and not the relation of the finite to the infinite as determined by God for God (ST 3.87). The groaning in the Spirit cannot be objectified or studied as a mere anthropological possibility. It is rather an experience of grace that takes one outside of oneself without the loss of self, an experience described as *ecstasy*. The human spirit is driven out of itself without losing itself (its rational structure). "'Ecstasy' means 'standing outside of oneself'—without ceasing to be oneself with all the elements which are united in the personal center."[19]

The ecstatic experience of Spiritual Presence does something that the human spirit cannot do for itself, namely, grasp unambiguous life. "Man in self-transcendence can reach for it, but he cannot grasp it, unless he is first grasped by it" (ST 3.112). As Tillich describes it, "the divine Spirit breaks into the human spirit; this does not mean that it rests there, but that it drives the human spirit out of itself. Faith as an ecstatic experience means that the 'in' of the divine Spirit is the 'out' of the human spirit" (ST 3.112). Ecstasy for Tillich "is the classical term for this state of being grasped by Spiritual Presence. It describes the human situation under the Spiritual Presence exactly" (ST 3.112). Ecstasy is not first a psychological state that can be studied or grasped. It is mirrored within human consciousness of the divine reality that drives us toward the Ultimate. The Ultimate is thus not one dimension among others but is rather their depth and horizon, "the ground of being of them all and the aim towards which they are self-transcendent" (ST 3.113). The Ultimate is the Spirit, who "elevates the person into the transcendent unity of the divine life and in so doing it reunites the estranged existence of the person with his essence" (ST 3.272). Tillich calls Paul's groaning too deep for words the "classical expression of the self-transcendence of life under all dimensions" (ST 3.87). It is characteristic of faith and of all prayer. Tillich thus maintains that the ecstasy of faith is profoundly revealed in the act of prayer. Ecstasy through unspeakable groans means that "every prayer is impossible for the human spirit" (ST 3.116–117). It involves "an ecstatic participation in the Christ who 'is the Spirit,' whereby one lives in the sphere of this Spiritual power" (ST 3.117).

One is not surprised to find Tillich defending speaking in tongues, writing to those who wish to "psychologize" this gift as a mere human capacity that they must in this case face the same criticism concerning the life of faith in general (ST 3.118). The implication here is that tongues is connected to something characteristic of faith itself, namely, an ecstatic groaning for the full unity of essence and existence in the Spiritual Presence. For Tillich, the groanings too deep for words thus implies a divine taking hold of the human spirit throughout the entire act of faith, throughout all of prayer. Ecstasy means that God transcends the cleavage between the praying subject and God as "object" of the prayer. Prayer makes God an object, but the object becomes subject as God "prays to himself through us" (ST 3.120). All prayer is ecstatic in some sense, revealing that God is the one who is experienced as both subject and object, transcending both: "Prayer is a possibility only in so far as the subject–object structure is overcome; hence, it is an ecstatic possibility," and ecstasy is thus the "essential character of prayer" (ST 3.120). This ecstatic experience of unambiguous life is eschatological: "The New Being is fragmentarily and anticipatorily present, but in so far as it is present it is so unambiguously" (ST 3.140).

Spiritual Community: The Unity of Diverse Tongues

The church is also at core a pneumatological reality for Tillich. Though not to be confused with Spiritual Community, the institutional church lives from this and manifests it, though imperfectly. Ecstasy for Tillich allows the church to manifest Spiritual Community right in the midst of ambiguous human structures (structure is not thereby abandoned). There is thus implied in ecstasy a resistance to any institutionalization of the Spirit or the reduction of the Spirit to moral action or psychological states. Tillich faults Christianity for early on abandoning the ecstatic character of faith in favor of "doctrinal or moral structure" or an institutionalization of the Spirit that seeks to replace charisma with ecclesiastical office (ST 3.117). Tillich, however, also warns that mindless ecstasy at the neglect of rational, moral, or institutional structure can be destructive to faith and must be avoided: "The Spiritual Presence is not an intoxicating substance, or a stimulus for psychological excitement" (ST 3.275). The participation of the community in all dimensions of its being in sacrament and Word remains important for encountering Spiritual Presence (ST 3.120). The sacrament "participates in the power of what it symbolizes, and therefore, it can be a medium of the Spirit" (ST 3.123). Similarly, the Word of God becomes such through the Spirit as its words "grasp the human spirit" (ST 3.124). Though legitimate as mediums of the Spirit, sacrament and Word still remain vital as guides and contexts for ecstasy. God is not bound to these mediums, but neither can they be replaced by inner spiritual illumination (ST 3.125–128). The church is thus to fight against chaotic and destructive ecstasy. True, we are to allow the deep groaning in the Spirit to help us to avoid a profane and reductionist institutionalization of faith, but we are also not to abandon structure altogether. For Tillich, ecstasy, "in its transcendence of the subject–object structure, is the great liberating power under the dimension of self-awareness" (ST 3.119). In support of revelatory self-awareness in relation to the other, Tillich wants to avoid a spiritual intoxication that represents an escape from the dimension of spirit with its burden of personal centeredness and responsibility. He writes: "He who prays earnestly is aware of his own situation and his neighbor's, but he sees it under the Spiritual Presence's influence and in the light of the divine direction of life's processes" (ST 3.119).

Tillich also wanted to avoid a realized eschatology through flights of ecstasy that seeks to escape entirely the conditions of finite existence so as to remove doubt entirely from faith. The "in spite of" characteristic of justification in the Spirit never leaves us as the church in this age (ST 3.167). "There is regenerative power in the churches, even in their miserable state" (ST 3.168). Experiences and expressions of Spiritual Presence are fraught with ambiguities and distortions. Yet, self-sacrificial love of Christ remains at the heart of ecstasy. He writes of Christ's love as "embodied in his being and radiating from him in a world in which agape was and is known only in ambiguous expressions" (ST 3.145). The pietists rightly knew in criticism of Protestant orthodoxy, that doctrinal accuracy could not accomplish the suppression of doubt, so they sought that through transcendent experiences of union with the infinite. Yet, such experiences cannot remove the distance between the finite self and the infinite. Doubt remains an element of faith. Indeed, "even the most immediate and intimate union with the divine, as in the bride-mysticism describing the union of the Christ and the soul, cannot bridge the infinite distance between the finite self and the infinite by which it is grasped" (ST 3.240). Yet, the ecstatic encounter with Spiritual Presence does offer a genuine grasping of unambiguous life. Such an experience of the Spiritual Presence can have extraordinary effects, such as "knowledge of strange tongues, penetration into the innermost thoughts of another person, and healing influence, even at a distance" (ST 3.115).

Ecstasy thus involves the healing of life and its structures rather than their abandonment. There is not to be a supernaturalistic dualism that abandons creation but rather the healing of creation in its implicit struggle by the universal Spirit for self-integration, growth, and self-transcendence in reaching for unambiguous life in the midst of finite estrangement (ST 3.31–32, 117–119). The Spiritual Presence is experienced in holistic ways, in all dimensions of human existence: "The multidimensional unity of life means that the impact of Spiritual Presence on the human spirit is *at the same time,* an impact on the psyche, the cells, and the physical elements that constitute man" (ST 3.276). This is not an "impact" in the causal sense, as though a divine supernatural force is coming at the human from the outside. Such would be to make the Spirit a finite and material participant in history, albeit an extraordinary one. Tillich rather seeks to understand the Spirit's effects in life as from the depths or ground of existence, within existence itself "as a presence which participates in the object of its impact" so as to transcend the category of finite causality (ST 3.276). Healing by faith is not to be confused with the autosuggestion of faith healers, though such suggestions can have certain healing effect (ST 3.278–279).

Tillich sees healing in Spiritual Presence as implicit in nature as graced by the Spirit. Grace does not destroy nature but rather unites it to the true essence that it seeks by grace and in its concrete existence to grasp: "The Spiritual Presence maintains the identity of the self without impoverishing the self, and it drives toward the alteration of the self without disrupting it" (ST 3.269). Of course, "God does not need to destroy this created world, which is good in its essential nature, in order to manifest himself in it" (ST 3.115, see also 114). As we have implied above, Tillich lifted up healing and regeneration as his overriding metaphor for salvation. Since the healing metaphor for salvation uniquely marks Wesleyan and pentecostal soteriologies, Tillich's soteriology would be in many ways friendly to the pentecostal cause.[20]

Pentecost is the model for describing key aspects of the church as living from Spiritual Community. Pentecost for Tillich is thus an event of new creation by the Spirit. This event implies the creation of community through the experience of ecstasy ("without ecstasy, there is no Spiritual Community" [ST 3.151]);

the creation of faith by the Spirit, which was nearly destroyed at Christ's crucifixion; the creation of love, which involves mutual service; the creation of unity
of diverse tongues (the reversal of Babel); and the missionary drive of those
grasped by the Spiritual Presence (ST 3.151–152). In the light of the universal
Spirit, Tillich will not confine Spiritual Community to the visible church. It is
"latent" in communities everywhere that are grasped by the Spiritual Presence
and manifest it; many "show the power of New Being in an impressive way"
(ST 3.153).

Tillich places a great deal of stress on the communal dimension of ecstasy
or life grasped by the Spiritual Presence. Ecstatic participation in the Spiritual
Presence is individual but not individualistic. One recalls that the "in" of the
divine Spirit is the "out" of the human spirit in acceptance of the other. Ecstasy
is the coming out of oneself for the sake of the other without disrupting or de-
stroying the self. This is for Tillich a profoundly moving experience of self-transcendence in the Spirit, but it is not to be confused with mere emotion or with
any other human faculty such as cognition or will (though it involves all three).
This communal bond through corporate self-transcendence and self-giving is the
work of the Spirit giving rise to faith and love. The ecstasy of faith and love does
not dissolve differences. It involves "the immense diversity of beings with regard to sex, race, age, nation, tradition, and character—typological as well as individual" (ST 3.157). Tillich saw the loss of Jesus' acceptance of the outcast in the
churches as their chief denial of Christ (ST 3.206). The unity of many "tongues"
is a unity in diversity in which otherness is respected and embraced.

Pentecostal Assessment

There is much that can be said from a pentecostal perspective concerning
Tillich's theology from the Third Article. His theology helps us to understand
how the Christ event fulfills the Spirit's work in all of creation. All being lives
from the New Being because all being lives from the Spiritual Presence. Yet,
Christ as the decisive and ultimate actualization of New Being is indissolubly united with Spiritual Presence for all times and places, so that one's being
grasped by New Being is being grasped in Christ, whether one knows this or
not. Tillich also highlights a participatory understanding of the Christ event
that creates a seamless connection between atonement and Pentecost. In atonement, the New Being in Christ participates fully in the estrangement and suffering of the creature and provides the focal point for our being grasped by New
Being in the midst of our estrangement. The "in spite of" characteristic of justification by faith is, therefore, not detached from life but is rather the ambiguous
grasping of unambiguous life. Faith as ecstatic participation in Spiritual Presence is pneumatological to the core. Tillich's fundamental concern is pentecos-

tal, namely, "How may the finite and estranged human vessel become grasped and directed by the divine Spirit?"[21]

There is also rich potential for dialogue with pentecostals in Tillich's ecstatic understanding of faith and life in the Spirit. J. Rodman Williams's assessment of Tillich's theology of the Third Article, the only one by a pentecostal or charismatic of which I am aware, praised Tillich's resistance to an institutionalization of the Spirit and openness to "ecstatic" experiences of the Spirit such as speaking in tongues. He also appreciated Tillich's stress on salvation and healing through the Spirit's presence within.[22] Referring to the charismatic or "neo-pentecostal" movement, he wrote that Tillich is "clearly an ally of all of us who are seeking to bear witness to the dynamic movement of the Spirit presently occurring."[23] His basic problem with Tillich, however, is his lifting up the universal "mutual immanence" between the divine Spirit with the human spirit as the basis for understanding Jesus' redemptive work, viewing the latter as manifesting universal salvation. Williams wants to reserve the salvific work of the Spirit to that which is received through conscious faith in Christ, "only for those who through faith in Jesus Christ are indwelt by Jesus Christ."[24] For Williams, Tillich "weights too much on the Spirit" as the point of departure rather than on the redemption initiated and made possible by Christ. In other words, Christ is not to be viewed as the central or decisive actualization of the universal Spiritual Presence in all wholeness wherever it is found; Christ is not to be identified from this reality. The Spiritual Presence is rather to be defined from Christ and his redemptive work, accessible only through conscious faith in him.[25]

This criticism is significant and would be shared by most Pentecostals. One can ask, however, in the context of rejecting salvific universalism, is it not still possible to affirm salvific "elements" in the experience of the Spirit of Christ that sustains humanity and through which they have their being (Acts 17:28)? Moreover, there is a growing recognition among pentecostal scholars of the need to integrate the redemptive and healing work of Christ more intimately with the Spirit at work in all of humanity, in all of creation.[26] In response to Williams, one might argue that Tillich is sensitive to the Old Testament understanding of the Spirit of God as intimately at work in creation including within the human spirit, to the point where Spirit and spirit can seem functionally one, though still distinct.[27] Tillich is clear that there is an ontological distinction between Spirit and spirit; the two are not simply to be identified. Yet, dialectically, they are one. Tillich helpfully couches this dialectical understanding within the language of infinite depth and horizon from which and to which the human spirit reaches. To see Christ as the ultimate revelation of the work of the divine Spirit in history represents an ancient christology that offers hope for redressing the one-sided emphasis on the Spirit's witness to the crucified and risen Christ. The crucified and risen Christ can then be seen as the fulfillment of the work of the Spirit in history in empathy with the suffering creation and in providing the power by which life is renewed and reaches implicitly for immortality. Pentecostal pneumatology can use Tillich as a resource for a renewal theology that overcomes dualistic supernaturalism or the neglect of a creation pneumatology as integral to the salvific and empowering work of the Spirit, including the Spirit's *charismata*.

Yet, is Tillich's christology tilted too far in the direction of the Third Article? Oneness Pentecostals also see Christ as the incarnation of God's "inner word," but view this inner word not as an eternal person but rather as God's inner mind or purpose. Otherwise, Christ is the incarnation of God in that Christ fully and decisively embodies the divine Spirit. The risen Christ is now identical with the Spirit.[28] How would their pneumatological christology differ from Tillich's? Though they would criticize Tillich's universalist implications (among other things), they would, I presume, find a definite affinity with his pneumatological christology. They are often accused of being too christocentric, but I have always suspected that their christocentrism was all about the Spirit, more so than I would be willing to accept as a trinitarian pentecostal. I appreciate the move of interpreting Christ from the vantage point of the work of the universal Spirit in creation, but it is the eternal Son who is incarnate in Christ; the Spirit mediates this incarnation and remains integral to the role of Jesus as the presence of the Son in flesh, bearing the Spirit and cooperating with the Spirit for our renewal. In quarreling with Tillich's pneumatological christology, however, I am in some sense (I believe!) engaging in an argument internal to the pentecostal movement.

More broadly, however, the role of Tillich's symbology problematically excludes any notion of the divine action in history, including creation, incarnation, resurrection, and Pentecost. These are not mere symbols that facilitate power-bearing meaning. Tom Driver rightly notes that even Tillich's notion of "power of Being" is not dynamic enough to support a dramatic understanding of the divine participation in the divine-human drama.[29] In a similar vein, Kevin Vanhoozer asks Hans Urs Balthasar's question as to "whether God can enter a drama that takes place in the world and play a part in it, without becoming mythological."[30] Tillich would alter this question to say "becoming finite" rather than "becoming mythological," since he has no problem with mythological language per se, since such is the indispensable language of religion. Tillich's point is rather that if this language is taken literally so that God really does become an actor in the drama, God becomes finite and one is trapped within a supernatural dualism. Are these the only alternatives: either a real divine action that turns God into a finite actor or a symbolic notion of salvation-historical events that reduces the language to mere transformative meanings? I find Tillich's notion of the Spirit as the living ground and horizon of self-transcending life to be promising (though limited) in significance, and I also agree that the narrative of the divine action is symbolic and not to be taken too literally. But I cannot merely reduce the divine action to power-bearing or transformative meanings within the person's ecstatic experience of the Spirit from the depths. Is it not possible for God to project Godself into the human drama as a real player in the developing drama without losing divine freedom and transcendence? Is it not possible to recognize the symbolic significance of the narrative without losing this insight?

Williams had a right to feel uneasy with Tillich's Spirit-centered theology, though not so much (in my view) for the reason he gives. The Spirit can certainly be a point of departure, but not to the point of so overshadowing the other two Articles that they are stripped of their capacity to depict a divine action in history outside the context of the human experience of self-transcendence. One cannot collapse the first two Articles into the third! After all, the Spirit is also the Spirit of the heavenly Father and of the eternal Son, dependent on them as they are on her. This means that incarnation is not merely a broken symbol of the eternal significance of the unity between Jesus and the Spiritual Presence. It metaphorically depicts the eternal Son in some actual sense becoming flesh for our salvation in cooperation with the eternal Spirit (the depth and horizon of creaturely life). There are real miracles to behold that no power-bearing meaning, no matter how inspirational, can in and of itself provide a sufficient substitute for.

Notes

1. See my development of this idea in Frank D. Macchia, *Baptized in the Spirit: A Global Pentecostal Theology* (Grand Rapids, MI: Zondervan, 2006).

2. As reported by Nels F. S. Ferré, "Tillich and the Nature of Transcendence," in *Paul Tillich: Retrospect and Future* (Nashville: Abingdon, 1966), 7–18 (11).

3. David H. Kelsey, *The Fabric of Paul Tillich's Theology,* (New Haven: Yale University Press, 1967), 82.

4. Ibid., 82–83. He points to this statement from Tillich: "The divine Spirit, or God, present to man's spirit, breaks into all history in revelatory experiences which have both a saving and transforming character" (*ST* 3.140).

5. Kelsey, *The Fabric of Paul Tillich's Theology,* 168.

6. Paul Tillich, *A History of Christian Thought: From Its Judaic and Hellenistic Origins to Existentialism* (New York: Simon and Schuster, 1967), 46.

7. Ferré, "Tillich and the Nature of Transcendence," 16.

8. I agree with Kelsey that in the term "depth" Tillich comes the closest to ontologically defining God's relation to creation. Kelly, *The Fabric of Paul Tillich's Theology,* 85.

9. Friedrich Schleiermacher, *On Religion: Speeches to Its Cultured Despisers* (New York: Cambridge University Press, 1996).

10. Paul Tillich, *Dynamics of Faith* (New York: Harper Brothers, 1958), 38–39.

11. Ibid., 14.

12. Tillich, *Dynamics of Faith*, 8.

13. Ibid., 7.

14. Ibid., 31.

15. Ibid., 7.

16. Ibid., 37.

17. This school of thought seeks to use Luther's understanding of faith as a living participation in Christ in order to connect with the Eastern Orthodox understanding of salvation as theosis. See Carl E. Braaten and Robert W. Jenson, eds., *Union with Christ: The New Finnish Interpretation of Luther* (Grand Rapids, MI: Eerdmans, 1998).

18. Paul Tillich, *The Shaking of the Foundations* (New York: Charles Scribner's Sons, 1955), 38.

19. Tillich, *Dynamics of Faith*, 7.

20. See Kimberly Alexander, *Pentecostal Healing: Models in Theology and Practice* (Journal of Pentecostal Theology Supplement) (Blandford Forum, UK: Deo, 2006).

21. See my development of this pneumatological soteriology (partly in dialogue with Tillich) in, Frank D. Macchia, *Justified in the Spirit: Creation, Redemption, and the Triune God* (Grand Rapids, MI: Eerdmans, 2010).

22. Though he does not prefer the term "ecstasy" to describe it. J. Rodman Williams, *Era of the Spirit* (Plainfield, NJ: Logos, 1971), 85–99.

23. Ibid., 96.

24. Ibid., 96–97.

25. Ibid.

26. One could mention here, for example, the work of Amos Yong. See Amos Yong, *Beyond the Impasse: Towards a Pneumatological Theology of Religions* (Grand Rapids, MI: Baker Academic, 2003), and his more recent *The Spirit of Creation: Modern Science and Divine Action in the Pentecostal-Charismatic Imagination* (Grand Rapids, MI: Eerdmans, 2011).

27. See my review of John R. Levison's excellent book, *Filled with the Spirit* (Grand Rapids, MI: Eerdmans, 2009). Frank D. Macchia, "The Spirit of Life and the Spirit of Immortality: An Appreciative Review of Levison's *Filled with the Spirit*," *Pneuma* 33:1 (2011): 69–78.

28. See Frank D. Macchia, "The Oneness-Trinitarian Pentecostal Dialogue: Exploring the Diversity of Apostolic Faith," *Harvard Theological Review* 103:3 (2010): 329–349.

29. Driver, *Patterns of Grace*, 30.

30. Hans Urs Balthasar, *Theo-Drama*, vol. 3: *Dramatis Personae: Persons in Christ* (San Francisco: Ignatius Press, 1992), 505; quoted in Kevin J. Vanhoozer, *Remythologizing Theology* (New York: Cambridge University Press, 2010), 2.

SEVEN

Pneumatological Participation

Embodiment, Sacramentality, and the
Multidimensional Unity of Life

ANDREAS NORDLANDER

The pentecostal tradition exhibits a curious tension between a distinct holistic affirmation of the material world, on the one hand, and an otherworldliness sometimes bordering on escapism, on the other. Though the factors playing into this tension are no doubt many and complex, I am going to suggest that one crucial factor is the failure of pentecostal theology, by and large, to develop a theology of creation adequate to nourish its spiritual practices, and to guard against the ever-present threat of gnostic dualism in one form or the other. But how should pentecostal theologians articulate such a theology of creation? Here I want to explore Paul Tillich's theology as a key resource for such a project, in particular three notions of *participation* to be found in his work: existential participation, universal participation, and ecstatic participation in New Being through the Spiritual Presence.

However, I shall also suggest that pentecostal theology should go beyond Tillich toward a more radical appreciation of the Spirit in creation; such a theology would be at once more general and more particular, since creation already implies what I call a pneumatological participation, which is general, even as a particular and concrete experience of its fullness—to which the pentecostal tradition witnesses—is available. I submit that this understanding implies a more consistent sacramental valuation of the material world than the one emerging from Tillich's writings and his basic philosophical-theological framework.

The Pentecostal Paradox

Initially, the paradoxical tension within the pentecostal tradition between the affirmation and the rejection of the world—of materiality, embodiment, culture and so forth—must be sketched. That the pentecostal tradition does in fact *operate* on the assumption of the goodness of the created world in general and the holism of the human being in particular, such that materiality and embodiment are to be affirmed and celebrated, is something that has recently been stressed by a number of scholars of Pentecostalism. In his attempt to delineate the basic pre-theoretical commitments embedded in pentecostal practice—its worldview, or social imaginary—James K. A. Smith makes this a fundamental point. He argues, for instance, that pentecostal openness to the Spirit's surprising operations *within* the material order, the role of the body in its "liturgical" practices, and its emphasis on bodily healing as well as on other material blessings "deconstructs" dualism and is "a testament to the very 'worldliness' of pentecostal theology."[1] At the same time, however, he recognizes that the implications of these elements of pentecostal practice have not been sufficiently appreciated even within the tradition itself.[2]

Another example is Margaret M. Poloma, who suggests that pentecostal healing practices contain a holistic worldview, recognizing "the intricate interweaving of soul, mind, body and spirit."[3] Reporting on her sociological research on the so-called Toronto Blessing in the 1990s, she says that the unusual somatic manifestations during prayer were often conceived of as "a kind of sacrament—signs that God was at work in those for whom the prayer was being offered. The primary 'work' that was believed to be underway was one of holistic healing."[4] Despite this tacit dynamic anthropology, however, Poloma also describes how Pentecostals have often been suspicious of standard medical science, and she suggests that Pentecostals need to develop their implicit holism such that the chasm between divine healing and medical science can be bridged.[5]

Smith and Poloma both clearly articulate a pentecostal holism, tending to affirm the entirety of creation as good, particularly including the material dimension, while also recognizing that this has often remained implicit in practice rather than explicit in preaching and doctrine. Indeed, it is arguable that pentecostal *theologizing* has more often than not been dualistic and rather suspicious of the various dimensions of embodied life. The reasons for this may be many: theoretical elaborations of experience always risk distorting its originary power and import, especially if they are articulated within a foreign theoretical framework. There is of course always a difference between living through an event and retrospectively reflecting on it, but some theoretical construals constitute not a development of the potentiality inherent in originary experience, but rather a distortion of it.[6] Different theological construals of the world may, quite simply, be better or worse at giving authentic voice to particular concrete experiences. For instance, might it be that the early pentecostal neglect to develop a sacramental vision of the world from its own roots in Wesleyan sacramental piety was a missed opportunity to acquire a theological vision of the world that would in fact have been conducive to an articulation of the pentecostal experience of the Spirit working in and through the material?[7] This question becomes especially pertinent if we call to mind pentecostal practices, such as the laying on of hands in prayer, the anointing with oil, as well as the use of prayer cloths and other material mediations of the Spirit's power—and yet we find no articulated sacramental theology; indeed, baptism and the Eucharist are commonly conceived of merely as acts of remembrance, obedience, and public declaration.[8]

Regardless of the other historical and contextual factors that have led to the paradoxical tension within pentecostal theology in this area, I believe there is a particular lacuna within pentecostal theology that has allowed it to often adopt less-than-conducive theological frameworks, and that has made it difficult to develop the affirmative holism of its spirituality with theological consistency: the absence of a well-developed theology of creation. Discussing the difficulty of pentecostals to achieve an integration between working for the kingdom that is already underway here and now, and waiting and praying for the kingdom yet to come (between the prophetic and the apocalyptic), Macchia confirms this diagnosis: "Part of the difficulty in reaching for such integration is that Pentecostals stress the redemptive work of the Son and the Spirit to the near exclusion of the first article of the creed, namely, God the Father, creator of heaven and earth."[9] This is made evident in Keith Warrington's recent survey of the content of pentecostal theology, in which most of the traditional theological *loci* are discussed, but which contains virtually nothing about creation.[10] Amos Yong, finally, considers pentecostal reflection on the theology and philosophy of nature to be still in an "embryonic stage."[11] As pentecostal theology now moves toward a systematic—and even philosophical—articulation of the faith that it lives, a central task is therefore to approach the theology of creation from a pentecostal perspective, making it possible to develop some of the life-affirming elements implicit in pentecostal practice in a more sustained and theologically balanced way.

Against this background, I now turn to Tillich's theology, which contains key resources for a pentecostal reflection on creation. In particular, he offers an antidualistic theology of life and its multidimensional unity, explicitly connecting it with pneumatology, one upshot of which is a broadly sacramental vision of the world.

Participation and Tillich's Theology of Life

The concept of participation has returned to the center in much recent theology. Having its provenance in Platonic philosophy, it was appropriated by Christian theologians, such as Augustine and Thomas Aquinas, as a way of articulating the relation between God the creator and the created world. To exist, said Aquinas, is to be related in a specific way to the source of all being, God, who continually gives creatures to be, and without which they would simply cease to exist: "God is essentially self-subsisting Being [*ipsum esse subsistens*] . . . Therefore all beings apart from God are not their own being, but are beings by participation."[12] This means that the whole of creation and each single creature stand in an existential relation to God—the world is in this way always already related to God. In David Burrell's pithy formulation: "The *esse* of creatures is an *esse-ad-creatorem* (their to-be is to-be-toward-the-creator)."[13]

Tillich adopts the framework of participation in his theology, in which it serves many different functions (cf. *ST* 1.177). Here I am primarily interested in how he uses it in three distinct ways, as he elaborates on existential, universal, and ecstatic participation.

Tillich's understanding of *existential participation*, which I shall only briefly consider, comes closest to the traditional understanding of participation.[14] He uses it in his discussion of God as creator, and therefore as related to the world, in the first volume of the *Systematic Theology*. The Christian doctrine of creation, says Tillich, does not primarily refer to a past event, but rather describes our unique relation of utter dependence upon "the creative ground of being," which is God. That God creates out of nothing—*ex nihilo*—signifies, negatively, that Christian theology rejects all forms of absolute dualism—there is ultimately nothing besides God in which we are rooted. But it also signifies, positively, that the power of being is implied in creatureliness, which is nothing but "participation in being-itself" (*ST* 1.253). This, then, is an existential participation without which creatures would simply not be.

Note that this way of understanding the creator-creature relationship, by way of philosophical concepts, is far from mere metaphysical abstraction, since Tillich argues that our participation in the very power of being—in the creative ground of existence—is what alone gives the ultimate courage to be in the face of the anxiety of finitude: "Ultimate courage is based upon participation in the ultimate power of being" (*ST*. 1.273).[15] For Tillich, as for Augustine before him, the doctrine of creation therefore has deep existential implications in the present.

The idea of a *universal participation* is also broached in the first volume of the *Systematic Theology*, under the rubric of "God as creating." This concept primarily signifies the way in which "man participates in the subhuman creature and vice versa" (*ST* 1.260), and, more generally, the interconnectedness of all things. Drawing here on the ancient symbol of the human being as the microcosmos, Tillich presciently gestures toward an ecological and holistic theology: "Here theology should learn from modern naturalism, which at this point can serve as an introduction to a half-forgotten theological truth. What happens in the microcosm happens by mutual participation in the macrocosmos, for being itself is one" (*ST* 1.261).

It is, however, in the third volume of the *Systematic Theology* that the topic of universal participation comes into full flowering, where it is often called the "multidimensional unity of life." Here Tillich embarks on a theological reading of the philosophy of life in true Continental style, where the concept of "life" swells to include the inorganic as well as the dimension of consciousness, and is intended to convey the unity, becoming, and process-character of all that is (*ST* 3.25–26). Under the concept of life, Tillich is thus really presenting a philosophical theology of nature.

Space constraints forbid me to delve into the intricacies of Tillich's philosophical theology of life at this point, so I shall just briefly mention what I take to be his salient points for the purposes of furthering the interaction between Tillichian and pentecostal theology.

First, what Tillich presents is a radically *nondualistic anthropology*—we are seamless wholes, which are also entirely woven into the fabric of nature. By contrast, a dualistic view of the human being, which separates material and spiritual parts, body and soul, "disrupts the multidimensional unity of life, especially the unity of the psychological and the spirit, thus making the dynamics of the human personality completely incomprehensible" (*ST* 3.26).

Second, this nondualistic anthropology is possible only because of a *nonreductionistic understanding of nature* (or life) in the first place—the fabric of nature includes many different dimensions and realms, some presupposing others, without being reducible to them. Indeed, Tillich seeks to provide "a solid basis for the rejection of all kinds of reductionist ontology," and understands reductive materialism as "an ontology of death" (*ST* 3.18–19). Rather, creativity is inherent in nature—life is "self-creative" such that it produces these different dimensions and, eventually the human being, in which all (known) dimensions are integrated; we are made of inorganic material, but we are also living, psychological, and spiritual creatures (*ST* 3.16–17, 21, 30–32).[16]

Third, the multidimensional unity of life—universal participation—means that what happens in one dimension impacts what happens in all the others as well. For instance, psychological disorder impacts the organic body, and vice versa. This has many interesting implications and is a fruitful framework within which to think about issues of health and disease, the local and the global, evolution, the rational and the aesthetic, and so forth. In the case of health and healing, for instance, Tillich concludes that "the correlate of the multidimensional unity of life is the multidimensional unity of healing" (*ST* 3.281).

I want to suggest that a doctrine like that of the multidimensional unity of life would underwrite the holism implicit in pentecostal practice; it fully affirms embodied life without in any way reducing the spiritual to the material. It recognizes that the body and what belongs to it is part of spiritual life, and that spiritual life is possible only on the basis of embodiment. The point is not that pentecostal theology should adopt a theoretical framework out of the blue, as it were, but rather that pentecostalism already implicitly operates on some such understanding of human beings—and by extension, of nature—their explicit theorizing notwithstanding.

Whereas theological treatises ordinarily address the topic of creation in connection with the first article, the doctrine of God, Tillich reserves his most extensive discussion of creation, in the sense of nature, for the fourth part of the "system," in order to tie it directly to the third article, the doctrine of the Spirit. The reason for this is evident: the theme of *ambiguity* runs through his entire theology of life, and indeed, the whole system—"this concept of life unites the two main qualifications of being *which underlies this whole system;* these two main qualifications of being are the essential and the existential" (*ST* 3.11–12, my italics; cf. *ST* 1.204). At its most basic, life is an ambiguous "mixture of essential and existential elements" (*ST*, 3,12, scare quotes omitted), and this plays itself out in all dimensions of life and is manifested in the constant presence of struggle (*ST*. 3.53). Thus, for instance, organic life goes out of itself in its desire for growth and continued life, but in order to do so it must negate other life—life lives on life. Or again, the development of personhood is possible only in relation with another human person, but at the same time it always involves some element of negating the other in the process of defining the self. Or finally, every cultural creation is the actualization of a potentiality over and against another— finite life implies finite possibilities and choices must be made. Thus, according to Tillich, self-creative and self-transcendent life in all its dimensions reaches for something it can nonetheless never attain in its own power—it reaches for unambiguous life, life beyond the polarities of essential goodness and existential estrangement, of subject and object, of potentiality and actuality. In short, all of life witnesses to a "quest" for fulfilment beyond ambiguity, and the stage is thus set for the third kind of participation—ecstatic participation in the unambiguous life of the Spiritual Presence.

Ecstatic Participation through the Spiritual Presence

According to Tillich's method of correlation, the philosophical analysis of life provides the question to which the theological doctrine of the Spiritual Presence is the answer. It is under the impact of the Spiritual Presence that the human spirit is driven out of itself and is grasped by the divine Spirit in an experience Tillich calls ecstasy—the Greek *ek-stasis* literally means to stand out from: "'Ecstasy' is the classical term for this state of being grasped by the Spiritual Presence" (*ST* 3.112). This refers to an experience—for it is an experience (*ST* 3.221)— of self-transcendence, which is different from the movement of self-transcendence inherent in life itself. For this is the work of the Spirit—as indicated by the expression "being grasped by"—it cannot be compelled, but is given—a grace—

and Tillich speaks of it as "created by the Spirit" (*ST* 3.118; cf. 3.211–212). This, then, is an "ecstatic participation . . . whereby one lives in the sphere of this Spiritual power" (*ST.* 3.117). In other words, what we are given in these kinds of experiences is what I would call a pneumatological participation, a Spirit-created ecstasy whereby we transcend ourselves and the ambiguities inherent in existence toward "the transcendent union of unambiguous life" (*ST* 3.140). What we participate in, when we participate in unambiguous life through the Spiritual Presence, is thus the conquest of the tension between essence and existence, that split which is ultimately responsible for our state of existential estrangement, according to Tillich. What the Spirit gives, albeit fragmentarily, is a foretaste of the reunion of human beings with God.

Ecstatic participation is a very wide concept in Tillich's theology; he discusses cases of being grasped by the Spiritual Presence that result in faith and regeneration—what Tillich calls participation in New Being (*ST* 3.222). But he also discusses many other ways in which human beings are grasped by the Spirit: through participation in the Spiritual Community; in acts of faith and love; in genuine prayer. Indeed, while the Spiritual Presence in Jesus as the Christ is the ultimate criterion of pneumatological participation for Tillich (*ST* 3.144), the experience is available in other cultures, religions, and periods. "The Spirit is present wherever the conquest of the subject–object split in man's existence occurs" (*ST* 3.212; cf. 3.92).

Christian appropriations of a participatory framework have always had to reckon with two different basic modes of participation, one of which refers to creation and the other to salvation. Augustine, for instance, speaks of a minimal form of existential participation (*minus esse*) and a fuller participation in God (*magis esse*), which results from conversion.[17] In a similar way, as we have seen, Tillich has recourse both to existential participation and to ecstatic participation, where the latter functions in the theological context of soteriology, including discussions of faith, regeneration, sanctification, and so forth, even though this is also considerably broadened to include many other phenomena.[18] But what is distinctive about Tillich's elaboration of the theme of participation—and this resonates with pentecostal sensibilities—is his explicitly pneumatological understanding of ecstatic participation—participation in New Being, or new life.

Two important corollaries follow from Tillich's understanding of this Spirit-created ecstatic participation: *First,* when a person is grasped by the Spirit, this impacts the whole person, because of the multidimensional unity of life. While the divine Spirit operates directly only on the human spirit, since the human spirit presupposes and includes all other dimensions they too are indirectly drawn into this pneumatological participation: "Because of the multidimensional unity of life, all dimensions, as they are effective in man, participate in the Spirit-created ecstasy" (ST 3.118; cf. 3.200–201). Because of universal participation, then, pneumatological participation extends in a sense to the entire world: "In order to be present in the human spirit, the Divine Spirit must be present in all the dimensions which are actual in man, and this means, in the universe" (ST 3.108). The point I wish to make is that, for Tillich, participation in the divine Spirit is in no way antithetical to the psychological, embodied, and material aspects of our existence; on the contrary, ecstatic participation embraces all these dimensions noncontrastively. Because of the multidimensional unity of life, pneumatological participation reinforces holism rather than dualism. Once more, this already resonates with pentecostal practice. What Tillich seems to offer, though, is a broader theology of nature, which theoretically undergirds a holistic anthropology through an understanding of the multidimensional unity of life, and in which, therefore, the ecstatic experience of the Spirit does not imply dualistic construals of the human being and the world. One may even suggest that existential participation, which follows from the doctrine of creation, is what grounds the multidimensional unity of life.[19] This means that our participation in the Spiritual Presence must impact the whole world, of which we are integral parts. Created *ex nihilo*, the world is an interwoven whole, and the Spirit's impact on one dimension affects all the others. Construed in this way, existential, universal, and ecstatic participation belong together. However, it should also be stressed that Tillich holds that the Spiritual Presence impacts all the different dimensions only "indirectly," which is to say only as they are related to the human spirit. There is in other words no room for the Spirit to directly impact the orders of nature in the absence of the human spirit (ST 3.118; 3.275–277). Tillich does not read creation pneumatologically, a crucial point, to which I shall return.

The *second* corollary concerns sacramentality. Grounded in his doctrine of the Spiritual Presence and in the multidimensional unity of life, Tillich develops a very broad understanding of what constitutes a sacrament: "The term denotes everything in which the Spiritual Presence has been experienced" (ST 3.121). Anything can, in principle, become a vehicle of ecstatic participation for human beings. Indeed, the particular sacraments of the Christian tradition only have meaning against this wider sacramental view, as it follows from the presence of the Spirit. This pneumatological sacramentality is itself closely related to the antidualistic anthropology, since it implies that the Spirit relates to all dimensions of human life. Says Tillich apropos of the increasing insignificance of the sacraments within Protestantism: "This development is rooted in a doctrine of man which has dualistic tendencies, and can only be overcome by an understanding of man's multidimensional unity. If the nature of man is conceived simply in terms of conscious self-awareness, of intellect and will, then only words, doctrinal and moral words, can bear the Spiritual Presence. No Spirit-bearing objects or acts, nothing sensuous which affects the unconscious, can be accepted" (*ST.* 3.121). This analysis coheres with pentecostal practice, which, as Macchia argues, contains "a unique kind of sacramental spirituality," operating on the assumption that more than intellectual cognition is involved in one's relation to God—the importance of embodiment and affectivity cannot be overstated.[20] But Tillich is right that this is at odds with the characteristically modern dualism Protestantism has often bought into, and which has also seeped into Pentecostalism. Rooted in the pentecostal tradition's experience of the Spirit, however, the possibility now opens up to develop a pneumatological sacramentality, in dialogue with Tillich, according to which the Spirit may be experienced through sacramental acts of various kinds. This would include the acts of baptism and Eucharist, the anointing with oil and the laying on of hands, as well as the practice of glossolalia, but would not be restricted to them. Such a pneumatological approach could reinvigorate the theological understanding of the traditional sacraments, but also enlarge the discussion to include a sacramental vision of the world grounded in the Spiritual Presence. However, this suggests going beyond Tillich in reading creation itself pneumatologically, rather than restricting the work of the Spirit to the economy of salvation.

Toward a Pentecostal Critical Appropriation

What I have suggested as a resource for pentecostal theology—the rich participatory framework and the world-affirming holism and sacramentality it implies—ignores other troubling issues with Tillich's general approach. This concerns his construal of essence and existence, in particular, which implies that God and humankind were once united and will be reunited in what he calls an "eschatological pan-en-theism" (*ST* 3.421)—the goal of the quest for unambiguous life. A consequence of this essentially Plotinian framework is the identification of creation and fall, as Tillich admits: "Fully developed creatureliness is fallen creatureliness" (*ST* 1.255). Because he understands creaturehood as a self-realization of the creature in separation from the divine essence, a rupture of the original unity, "creaturely freedom is the point at which creation and fall coincide" (*ST* 1.256). Paradoxically, then, creation is affirmed as (essentially) good, even though it is *necessarily* fallen. Its goodness seems at times to be identified with human freedom; but simply to exist is to be estranged from God.[21]

Against this background, existential participation in the ground of being as a result of creation is already tainted with a certain negativity (in virtue of being precisely a *participation* in the source, and not an *identity* with the source). Consequently, the ecstatic participation created by the Spirit comes to be seen as a means of progressively overcoming the ambiguous conditions of existence, which could be read as overcoming creaturehood itself, insofar as being a creature means to have fallen into existence. Let me hasten to add that Tillich at several places denies this implication, insisting, for instance, that we do not conquer estrangement by overcoming finitude, but by the presence of being itself within the finite (*ST* 1.254; cf. 1.192–204), and that ecstatic participation does not rupture or deny created structures, but leads them to fulfilment (*ST* 3.114). Nonetheless, this is clearly a point at which Tillich's system shows considerable internal tension as he seeks to affirm the goodness of the created world but also a philosophical framework that at least suggests otherwise. This is nowhere clearer than in his eschatology, which is a sometimes rather tortuous attempt to balance these two incongruent perspectives (*ST* 3.394–423).

This philosophical framework seems to compromise the unqualified affirmation of the goodness of created existence that the doctrine of creation was originally meant to provide.[22] In this case, the correlational method demonstrates its vulnerability; one has the impression that the existentialist analysis of the human condition rather firmly governs the ways in which the theological response is fleshed out. One need not, however, accept Tillich's philosophical underpinnings in order to appreciate his insights into the structure of participation. The very idea that the Spirit is the creator and agent of participation is highly suggestive. But for the reasons given above, I believe that pentecostal theology would do well to broaden Tillich's notion of pneumatological participation to include the theology of creation proper, which could then lead to a reconfiguration of the whole framework in the direction of a still more unreserved affirmation of created existence—*qua* existence.

What do I mean by this? Simply that a fully trinitarian theology would give a pneumatological reading of creation, not only of salvation; the Spirit of God is at work also in the creation of the world—hovering over the face of the deep, the *Creator Spiritus*.[23] Whereas Tillich, as we have seen, refuses to connect ecstatic participation through the Spiritual Presence with existential participation in the creative ground of being, some pentecostal theologians—notably Amos Yong—are moving in this direction. Reading creation pneumatologically implies a more general working of the Spirit in creation in relation to Tillich's more restricted understanding of the Spirit in ecstatic participation. To the more traditional or Thomistic understanding of existential participation in causal terms, and to Tillich's understanding of it as sharing in the power of being, pentecostal theology would add a pneumatological dimension implied in creation: simply to be is already to be under the impact of the Spirit, who is the breath of God, giving life to all.

But if pentecostal theology has begun to open for a wider understanding of the Spirit in creation, it is also committed to a more particular and concrete understanding of the work of the Spirit in the individual, and in the ecclesial community, than Tillich's doctrine of ecstatic participation seems to allow. The experience of Spirit baptism is what constitutes a challenge at this point. For even if the Spirit is seen to operate in creation, and in different cultural and even religious contexts, pentecostals take Spirit baptism—itself a participatory metaphor[24]—to be a specific experience, attended by concrete signs, and initiating a closer walk with God as well as an empowerment for witness. While this experience could well be described as ecstatic, it would be far-fetched to describe it as a fragmentary overcoming of the ambiguities inherent in existence. In short, the Tillichian theoretical framework does not, as it stands and on its own, seem particularly conducive to an articulation of the pentecostal experience of the Spirit. For though Pentecostals may have oftentimes understood the experience of the Spirit in a too circumscribed and particularist way, a theological articulation seeking to be faithful to the phenomenon itself would have to understand it as more than the ultimate criterion validating similar types of experience in any number of contexts.

Moreover, and related to this, while Tillich understands ecstatic participation to be paradigmatically exemplified in Jesus as the Christ, it carries no necessary relation to the Christ and could in principle be equally well instantiated in other contexts. Consequently, the criteria for knowing whether one is in the grip of the Spirit are extremely vague and general, and those seeking a richer experience of life in the Spirit are informed that they are already living it: "He who is ultimately concerned about his state of estrangement and of the possibility of reunion with the ground and aim of his being is already in the grip of the Spiritual Presence. In this situation the question, What shall I do to receive the divine Spirit? is meaningless because the real answer is already given and any further answer would distort it" (ST 3.223; cf. 3.111–120). Surely such an approach is contrary to pentecostal sensibilities. Witnessing to a more concrete experience of the Spirit's fullness, the pentecostal response would more likely be an invitation to pray and tarry awhile in the upper room. Pentecostals would likely agree with Tillich that "existential seriousness" may indeed be evidence of the impact of the Spiritual Presence, but it is not enough—it is only an invitation to come further along.

The point I wish to make is that pentecostal theology should have at once a wider and a more restricted understanding of the work of the Spirit: wider in that the Spirit is at work in all creation; more restricted in that it flows out of a tradition witnessing to a particular way of being grasped by the Spirit, closely related to the Christian community and its way of faith. Pentecostal theology, in affirming the Spiritual Presence both generally in creation and specifically in the Christian life, would be able to see the work of the Spirit in creation and in culture, as well as in the more intense or ecstatic participation to which Spirit baptism testifies.

All of this, in closing, relates to the pneumatological understanding of sacramentality, as I have intimated above. The broadening of pneumatological participation to include the economy of creation, as well as salvation, lays the ground for a pneumatological sacramentality in tune with pentecostal practice, even as it goes further: sacramentality is seen to be not only salvific, but creational, not only instrumental, but ontological.[25] The Spiritual Presence, the *Creator Spiritus*, makes the whole world a potential sacrament.

Notes

1. James K. A. Smith, *Thinking in Tongues: Pentecostal Contributions to Christian Philosophy*, Pentecostal Manifestos 2 (Grand Rapids, MI: Eerdmans, 2010), 39–43.

2. Ibid., 42–46, 60–61.

3. Margaret M. Poloma, "Divine Healing, Religious Revivals, and Contemporary Pentecostalism: A North American Perspective," in *The Spirit in the World: Emerging Pentecostal Theologies in Global Contexts,* ed. Veli-Matti Kärkkäinen (Grand Rapids, MI: Eerdmans, 2009), 27.

4. Ibid., 33.

5. Ibid., 29.

6. Such an understanding is what drives various hermeneutically sensitive phenomenologies, especially in the wake of Heidegger. See, e.g., his introductory presentation of the concepts of *phenomenon* and *logos* in *Being and Time,* trans. John Macquarrie and Edward Robinson (New York: Harper and Row, 1962), 49–63.

7. On the Weselyan roots of the Pentecostal movement, see Donald W. Dayton, *Theological Roots of Pentecostalism* (Metuchen, NJ: Hendrickson, 1987), esp. 35–54.

8. Keith Warrington, *Pentecostal Theology: A Theology of Encounter* (London: T and T Clark, 2008), 161–169; Frank Macchia, "Tongues as a Sign: Towards a Sacramental Understanding of Pentecostal Experience," *Pneuma* 15:1 (Spring 1993): 61–76. One could also investigate the influence of other theological frameworks, such as fundamentalism, evangelicalism, and dispensationalism, on pentecostal theology, and which elements of pentecostal experience this influence has tended to underwrite as well as to suppress.

9. Frank Macchia, *Baptized in the Spirit: A Global Pentecostal Theology* (Grand Rapids, MI: Zondervan, 2006), 279.

10. Warrington, *Pentecostal Theology*. To be clear, I do not take this to be an omission by Warrington, but simply a reflection of the state of pentecostal theology.

11. Amos Yong, *The Spirit Poured Out on All Flesh: Pentecostalism and the Possibility of Global Theology* (Grand Rapids, MI: Baker Academic, 2005), 269. In this work Yong begins to elaborate what he calls a "pneumatological theology of creation," including a highly suggestive reading of the Genesis narrative.

12. Thomas Aquinas, *The Summa Theologica of St. Thomas Aquinas.* Trans. the Fathers of the English Dominican Province. (Notre Dame, IN: Christian Classics, 1948) 1a, q. 44, art. 1.

13. David Burrell, *Faith and Freedom: An Interfaith Perspective* (Oxford: Blackwell, 2004), xx–xxi. Note that this "existential" rendition of participation represents a Christian development of the Platonic notion of a "formal" participation, under the influence of the Christian doctrine of creation. Whereas formal participation seeks to answer the question of *what* a thing is (*quid est*), existential participation seek to answer the deeper question, never addressed by Plato, of *why* a thing is, if it exists in the first place (*an est*). For helpful discussions of this, see Jacob H. Sherman, "A Genealogy of Participation," in *The Participatory Turn: Spirituality, Mysticism and Religious Studies*, ed. Jorge N. Ferrer and Jacob H. Sherman (Albany, NY: State University of New York Press, 2008); and Jan Aertsen, *Nature and Creature: Thomas Aquinas' Way of Thought* (Leiden: Brill, 1988), 7–53.

14. There are important differences, however: Augustine and Thomas would not have explicated participation in reciprocal terms, as does Tillich—and this follows from his pan-en-theistic understanding of the relation between God and creation. However, there is no space here to further consider this issue.

15. See also *The Courage to Be* (New Haven, CT: Yale University Press, 1952), especially ch. 6. Writes Tillich: "Every courage to be has an open or hidden religious root" (156).

16. This understanding of nature bears strong affinities with the views of Teilhard de Chardin, which Tillich acknowledges in the preface, and therefore also with an entire tradition of Continental philosophical biology since Kant. This also means that there is an affinity with Merleau-Ponty, and through him with exciting contemporary formulations within the life and mind sciences—such as the work of Evan Thompson. Today this general approach, often called *emergentism*, is continually gaining scientific and philosophical momentum. That Tillich's theology of life is in tune with these developments is an additional reason why he is an interesting dialogue partner for contemporary pentecostal theology. For an introduction to these issues, see Evan Thompson, *Mind in Life: Biology, Phenomenology and the Sciences of Mind* (Cambridge, MA: Belknap Press, Harvard University Press, 2007); and Philip Clayton, *Mind and Emergence: From Quantum to Consciousness* (Oxford: Oxford University Press, 2004). For a pentecostal interaction with emergence theory, see Amos Yong, *The Spirit of Creation: Modern Science and Divine Action in the Pentecostal-Charismatic Imagination*, Pentecostal Manifestos 4 (Grand Rapids, MI: Eerdmans, 2011); and Nimi Wariboko, *The Pentecostal Principle: Ethical Methodology in New Spirit*, Pentecostal Manifestos 5 (Grand Rapids, MI: Eerdmans, 2012).

17. An excellent elaboration of this theme is found in Emelie Zum Brunn, *St. Augustine: Being and Nothingness* (New York: Paragon House, 1988).

18. It seems that the category of soteriology, vis-à-vis Tillich's work, could include all those experiences in which ecstatic participation occurs, whether within a Christian context or not, since they all point toward the ultimate eschatological union.

19. Etienne Gilson makes a similar point from a Thomistic perspective: "Each and every man can share in the common good of his species, and nothing that is human remains foreign to him. Nay, nothing that *is*, is foreign to him. A member of the universal brotherhood of being." *Being and Some Philosophers*, 2nd ed. (Toronto: Pontifical Institute of Medieval Studies, 1952), 186–187.

20. Macchia, "Tongues as a Sign," 71. Macchia argues that the practice of glossolalia is a privileged expression of this sacramental spirituality. The point here should not be

to deny the urgent need of a cognitive or intellectual strengthening of many pentecostal communities, but rather that such should never be construed dualistically or perceived as taking the place of its indigenous emphasis of relating to God with one's whole being.

21. Cf. Oswald Bayer's critique in "Tillich as a Systematic Theologian," in Russell Re Manning, ed., *The Cambridge Companion to Paul Tillich* (Cambridge: Cambridge University Press, 2009), 24.

22. See Gerhard May, *Creatio ex Nihilo: The Doctrine of "Creation out of Nothing" in Early Christian Thought* (Edinburgh: T and T Clark, 1994).

23. For some critical remarks about this concept, which need to be kept in mind, see Simon Chan, *Pentecostal Theology and the Christian Spiritual Tradition,* Journal of Pentecostal Theology Supplement Series 21 (London: Sheffield Academic Press, 2000), 111–114.

24. Something that Macchia draws attention to. *Baptized in the Spirit*, 32, 45.

25. This is important in view of the observation that "the pneumatological dimension of sacramental theology is still largely underdeveloped." Wolfgang Vondey and Chris W. Green, "Between This and That: Reality and Sacramentality in the Pentecostal Worldview," *Journal of Pentecostal Theology* 19 (2010): 264.

EIGHT

Tillich's Sacramental Spirituality in a New Key

A Feminist Pentecostal Proposal

LISA P. STEPHENSON

Frederick Parrella has suggested that in view of the focus of Tillich's Spiritual Presence on the experience of being grasped by the Spirit—rather than intellectual assent and doctrinal formulations—Tillich's treatment of the divine Spirit is in itself spirituality as well as theology.[1]

Working from this perspective, this chapter will explore the Tillichian notion of Spiritual Presence as a form of spirituality and bring it into dialogue with a feminist pentecostal spirituality. On the one hand, Tillich's sacramental spirituality enhances and expands several values of a feminist pentecostal spirituality. On the other hand, because Tillich died just as second-wave feminism and academic Christian feminist theology were emerging, he was never able to revisit his theology in light of feminists' concerns and priorities. Therefore, the feminist pentecostal spirituality that emerges in this chapter offers Tillich and his theological legacy an example of how to develop his theology of Spiritual Presence beyond his initial concerns to encompass a feminist perspective.[2]

Because a theoretical articulation of a feminist pentecostal spirituality does not exist—and thus this chapter represents an initial articulation of such—I will proceed by maintaining some of the traditional values of pentecostal spirituality while integrating several core values of feminist spirituality.[3] To present a definitive list of characteristics for either one of these types of spirituality portends either naivety or arrogance. In order to avoid both of these pitfalls, I suggest below some of the central concerns and values of Pentecostals and feminists that are *representative* of each spirituality respectively. Next, I will expound on some of the central characteristics of the sacramental aspects of Tillich's spirituality. Finally, I will outline a feminist pentecostal spirituality that is informed by Tillich's sacramental spirituality, and demonstrate how his spirituality can extend beyond his initial articulation.

Pentecostal and Feminist Spirituality

To date, the subject of pentecostal spirituality has received its fair share of attention. Among the many who offer characterizations, Russell Spittler suggests that five implicit values govern pentecostal spirituality. First, there is an emphasis on individual experience, which places great significance on one's own spiritual encounter with God. This encounter is usually shared by means of personal testimony. Second, there is an emphasis on orality. Oral tradition has held much weight among Pentecostals, and the oral nature of Pentecostals' liturgy is overwhelming. This latter characteristic is due in large part to the emphasis Pentecostals place on the gifts of the Spirit, many of which are oral. Third, there is an emphasis on spontaneity, which is a consequence of the unpredictability of the Spirit. When attempting to follow the Spirit's lead, one must be free of a rigid order or schedule that would constrain the movement of the Spirit. Fourth, there is an emphasis on otherworldliness. The "real" world is the eternal one, not the earthly one. Finally, there is an emphasis on biblical authority. Pentecostals are committed to the authoritative role of scripture in their lives and in their doctrine. Spittler maintains that these values coalesce in a variety of ways and are exemplified in a multitude of stereotypical pentecostal practices.[4]

Like pentecostal spirituality, feminist spirituality has also acquired its fair share of scholarship. In fact, Nicola Slee suggests that much of feminists' thinking on the Spirit can be found in feminist spirituality, rather than in traditional abstract doctrinal reflection on the Spirit.[5] Feminist spirituality is a term that encompasses a broad movement finding expression in all of the major world religions, including movements such as paganism and Wicca. Consequently, there is no *single* feminist spirituality, though one could point to certain trends or emphases that are pervasive enough to warrant their use as descriptors.[6]

Sandra Schneiders suggests that there are five salient characteristics of feminist spirituality.[7] First, it is rooted in and oriented toward women's experience, especially that of empowerment and disempowerment. This is largely communicated through storytelling, as women regard their own experiences to be significant. Women find the sharing of personal experience to be a technique for consciousness-raising and a source of mutual support. Second, it is deeply concerned with what has been dichotomized by patriarchal religion. Feminists are concerned with rehabilitating what has been regarded as inferior and reappropriating what has been alienated, especially that of body and spirit. Third, and closely related to the second emphasis, feminist spirituality expresses a profound concern for nonhuman nature. Feminists purport that there is an intrinsic connection between the oppression and exploitation of women and that of nature. In order to contribute to a truly renewed and livable world, a spirituality that values women *and* all that has been "feminized" must emerge. Fourth, it rejects cerebral, rationalistic, and abstract approaches to religious participation in favor of rituals that are participative, inclusive, life-enhancing, and joyful. Consequently, feminists choose to organize themselves religiously in communities that are inclusive and participative. Fifth, it is committed to the intrinsic relationship between personal growth and transformation and a politics of social justice. For feminists the "personal is political," meaning that the personal problems women have faced are linked to larger, structural issues that must be transformed, and that this larger transformation is only possible through personal transformation. Thus, feminist spirituality starts with a commitment that faces both inward and outward simultaneously.

As noted above, there can be a fusion of pentecostal spirituality with feminist spirituality. The result is a feminist pentecostal spirituality that maintains the traditional pentecostal emphasis on 1) individual experience, but with particular attention to women's spiritual encounters; 2) orality, but with particular attention to women's voices; 3) otherworldliness, but realizes such spirituality impinges on the thisworldly dimension, which necessitates personal and structural transformation especially as it relates to the injustices done to women and nonhuman nature. The way in which such a pentecostal spirituality can be embodied will be demonstrated below.

Tillich's Sacramental Spirituality

Fundamental to Tillich's notion of Spiritual Presence (and thus of his spirituality) is the sacramental element.[8] Tillich claims that there are two modes of communication in relation to the Spiritual Presence and through which the Spiritual Presence is effective: sacrament and word. Objects that are vehicles of the Spiritual Presence become sacramental materials and elements in a sacramental act. Tillich goes so far as to say that the sacrament is the medium of the Spiritual Presence, and the latter cannot be received without the former. "God grasps every side of the human being through every medium" (*ST* 3:120–122). It is here that the second portion of Tillich's formula "Protestant principle and Catholic substance" emerges strongly. The sacramental aspect to Tillich's spirituality expresses his appreciation and desire for Catholicism's emphasis on the concrete embodiment of the Spiritual Presence (i.e., "Catholic substance").[9] In order for Protestants to rediscover the sacramental sphere, they must realize that objects can become the bearers of transcendent power and meaning.

There are several governing ideas to Tillich's notion of sacrament. First, he proposes that the concept contains three meanings. In its largest sense, it refers to everything in which the Spiritual Presence has been experienced. In a narrower sense, it refers to particular objects and acts in which a spiritual community experiences the Spiritual Presence. In its narrowest sense, it refers to the traditional "sacraments" in the performance of which the spiritual community actualizes itself (*ST* 3:121).

Second, there is a necessary relationship between the idea and the material element, which Tillich calls a realistic interpretation of the sacramental element. This stands in contradistinction to a symbolic-metaphoric interpretation—in which there is no intrinsic relationship posited—and a ritualistic interpretation—in which the relationship is accidental.[10] Third, and following from the second point, because the sacramental material is intrinsically related to what it expresses, it is a symbol rather than a sign. As a symbol, it has inherent qualities that make it suitable to its symbolic function and irreplaceable. As a symbol, it participates in the power of what it symbolizes and thus can be a medium of the Spirit. However, Tillich is mindful to note that the inherent qualities of objects do not *create* a sacrament but merely allow such objects to become *bearers* of sacramental power (*ST* 3:122–123).[11]

Finally, in principle, every finite object possesses sacramental potential. Every object can be the bearer of a transcendent power and integrally related to salvation history. Nonetheless, all objects are not sacraments in actual existence, because of their separation from the divine. If we were to see the holy in every reality, then the Kingdom of God would be completely realized. It is not, and thus we do not. Because of the impending coming of the Kingdom of God, the holy is seen only in special places and contexts. In these instances, the holiness that appears is essentially a representation of what is possible in everything and in every place. Every sacrament points to the universality of the sacramental principle.[12]

The other medium of the Spiritual Presence is the word. Human words that communicate the Spiritual Presence become the Word of God. This includes written and spoken words. The Bible is a potential medium, but it does not become the Word of God until it is actualized (i.e., it grasps the spirit of humans). This potentiality is true of other literature as well, though Tillich ascribes a primacy of place to the Bible as the Spirit's most important medium in the Western tradition. Likewise, whenever spoken words become the medium of the Spirit whereby the Spirit enters the spirit of someone, those words become the Word of God. This can occur in something as formal as a sermon or as mundane as an ordinary conversation. As Tillich notes, this enlarges indefinitely the number of words that can become the Word of God. Yet, he does propose that the biblical words are the criterion against which one must measure all other words in order to determine if they are the Word of God (*ST* 3:120–121, 124–125).

Tillich maintains that word has a sacramental quality to it. A word is both a natural phenomenon (i.e., word as breath or sound) and the bearer of meaning.

When the relationship between the word as natural phenomenon and as a bearer of meaning is understood from the perspective of a realistic interpretation, it implies that the sound and meaning are "bound together in such a way that the natural power of words becomes the necessary bearer of its power of meaning, so that the one is not possible without the other. Where this is asserted, words by their natural power are potential bearers of a transcendent power and are suitable for sacramental usage."[13]

However, the distinction between word and object is not as precise as Tillich presents. Words are dependent upon objects to exist. They are formed and communicated by virtue of their connection with some material item. Written words require pen, paper, and hands. Spoken words require lungs, vocal cords, and a mouth. In essence, they both require bodies. While Tillich presents word and sacrament as two different modes of communication of the Spiritual Presence, word relies upon some form of concrete embodiment in order to be expressed and received. Tillich grants that the word is implicit in the sacramental object, but the same is conversely true. The sacramental object is implicit in the word. This qualification will become important below.

Sacrament, Spirit, and Women: A Feminist Pentecostal Spirituality

While there are many merits to Tillich's sacramental spirituality, he falls short of realizing the implications of it for a feminist spirituality. Nonetheless, the potential is there. Below I will employ Tillich's sacramental spirituality within a feminist pentecostal spirituality. Tillich's theology offers a feminist pentecostal spirituality a sacramental orientation that enhances and expands several fundamental values as articulated by feminists and Pentecostals. In turn, the feminist pentecostal spirituality that emerges in this chapter advances Tillich's spirituality to encompass significant feminist concerns that initially he neglected.

Orality and Embodiment

I want to begin by focusing primarily on the oral nature of a feminist pentecostal spirituality, recognizing that it also involves individual experience. One's encounter with the Spirit is closely connected with pentecostalism's orality, both in contributing to it (i.e., one's encounter with the Spirit leads to an oral expression) and being affected by it (i.e., one encounters the Spirit because of it). That there is an oral character to pentecostal spirituality is undeniable, especially within a worship service.[14] Through Tillich's understanding of words as sacraments of the Spiritual Presence, human words have the potential to become the Word of God. In view of the orality of feminist pentecostal spirituality, this means that every prayer, prophecy, testimony, song, sermon, word of wisdom or knowledge, and any other conceivable oral activity that may take place among Pentecostals has the potential to become a sacrament of the Spiritual Presence.[15] Daniel Albrecht hints at this sacramental nature of the pentecostal worship service when he refers to the iconic dynamic of the ritual sounds that are present within it. He suggests that Pentecostals create sounds to surround the worshipper in a way analogous to the distribution of icons around Eastern Orthodox sanctuaries to visually surround the worshippers. In this way, the oral elements in a pentecostal service serve as auditory icons. They are windows to the divine; intersections between the finite and the infinite; sacraments of the Spiritual Presence.[16]

There is a twofold implication of thinking about the oral elements of a pentecostal service as sacraments. First, Tillich's insistence on a realistic interpretation of sacraments means that the words themselves are not incidental. Rather, there is a necessary relationship between them and the sacrament, as they are the bearers of power and meaning. This implies that the particular content of the oral events within pentecostalism matters. It is not just significant that an oral event takes place, but the very words that comprise that event and how they are received by or grasp the human spirit are important.

Second, it challenges the traditional Protestant focus on the sermon as the apex of the service, of which Pentecostals can at times be guilty. While the sermon has the potential to be the Word of God for the people of God, Tillich's point is that this potential can also be realized in any of the other oral events that might take place during the service. All words can become mediums of the Spirit. All words can become the Word of God. Consequently, Pentecostals should resist the urge to elevate the sermon to a priority of place and embrace the multiplicity of orality that can emerge within a service. These other oral events are just as significant and potentially sacramental.

When the oral nature of a feminist pentecostal spirituality is viewed as sacramental, valuing orality includes valuing embodiment. As mentioned above, the word relies on some concrete form of embodiment. A focus on orality alone can give rise to a bifurcation between the word itself and the body from which it is emanating. But there is room within a sacramental spirituality—and thus within a feminist pentecostal spirituality—for a focus on the body as a location of the Spiritual Presence.

In point of fact, the Acts narratives echo this understanding. The point of the outpouring of the Spirit is not just the manifestation of the gifts of the Spirit (i.e., orality), but also from what *bodies* these gifts of the Spirit emerge from. It is not significant merely that God's Spirit is poured out, but upon *whom* it is poured. This is evident in Acts 2 when the social categories listed in the Joel citation deliberately reflect those who traditionally had nothing to say in society:

young people, women, slaves, and maidens.[17] This is also evident in Acts 8, in the instance of the Samaritans, and in Acts 10, with respect to the Gentiles. In all three of these instances, the true marvel is not that the Spirit is received, but that *these* particular people have received the Spirit. They are the ones that God has chosen to pour his Spirit upon.

Thus, from a sacramental perspective, Pentecostals have visual icons in addition to the auditory ones. Albrecht notes this phenomenon and claims that among other objects, Pentecostals' visual icons include fellow believers. In a service, Pentecostals are not surrounded by icons fashioned in wood and plaster, but rather icons that are living, active, human, and, therefore, embodied.[18] Such an approach has implications for the problem of sainthood, which Tillich himself remarked that Protestantism should rethink. He suggested that a saint should not refer to one who achieves personal perfection, but to one who is transparent for the ground of being which is revealed through him or her (*ST* 1:121–122). Perhaps Pentecostals are, unwittingly, on their way to a theology of sainthood through the means of fellow believers as sacraments. In light of this, saints are those who are mediums of the Spiritual Presence for others.

From a feminist perspective, viewing the oral aspects of pentecostal spirituality as sacramental provides women opportunities both to experience empowerment and to communicate this experience. When women's voices and bodies are sacramental they are affirmed as sites of the divine. The sacramental element puts all persons within the community on an equal playing field, because each individual has the potential to become a sacrament. There is no priority of persons. There is no exclusion of those who are weak or powerless. The Spirit usurps social and ecclesial rights, privileges, and positions.

Moreover, this understanding of orality provides an opportunity for women to gain access to power in unofficial ways. Women may not have a central voice in some matters of the church, but they are defining pentecostal spirituality as they are frequently the ones whose voices and bodies are being used by the Spiritual Presence. The fact that most pentecostal pastors are male becomes somewhat insignificant for pentecostal spirituality because women's voices and bodies can be sacramental. Their voices are heard and valued, even though they may not possess the titles.

Furthermore, women sharing their testimonies is not just a technique for consciousness-raising or a source of mutual support, but also a potential medium of the Spiritual Presence. Viewed from this perspective, personal testimonies take on even greater significance, for both the individual and the community. Women can communicate their experiences of empowerment and act as bearers of the empowering presence of the Spirit for others when their words become the Word of God.

Viewing the oral aspects of feminist pentecostal spirituality as sacramental also provides an opportunity for women's expressions of disempowerment to be viewed and experienced as more than mere complaint. If *all* forms of orality are considered to be potential sacraments, then it is not in the edifying words alone that the Spiritual Presence can be encountered, but in the critical ones as well. In particular, the prophetic voices of women who express conscious anger at present conditions of injustice can be sacramental too. In a sacramental spirituality, when women voice their disempowerment, the Spirit can still be present.

From a feminist perspective, recognizing that orality includes embodiment joins two traditionally dichotomized realities: that of body and spirit. Traditionally, the body has been considered inferior to the spirit. But a sacramental spirituality does not allow one to consider the body as inferior or to alienate it from one's spirituality, because it is a medium of the Spiritual Presence. Within Pentecostalism, overcoming traditional dichotomized realities goes even further than just body and spirit, because frequently the Word of God is uttered forth in a female voice, from a female body. Not only are body and spirit joined, but women and spirit are joined. This move acknowledges that female bodies can be sacraments of the Spiritual Presence; beings who reflect the Ground of Being; fellow believers who may in fact be saints.

Individual Experience and Community

Tillich's sacramental spirituality urges feminist Pentecostals to move from individual experience to the communal experience. The Spiritual Presence in and through others necessitates community. On the one hand, the Spiritual Presence in an individual is significant for *others*. What one has experienced is important not just for oneself, but for the whole community. For example, it is in one's sharing through personal testimony that one's words can become sacramental and through which others encounter the Spiritual Presence. The power of this individual experience, then, is not just for one's self, but for the community. On the other hand, the Spiritual Presence in others is significant for the *individual*. One cannot be dependent on individual experience alone to fully encounter God. It is presumptuous and shortsighted to discount other persons' individual experience as a medium of the Spiritual Presence for one's self. An emphasis on individual experience must also be an emphasis on community.

And yet feminist pentecostal spirituality would push the communal aspect beyond just human persons to include the whole of creation. The bodies that can function as sacraments are not limited to human bodies, but include nonhuman bodies. Humans are part of a cosmic community, and the nonhuman bodies that help comprise that community alongside of humans also have the potential to be sacraments. While a sacramental approach alone is vulnerable to engendering a utilitarian attitude toward nonhuman nature, it does express the symbolic importance of each and every body on earth. Ultimately a feminist spirituality upholds the intrinsic value of nonhuman nature, apart from its sacramental potential. But, as at least one feminist has noted, this does not discount a sacramental approach as a way to begin to change exploitive attitudes toward nature.[19]

Otherworldliness and Thisworldliness

When considering otherworldliness through the sacramental lens, the eschatological tension is accentuated. This occurs through the energizing and criticizing principle that pertains to sacraments. As one experiences the sacramental, one is enabled to momentarily experience the holy (i.e., energizing principle) because the finite becomes a bearer of transcendent power. Yet this experience is a reminder of nature's separation from the divine (i.e., criticizing principle) because the holy is only seen in special places and contexts. The sacramental experience is a unique one, not simultaneously realized in everything and in every place. Thus, sacraments themselves embody the eschatological tension of the already/not yet. When Pentecostals' experience of the Spiritual Presence is understood as a sacrament, the sacramental element energizes the community, but also critiques it from getting too comfortable with the present as it exists. There is more to be realized.

And yet, ironically, the emphasis on otherworldliness emerges by means of *this* world. The sacramental principle implies that one need not completely abandon this world for the next. Until the Kingdom of God is completely realized, persons are dependent upon the present world to experience the Spiritual Presence.

This focus on thisworldliness gives rise to a "negative sacramentalism." This phrase, used by Sallie McFague, focuses on the ways in which the earth and its many bodies do not manifest the Spiritual Presence, but rather are signs of human sin and destruction. They are not expressions of the divine, but of human neglect and oppression. Negative sacramentalism focuses not on "their use to help us in our religious pilgrimage but on our misuse of them, our refusal to acknowledge these bodies as valuable in and for themselves and to God."[20] Consequently, when focused on thisworldliness, Christian spirituality should include a focus on the care of bodies—human and nonhuman. A sacramental spirituality is not just for personal growth and transformation, but ultimately for the purpose of seeking justice within society's structures in anticipation of the renewal of creation itself.

In this chapter, I have outlined a feminist pentecostal spirituality that embraces several of the core values of pentecostal spirituality and feminist spirituality, while utilizing Tillich's sacramental spirituality to reorient these values. In doing so, I have expanded the boundaries of a feminist pentecostal spirituality further, as well as embodied Tillich's sacramental spirituality in ways that he never did. Of course the real goal is not the articulation of a sacramental feminist pentecostal spirituality but an embracement of it as a commonplace lived experience among Pentecostals, as well as all those who desire to abide with the Spiritual Presence.

Notes

1. Frederick J. Parrella, "Tillich's Theology of the Concrete Spirit," in *The Cambridge Companion to Paul Tillich*, ed. Russell Re Manning (Cambridge: Cambridge University Press, 2009), 88–89; Parrella, "Tillich and Contemporary Spirituality," in *Paul Tillich: A New Catholic Assessment*, ed. Raymond F. Bulman and Frederick J. Parrella (Collegeville: Liturgical Press, 1994), 241–267. The spirituality referred to in this chapter is that of a lived experience. This type of spirituality is a "conscious involvement in the project of life integration through self-transcendence toward the ultimate value one perceives." In the instance of Christian spirituality, ultimate value is the triune God. See Sandra M. Schneiders, "Christian Spirituality: Definition, Methods and Types," in *The New Westminster Dictionary of Christian Spirituality*, ed. Philip Sheldrake (Louisville: Westminster John Knox Press, 2005), 1–2.

2. Feminist theology's engagement with Tillich's thought has been both positive and negative. Rachel Sophia Baard does an excellent job of surveying both types of feminist responses in her essay "Tillich and Feminism," in *The Cambridge Companion to Paul Tillich*, 273–287. In particular, Mary Ann Stenger claims that feminist spirituality can be enhanced with an engagement of Tillich by emphasizing more fully than he does the implications of the Spiritual Presence for individual self-realization, interdependence and community, the struggle for justice for all peoples, and our ecological unity. Part of my effort in this chapter is to realize this engagement. See Mary Ann Stenger, "Paul Tillich and the Feminist Critique of Roman Catholic Theology," in *Paul Tillich: A New Catholic Assessment*, 183–185.

3. Andrea Hollingsworth is the closest example of an articulation of a feminist pentecostal spirituality in her article "Spirit and Voice: Toward a Feminist Pentecostal Pneumatology," *Pneuma* 29 (2007): 189–213. However, her focus is on proposing a constructive feminist pentecostal pneumatology rather than a feminist pentecostal spirituality per se—though she does focus on pentecostal spirituality in order to achieve this construction.

4. R. P. Spittler, "Pentecostal and Charismatic Spirituality," in *The New International Dictionary of Pentecostal and Charismatic Movements*, ed. Stanley M. Burgess (Grand Rapids, MI: Zondervan, 2003), 1096–1102. Spittler acknowledges that the facets he highlights are those largely expressed in the North American context. He rightly notes that there "is a geography of spirituality: this analysis needs adjustment for other cultures" (1097).

5. "Feminist spirituality" is distinct from "women's spirituality." The former is a more recent phenomenon that arises from the consciousness of women's oppression and the commitment to overcome it, whereas the latter refers to women's tradition of spiri-

tuality more generally. See Anne Carr, "On Feminist Spirituality," *Horizons* 9:1 (Spring 1982): 96–103; Nicola Slee, "The Holy Spirit and Spirituality," in *The Cambridge Companion to Feminist Theology,* ed. Susan Frank Parsons (Cambridge: Cambridge University Press, 2002), 171–189.

6. Slee, "The Holy Spirit and Spirituality," 175–179.

7. Sandra M. Schneiders, "Feminist Spirituality: Christian Alternative or Alternative to Christianity?," in *Women's Spirituality: Resources for Christian Development,* 2nd ed., ed. Joann Wolski Conn (New York: Paulist Press, 1996), 30–67. Cf. Slee, "The Holy Spirit and Spirituality," 179–182. While I employ a definition of *feminist* spirituality, I do not intend for this perspective to be either exclusive or exhaustive of other forms of women's spirituality (e.g., womanist spirituality).

8. Maxwell E. Johnson claims that Tillich adopts a sacramental approach as the basis for his entire system of thought. He says, "Tillich does not *have* a sacramental theology; his theology itself *is* sacramental, based on a particular vision of reality ontologically related to that mystery which is the ground and power of being itself." Maxwell E. Johnson, "The Place of the Sacraments in the Theology of Paul Tillich," *Worship* 63:1 (January 1989): 17–31.

9. However, this should be held in tension with Protestantism's prophetic critique against any final authority that takes upon itself an infinite claim (i.e., Protestant principle). Tillich clarifies the dialectical relationship between the Protestant principle and the Catholic substance in his article "Permanent Significance of the Catholic Church for Protestantism," *Dialog* 1:3 (Summer 1962): 22–25.

10. Paul Tillich, *The Protestant Era* (Chicago: University of Chicago Press, 1948), 95–96.

11. See also Tillich's explication of the meaning of symbols in *Dynamics of Faith* (New York: Harper and Row, 1957), 41–43.

12. Tillich, *The Protestant Era,* 110–111.

13. Tillich, *The Protestant Era,* 98.

14. David Daniels expounds on sound as a primary marker of early Pentecostal identity in "Gotta Moan Sometime": A Sonic Exploration of Earwitnesses to Early Pentecostal Sound in North America," *Pneuma* 30 (2008): 5–32.

15. Cf. Macchia, "Sighs Too Deep for Words: Toward a Theology of Glossolalia," 47–73; Macchia, "Tongues as a Sign: Towards a Sacramental Understanding of Pentecostal Experience," 61–76.

16. Daniel E. Albrecht, "Pentecostal Spirituality: Looking Through the Lens of Ritual," *PNEUMA* 14:2 (Fall 1992): 107–114. For a more detailed study on the intersection of ritual and pentecostal spirituality, see Albrecht's *Rites in the Spirit: A Ritual Approach to Pentecostal/Charismatic Spirituality* (Sheffield: Sheffield Academic Press, 1999).

17. The one exception is the mention of the elderly. See Matthias Wenk, "The Fullness of the Spirit: Pentecostalism and the Spirit," *Evangel* 21:2 (Summer 2003): 43.

18. Albrecht, "Pentecostal Spirituality," 110–114.

19. Sallie McFague, *The Body of God* (Minneapolis: Fortress Press, 1993), 182–185.

20. McFague, *The Body of God,* 186.

NINE

Political Theology from Tillich to Pentecostalism in Africa

NIMI WARIBOKO

In Africa, politics is a process of power-exchange. It is akin to warfare with clear, concrete definition of friends and enemies. The political is the militant site of the agonistic transfer and control of power. The possession and deployment of power is the key to extracting and allocating resources from the *common* that are needed to live a full human life. Both process and site are presumed to be pervaded by *spiritual presences*. Politics is a spiritual warfare; a struggle between one *power of being* against another, which determines the "who" of the contestants' humanity. The spiritual is the inner dynamics of politics in all spheres of society, public life.

This chapter investigates how the logic and dynamics of forms of political power are related to the dimensions of spiritual life. It also demonstrates how power and spirit are related to the conception of the political. A contextual African pentecostal political theology is then revealed from the complex nexus of power, political site, and spiritual presences. Tillich's notions of *power of being* and Spiritual Presence provide a useful framework to organize the data and to trace the contours of the emerging political theology. In this mutually critical engagement with the African data, Tillichian political theology is enriched and extended. There is a deep affinity between African pentecostal political theology and that of Paul Tillich: politics is a mode of power of being. This intersection raises the question: What is the fate or nature of political theology in the pentecostal moment, that is, in a post–Protestant-Catholic moment?

The rest of this chapter unfolds in four sections, including the conclusion. Immediately following this introduction I offer a targeted overview of Tillich's political theology in terms of its ontological and existential elements, showing the central role of his notion of Spiritual Presence (his peculiar designation of the Holy Spirit) as the link between them. The second section investigates both the ontological and existential elements of political life (what I prefer to call the "political") in Africa. How the political is critiqued, addressed, and deployed by African Pentecostals, and how it is itself grasped by the Spiritual Presence when the Spirit is invited as an *answer* to the ambiguities and existential questions of social life, is the focus of the third section. The discussions in this section pivot around *political spirituality,* which is conceptualized as the quest for (harmony between) power and meaning in the political, the common coexistence where *being* and *being-with* are always at stake. In the concluding section, I offer a perspective on the nature of political theology in the pentecostal moment.

Before going further, it is important to remark that the dialogue with Tillich does not mean that the terms of the engagement will be defined solely by a disproportional elaboration on Tillich's work; putting an emphasis on Pentecostalism and incorporating Tillichian theology for insight is one way of engaging with Tillich's theology. My approach here is to use Tillichian categories to illuminate the African data, even as I deploy them to enrich and complexify Tillich's philosophical and theological analysis.

Tillich's Political Theology

Tillich's political theology is a theorization of political existence that simultaneously embraces the complexity and weight of socially imposed sufferings and the relation of such to the structures and elements of social existence and society's orientation to the Unconditional. It is a product of philosophical and cultural analysis of social situation and ontology.[1] It is a disciplined reflection on and a search for "encounters where love and justice become creatively one."[2] The ethical vision carried by his political theology is the manifestation, the unconcealment of justice "etched into the order of things," chiseled into the very ontological conditioning of social life, etched into the power of being.

The best entry point into Tillich's political theology is his notion of power. Tillich's theory of power moves in multiple intercalated grooves. In a 1931 essay he distinguished between force, might, and power.[3] Force refers to the compulsion deployed by one entity (usually a governing center) on another to break its resistance, will. Might (which later became power of being) is the dynamic of all things to maintain themselves in existence, to stay in relational encounters with other existents, and to go beyond themselves and come back to themselves. Simply put, it is the dynamic of individuation and participation that does not destroy the existent's particular center of being. He sums it up in this way:

> Might, as a general term embracing nature and man, appears in the force of a wave rushing into the land and ebbing; as well as in the unfolding strength of a tree, which overshadows others until it is itself overshadowed; in the prominent position of an animal in the herd, which another will perhaps soon contest; in the impression of the adult on the small child and the mutual dependence of the adult on the child.[4]

What then is power? "Power is might on the level of social existence."[5] Social existence, according to Tillich, is a constantly changing balance, a dialectic of tension, agonism, strife, rhythms, etc. Social existence is a struggle (Latin, *agon*) of mights in encounters.

Tillich's threefold notion of power at once captures the meaning of the political as the being, processes, and practices of social control (domination). The political is about the ontological conditioning of existence, the agonistic and cooperative interplays of power of being. Tillich here facilitates our understanding of *political* as the human organizing of agonistic power, as the way humans organize power in social life.

The next groove in which Tillich's thought moves is the notion of power of being. Every human being has the power of being, the capacity to resist nonbeing. It refers to the "self-affirmation of life in its self-transcending dynamics, overcoming internal and external resistance."[6] In this view of power as constitutive of being, it is seen as not exclusively concentrated at a single place but as interactive. Though it is commonly available to all human beings, power is differently actualized, and every social intercourse involves the exercise of power. This is so because every interaction involves self-affirmation; the exercise of power is always limited by the presence of others who should not be treated as objects and whose intrinsic claims of self-worth are readily asserted even if they are not respected. Every social encounter represents a site of power, is a site of the political, and hence is embedded in and draws from the human organizing of agonistic power, to use Mark Lewis Taylor's words.[7]

The third groove of Tillich's thought on politics and power is that of justice. He claims that this human organizing of agonistic power harbors an unavoidable demand of justice—a demand that may be suppressed by force or compulsion, but does not totally disappear. Every social encounter demands the actualization of potentialities, the power of being, of those involved. The justice that is demanded in such an interaction is grounded in the power of being that is itself anchored in *Being-Itself,* God. The claim of justice—the call not to suppress the actualization of being—is raised either silently or vocally.[8] Once again, Tillich facilitates our understanding of the agonistic nature of social existence, the intrinsic capability of all humans to resist dehumanization, to affirm their being and resist nonbeing, and to uphold the intrinsic claim of justice in all social encounters or communities.

It is in social encounters that a person becomes a *person* in a community, which is always only defined in relationship to justice. This brings us to the communal dynamic, the transformative matrix of the political or political thinking. "The roots of political thought must be sought in human existence itself. Without having a picture of man, of his powers and tensions, it is impossible to make any statement about the bases of political existence or thought."[9] According to Tillich, there are two roots of political consciousness. They are (a) the romanticizing and reverence of origin and history of a group or community and (b) the expectation of the new.[10] In the breast of human beings there is usually a deep connection to place of origin and shared land. This characteristic connection is expressed in politics as conservatism, a leaning back to a mythologized past. In the same deep place of the citizen there is the expectation of the new, the not-yet, growth, and progress. Politics, or rather the political, exploits and feeds off the community's attachment to or struggle with these forces. Though the two tend to grow together, in general we can discern either direction with respect to how society is organized at any given time.

It is against the background of this expansive notion of politics as encounters of power of being that we can best understand Tillich's notion of the Spiritual Presence. According to Tillich, political existence is pervaded by the will to grasp the Unconditional, a society's ultimate concern. The Unconditional is at work in the community's pursuit of love and justice, in the "cultural self-creativity of life," in the meaning-giving orientation of ordinary life, and in the forward-leaning thrust of human beings to reach the not-yet. The Spiritual Presence traces, fosters, and connects both the cultural creative actions of individuals and groups and the norms operating throughout the political sphere to the "Unconditioned within meaning-fulfilling existential relationships."[11] The Spiritual Presence works to enable the experience of the ultimate concern as consciously expressed through:

1) Creative encounters of love and justice.
2) Continual orientation to the Protestant principle, which attacks and exposes claims by any finite person or institution claiming to be infinite, final, or ultimate.
3) Empowering the theonomous development of culture and the community of *New Being* (Jesus the Christ) (*ST* 1:147–148).
4) Enabling individuals and groups to respond to the demand of the *moral imperative,* to become a *person* within a community of persons.[12] This is "the demand to become actually what one is essentially and therefore potentially. It is the power of man's being, given to him by nature, which he shall actualize in time and space. His true being shall become his actual being. . . ."[13]

It is not only the Spirit that is present in the moral-cultural situation or the political sphere, but there is also the *demonic.* The demonic, according to Tillich, comprises ambiguous, destructive finite forces, dynamics, and institutions that falsely claim ultimacy and resist a person's experience of the moral imperative and ultimate meaningfulness in complex social unity (community). These must be resisted as a threat to being, community, and human flourishing.

In the next two sections we will explicate grassroots pentecostal theology based on my participant observations in Nigeria and discussions with African Pentecostals in Africa, North America, and Jamaica. As we will demonstrate, this line of grassroots pentecostal political thought opens up the possibility of a different idea of the intersection of politics and theology. The sections will exemplify how the grassroots lines of thought meet, cross, bend, and layer with Tillich's understanding of power, spiritual presences, and the appearance of the new. The two sections together provide a conceptual field where pentecostal ideas and Tillich's theology are thought together by reflecting on the notions of the political and spiritual warfare. The purpose of tracing the grassroots meaning of the political as it is imbricated in the practices of spiritual warfare is to investigate how people whose power of being is pushed and weighed down by socially imposed sufferings do not stay on the *ground* but instead keep bubbling up to the surface as if through the promise and portentous power of grace.

The Political in Africa

We begin by describing the African Pentecostals' conceptualization of politics and then give a sense of their view of politics as worked out in their spirituality. We will not get very far if we look for a conception of politics that is restricted to citizens' participation in party organizations, political protests, and periodic elections.[14] Neither are we to understand African pentecostal theology if we are only interested in committed actions to overthrow a government or revolutionize state power. The political views of African Pentecostals are also not discernible at the level of structure and dynamics of state power and entities. The primary focus is on the nonentitative reality of politics. Politics, the act of being-with, the ex-position of beings to one another, shows two sides in the African conception: the underlying reality (nonentitative) and the entitative reality. All beings, holders of political offices and those they dominate, share in the underlying reality, but not all share in the same entitative reality. Pentecostals largely conceive of politics nonentitatively, though this does not mean entitative politics is excluded. The nonentitative is the formless reality that takes the shape of the "appearance," which assumes a form and becomes finite or determinate so as to exist, either dominating others and imposing suffering on them or working for the common good. In this nonentitative conception, politics is part of "becoming-itself." Any actuality of the nonentitative component, any actuality in concrescence, can be surpassed as it undergoes further stages of actualization while firmly grounded in the underlying activity. Politics is an ongoing fulfillment of potentiality insofar as it exists potentially.

Scholars such as Ogbu Kalu and Ruth Marshall have rightly approached the investigation of the African pentecostal political theology by focusing on this underlying reality. Kalu calls it "the magical substratum that underpins the political culture."[15] The political engagement of African Pentecostals thus involves looking "beneath the structures of the public spheres to address the spirits that govern them. This theme opens up the possibility for examining both the overt and covert dimensions of political engagement. In Africa the sacralization of the cosmos legitimates the political space and the dynamics of the political culture. The rulers and the ruled often act from a sense of the presence and ultimateness of the spiritual forces."[16]

African Pentecostals' well-noted language of spiritual domination or hindrance to individual and national development gestures to a deft recognition of the rich substratum of political and economic behavior, serving as "a critical rhetoric against power" that portrays political leaders as "possessed and empowered by the spirits that they worship in secret."[17] Spiritual warfare as an engagement with the nonentitative dimension of politics is a form of critique of corrupt political power and also a form of resistance. As Ruth Fratani-Marshall puts it: "In its engagement with local forms of knowledge and practice it develops an ongoing critical debate about government, one which not only indicts the immorality and inequality at the heart of domination, but does this by using a language and imagery that resonates in the imagination of the dominated."[18]

Though Kalu and Marshall are on the right track, their works do not go far enough in understanding the nature of the nonentitative dimension of politics.[19] They have restricted its meaning to only the spiritual substratum and ignored the political as the *ontologically constitutive* dimension of being-together. Just as the political cannot be restricted to certain types of entities, it cannot be limited to a spiritual substratum either. It must be conceived as constituting being, enabling and constraining practices, and the *contexture* of being-with. It is always marked by agonistic strivings and tensions. Scholars investigating African pentecostal political thought have tended to neglect the political as the human organizing of agonistic power in society through practices, and "as the dimension that is inherent to every human society and that determines our very ontological condition."[20] They have failed to bring to bear on their analyses the historical and social practices that encompass Pentecostals and non-Pentecostals alike, or to foreground any form of political praxis. Actors in a political setting are encompassed by, caught up in, and surrounded by complex practices that constitute their contexture and exercise powers over their thought and actions as they themselves keep the practices ongoing by their very being-together. This is the site of the social, according to Theodore Schatzki. The "site of the social" is the setting, the contexture, in which practices, actions, are presented, where they actually become actions. It is the embedding milieu or medium in and amid which social life (human actions, interactions, and coexistence) transpires.[21]

African Pentecostals struggle to shape this site of the social, the contexture in which social life hangs together, in which practices cluster and congeal to produce domination, oppression, and derailment of destiny. They consider this site as too important to be ignored or to be left for politicians and the spirits that empower them. For the Pentecostals the political is very pervasive, and it is enmeshed in, strives in, and emerges (spectrally and concretely, if you like) from the very hanging-together of being and practices. The practices that are constitutive of being and that trace the ontological constitution of human beings in Africa are imbricated with what Achille Mbembe names as *necropolitics* and *necropower*.[22]

The dimension of necropolitics and necropower is very important in understanding the structure, logic, and dynamics of African pentecostal political spirituality as it is located within the full array of social complexity of the ever-ongoing economic, political, and legitimacy crises in the continent. Spirituality becomes, among other things, a weighing-in against the deadly structures and dynamics of being; an agonistic contestation of the concentric contextures and their accompanying powers that generate, structure, and animate human socialities in ways that organize death and dying, destroy destinies and hopes, and impose social suffering.

We have so far shown the "fundamental structures" of the conceptualization of politics by Pentecostals in Africa. It is both entitative and nonentitative. The latter dimension points not only to the magical substratum of culture, but also to the very social and historical practices that constitute human beings. These dimensions of the political go *pari passu* with the Pentecostals' conceptualization of power. Somewhat homologous to the entitative notion of the political is the juridical model of power, referring to law and sovereignty that stand or rule over citizens and negatively constrain their actions. There is also biopolitical notion of power, the ways of technologies of control and constraint that work in circuitous, multiple, and network manner across sites, domains, and contextures of social existence. Power disseminates itself into the interstices of life, shaping all of life, pervading structures for the production and reproduction of livingness. Although these two forms of power are distinguishable for analytical purposes, they often dwell and operate together in the agonistic context of ordering and ordered life. Power works through micro- and macro-relations.

Why is this dual understanding of power important? Political spirituality, as we shall see, is not limited to the obvious resistance against power as repression ("power over"), but is also against power's productive networked mode. The acknowledgment of organizing matrices and processes of power and of the pentecostal Christian enmeshment in the enveloping system of power is the necessary first step for calling upon and inscribing the divine who sees, watches, and surveys all sites of existence. This acknowledgment is also necessary for the special spiritual attention many African Pentecostals pay to micro-relations (such as household "enemies," everyday relations with family members, neighbors, and coworkers) and the possibility of evil everywhere. The "enemy" of one's human flourishing may just be embedded in one's mundane relations! This calls for constant vigilance.

One way of weighing-in—that is, resisting this networked power—is the countergeneration of collective power. This power that is only a potential comes to life, is actualized, when the members of a corporate body act in concert. It happens when the believers "stand up" together and act for their common good. According to Hannah Arendt, "power corresponds to the human ability not just to act, but to act in concert. Power is never the property of an individual; it belongs to the group and remains in existence only so long as the group keeps together."[23]

Pentecostals in Africa refer to this collective as "corporate anointing." The social practice of many believers coming together in their tens, hundreds, and thousands to pray for hours, often into the night, is not only about fighting the devil, but also about an understanding of how power is generated and deployed.[24] This praxis reflects the fundamental understanding of power as generated and sustained in a network of persons and within the internal and immanent social dynamic of the community and its immediate and remote larger contexts.

A critical issue in the contestation for power is the struggle over sovereignty. According to the pentecostal imaginary, there are basically three authorities vying for sovereignty over the life of the citizens in the political: the corrupt postcolonial state, Satan and his cohorts, and God. Pentecostals see themselves as securing God's sovereignty over their lives and their nations. Commenting on the issue of sovereignty in the pentecostal imaginary in Nigeria, Ruth Marshall states, "The original impulse of the Born-Again revolution in Nigeria responded to the urgent desire to institute forms of sovereignty that would redeem the individual and collective past from a history of subjection and auto-destruction, and rescue the individual and the nation from the experience of radical uncertainty and loss of control over the present and future."[25]

Let us take a moment to summarize what we have found so far in our analysis of African pentecostal understanding of politics:

1) Politics is understood both entitatively and nonentitatively. The latter dimension points not only to the magical substratum of culture, but also to the very social and historical practices that constitute human beings.

2) Power operates both in juridical and networked modes.

3) Hence resistance to power involves both contesting notions of sovereignty and law and the generation of collective forces to counter insidious operations of power in micro-relations.

4) The political is an encounter and struggle between persons, each with his/her own power of being. The encounter is agonistic and determines the "who" of the contestants.

To this list we need to add that the political is suffused with spectrality (ghosts and spirits). There is the spectral presence of the physically dead and those living-dead wrestling under the weight of socially imposed sufferings. In addition, the highly charged and energized sites of politics are haunted by past atrocities inflicted on the poor and marginalized, their awful pains, and their un-answered cries for justice.

Finally, politics is warfare in Africa. There is an overemphasis on capturing political power and an intense fear of losing to rival parties. For this reason, po-litical competition assumes the character of warfare and has become a zero-sum game, "an anarchy of dedicated self-seeking."[26] The leaders are often engrossed in a struggle for survival. Most importantly, the tendency is to use state power for the accumulation of capital/wealth. Politicians and bureaucrats use state power to create or strengthen their material base.[27] In this highly statist economy and warring polity, economic success and personal security and welfare depend on access to state power. [28]

Given these various characterizations of politics and power in Africa, it is little wonder that political spirituality takes on the character of warfare, involves complexly structured intensification of life, and is dedicated to seeking divine intervention in everyday interactions. We have given the context in which pen-tecostal political theology is forged in Africa and will now investigate how this context shapes political spirituality.

The context is one in which identities are defined along the lines of friend/ enemy distinction with its unsurprising Schmittian reductive appeal to vio-lence.[29] There is a basic assumption of violence in such relationality and the pos-sibility of relating to one's enemies in nonviolent spiritual terms in prayers is etiolated. In this charged context of *agonistic spirituality*, all the significant con-cepts in the pentecostal understanding of the political are theologized secular concepts. To put it more accurately, it is a milieu in which the secular is theologized and the theological secularized and the private realm publicized and the public privatized.

Political Theology as Grace-filled Warfare

Needless to say, the beginning of wisdom in African pentecostal political spirituality is an agent's clear definition of friends and enemies, and a rigorous evaluation of the power (capabilities, "firepower") on each side and the power political agents can access when needed. In the pentecostal imagination that sees a person's problems, sickness, failures, and misfortunes as caused by a demon or by another person under the influence of Satan or evil spirit, there is often a clear distinction between a friend and an enemy. Each person judges or is free to consider the other, the adversary, the enemy, as a threat to his or her life, way of life, well-being, or existence who must be resisted, fought, or placated to preserve one's well-being or to progress through life. (Of course, this point of view has *Schmittian* implications for political spirituality.) Thus, political spirituality as a way of claiming a stake in a hostile world, imposing one's "acquired" sovereignty (from Jesus, the *superpower*) on daily events, as a pattern of defending one's turf in the agonistic power exchanges in order to safeguard one's *being* and to significantly and meaningfully elevate one's level of flourishment, is a form of warfare. Though the weapons are not carnal, only mighty in God for the pulling down of strongholds, it is nonetheless warfare. It is spiritual warfare!

Spiritual warfare is that special mode and mood of prayers, fasting, speaking in tongues, confession of sin, spiritual mapping, deliverance, and prophetic utterances calculated to initiate the new, usher in freedom, and promote human flourishing. Spiritual warfare is a way of discerning and critically reflecting, contesting, and resisting the play of powers in the ontological conditioning of being, the forces weighing down on current life, and the agonistic tensions dragging bodies to increased vulnerability of death by exclusion from centers of life-enhancing supports.

Spiritual warfare is a special engagement with the grace of God and a moment of an intense *dwelling* in the grace of God and in the embrace of the Holy Spirit. For African Pentecostals grace is an agent, a source of empowerment, a veritable ally. Grace is surplus power over personal and social sins. It is an excess *beyond* their surplus suffering and an intensification of life-enhancement, life-giving nourishment over the great vulnerability to premature death that is their lot.

Spiritual warfare is also a "hand-to-hand" combat with the forces of "darkness" to overcome poverty and establish the "who" of the person. Poverty is being at the edge of being, the edge of nonexistence, with the weight of one's being jabbed more often by the jagged edges and boundary of finitude than is the case for those living in privilege. Hannah Arendt once compared poverty to darkness. The presence of the poor is covered in the *polis*. Their "who" is covered in the darkness of nonrecognition. This darkness weighs on the poor as the dews of the night weigh on the fleece of the lamb tethered outside before the dawn of its sacrifice. Poverty is heavy. Engaging in spiritual warfare and doing so in the collective gathering of the church-polis is one way the poor show the "who" of their individuality in the world of appearance.

Given the preceding discussions, it is germane to argue that the praxis of spiritual warfare is creating a way of being. Or one may well say spiritual warfare arose and is sustained from a specific way of being, a way of "broadening and deepening being."[30]

Outline of a Pentecostal Political Theology

The title of this chapter, "Political Theology from Tillich to Pentecostalism in Africa," was chosen to indicate the kind of reflection I am offering. I have read African pentecostal political praxis through the lens of Tillichian theology, even as I supplemented the reading with practice theory. Tillich's notions of *power of being* and spiritual presence provided a useful framework to organize the data and to trace the contours of the emerging African pentecostal political theology. In a very fundamental sense, politics in Africa is a spiritual warfare; a struggle of one *power of being* against another, which determines the "who" of the contestants' humanity. The spiritual is the inner dynamics of politics in all spheres of society, of public life.

The reflection was also geared to illuminate Tillich's treatment of power and might through pentecostal understanding of spiritual warfare and "corporate anointing." African pentecostal praxis reflects the fundamental understanding of power as generated and sustained in a network of persons and within the internal and immanent social dynamic of the community. This is akin to Tillich's notion of power as might at the level of social existence; but these persons' conception and use of it in everyday life deepens our understanding of Tillich's insights. The African Pentecostals' understanding of power of being and their deployment of it in political struggles in the form of spiritual might facilitates our understanding of Tillich's threefold notion of power in relation to politics. We may now consider the threefold notion to be envisioning politics as the human organizing of agonistic power, as the way humans organize power in social life. There is something more. For African Pentecostals, the political is about the ontological conditioning of existence, the agonistic and cooperative interplays of power of being. This is an aspect of politics many Tillichian scholars do not usually emphasize in their analysis of contemporary struggles for social justice, though Tillich was noted for his ontological analysis.

Let us now show how the interaction between Tillichian theology and African pentecostal theology unfolded together in the preceding pages. First, we analyzed the political orientation of African Pentecostals in terms of the ontological and existential elements that inform not only Tillich's political theology, but also the entirety of his theology system. Second, in his mutually critical correlative method the Holy Spirit is the answer to the existential questions of life. For Tillich, life is actualization of being. We demonstrated through our analysis of spiritual warfare how the power of the infinite Holy Spirit is invited and accessed to deal with the ambiguities of life in the concrete finite order and for vanquishing obstacles that thwart the actualization of potentials.

Finally, Tillich's view of power, which is very agonistic, appropriately informed our treatment of the political, which foregrounds our turn to spiritual warfare. In the practice of spiritual warfare there is union of power and meaning as the *theology of the concrete spirit*. In Tillich's theology, the Spirit is the unity of power and meaning. "This unity is made actual, real and concrete *in* life *as* Spirit."[31] This unity, according to Frederick Parrella, serves "as ground and model of life, particularly the life of the human spirit."[32] In the pentecostal way of being, the finite believer becomes a concrete sacrament or vessel of the Holy Spirit, even as the Spirit is "the ground, ideal and destiny of [his or her] concrete life."[33] As Tillich himself puts it, "the Spiritual Presence cannot be received without a sacramental element, however hidden the latter may be" (*ST* 3:122).

The key points to our theology-of-culture approach to pentecostal political theology set within the dynamics of the unfolding of social being are presented below as a summary of this chapter.

1) The political. The meaning of politics is deepened and broadened to *the political*. The political is about how power is organized in society and how it is ontologically constitutive of being.
2) Power. Power is pervasive and permeates all social encounters. It is both concentrated at a center and also networked.
3) Spiritual presence. The processes and sites of the political are permeated by spiritual presences. These aid, haunt, or resist the operations of the political.
4) Thirst for justice. The arc of the political bends toward justice for the actualization of power of being. Thus there is thirsting for some kind of creative encounter of love and justice between God and human beings, and between human beings. The quest for justice is partly driven by the efforts to establish the "who" of the persons. "Another way to see justice and love as principles [that is, operating powers that 'move social groups and individual

agents in society towards a way of being that is ethical'] is to say that they are for Tillich modes of power of being. They are the forming power and uniting power of being, respectively. In *Love, Power and Justice* the middle term of his title suggests that the other two terms are ways of expressing that power."[34]

5) Moral imperative. The political carries a moral imperative, whether it is acknowledged or suppressed or neither. There is a demand on every man and woman to actualize his or her potentials, to become a person in a community. In the practice of spiritual warfare this demand is boldly put before the social-political system, the satanic realm, and God.

6) Unconditional. There is a meaning-seeking and teleological orientation to the Unconditional.

7) Way of being. Political spirituality is a way of being, a *transimmanental* mode of relating to the agonistic political.

On the whole, pentecostal political theology as a theorization of the political (the organizing and generative principles of power in any society[35]) relates the complexity and pains, and the promise and hope of social living, to the spiritual depths (God, Unconditional) of political existence and to the spiritual presences that pervade and haunt intersubjective relations, and discerns the possibility of encounters between persons where "love and justice become creatively one." Its aim is to nurture the kind of social life in which the Unconditional radiates into politics for the transformation of society and flourishing of free persons who are *true beings* in a community of persons. It also aims to set limits to the power of the state, to not concede the political realm to the state, by articulating the reality of the church both as a body and soul of society.[36] The proper delineation and explication of this kind of political theology of pentecostal community will always demand not only keen theological and ethical insights, but also prodigious labor in philosophical and cultural analysis if politics is to promote human flourishing.

Notes

1. See Mark Lewis Taylor, "Tillich's Ethics: Between Politics and Ontology," in *The Cambridge Companion to Paul Tillich,* ed. Russell Re Manning (Cambridge: Cambridge University Press, 2009), 189–191.

2. Grace Cali, *Paul Tillich: First-Hand: A Memoir of the Harvard Years* (Chicago: Exploration Press, 1996), 93.

3. Paul Tillich, "The Problem of Power: Attempt at a Philosophical Interpretation," in *The Interpretation of History* (New York: Charles Scribner's Sons, 1936), 181–194.

4. Tillich, "Problem of Power," 183.

5. Ibid.

6. Paul Tillich, *Love, Power and Justice: Ontological Analyses and Ethical Applications* (London: Oxford University Press, 1954), 37.

7. For an excellent discussion of the political, see Mark Lewis Taylor, *The Theological and the Political: On the Weight of the World* (Minneapolis: Fortress Press, 2011).

8. Tillich, *Love, Power and Justice*, 62, 63.

9. Paul Tillich, "The Two Roots of Political Thinking," in *Interpretation of History*, 203–204.

10. Ibid., 203–215. See also Paul Tillich, *The Socialist Decision*, trans. Franklin Sherman (New York: Harper and Row, 1977 [1933]).

11. Paul Tillich, *The System of the Sciences According to Objects and Methods*, trans. Paul Wiebe (East Brunswick, NJ: Associated University Press, 1982 [1923]), 203.

12. Paul Tillich, *Morality and Beyond* (Louisville: Westminster John Knox Press, 1963), 19.

13. Ibid., 20.

14. For example, see Kevin O'Neil, *City of God: Christian Citizenship in Postwar Guatemala* (Los Angeles: University of California Press, 2009).

15. Ogbu Kalu, *African Pentecostalism: An Introduction* (New York: Oxford University Press, 2008), 199.

16. Ibid., 200–201; see also 199, 202.

17. Ibid., 211.

18. Ruth Fratani-Marshall, "Mediating the Global and Local in Nigerian Pentecostalism," *Journal of Religion in Africa* 28:3 (1998): 278–315, esp. 306–307, quoted in Kalu, *African Pentecostalism*, 216.

19. This shortcoming is principally attributable to their conceptualization of the political. I have noticed it because I consider the political to also encompass the human organizing of agonistic power in society through practices, which are nonentitative. This way of formulating the political is indebted to secular theorists like Chantal Mouffe, Theodore R. Schatzki, and nonpentecostal political theologian Mark Lewis Taylor, just to name a few.

20. Chantal Mouffe, *The Return of the Political* (New York: Verso, 1993), 3, quoted in Taylor, *Theological and the Political*, 67.

21. The ontological or instituting power of politics is best understood through what philosopher Theodore Schatzki has called contexture, "the setting or backdrop that envelops and determines phenomena." Theodore R. Schatzki, *The Site of the Social: A Philosophical Account of the Constitution of Social Life and Change* (University Park: Pennsylvania State University Press, 2002), 53.

22. "I have put forward the notion of necropolitics and necropower to account for the various ways in which, in our contemporary world, weapons are deployed in the interest of maximum destruction of persons and the creation of death-worlds, new and unique forms of social existence in which vast populations are subjected to conditions of life conferring upon them the status of living dead." Achille Mbembe, "Necropolitics," trans. Libby Meinthes, *Public Culture* 15:1 (2003): 40, quoted in Taylor, *Theological and the Political*, 67.

23. Hannah Arendt, *On Violence* (New York: Harcourt Brace Jovanovich, 1969), 44. See also Keith Breen, "Violence and Power: A Critique of Hannah Arendt on the Political," *Philosophy and Social Criticism* 33:3 (2007):343–372.

24. An understanding any political theorist can tease out from their spiritual practices.

25. Marshall, *Political Spiritualities,* 236. For her further discussions on sovereignty and Pentecostalism, see 169–171, 198, 206–208, 233–234.

26. Claude Ake, *Democracy and Development in Africa* (Washington, DC: Brookings Institution, 1996), 129.

27. Segun Osoba, "Corruption in Nigeria: Historical Perspectives," *Review of African Political Economy* 23:69 (1996): 371–386.

28. Ake, *Democracy and Development in Africa,* 7.

29. Carl Schmitt, *The Concept of the Political,* trans. George Schwab (Chicago: University of Chicago Press, 1996).

30. Mark Lewis Taylor, *Religion, Politics, and the Christian Right: Post 9/11 Powers and American Empire* (Minneapolis: Fortress Press, 2005), 97.

31. Frederick J. Parrella, "Tillich's Theology of the Concrete Spirit," in *Cambridge Companion to Paul Tillich,* 79.

32. Ibid., 86.

33. Ibid.

34. Taylor, "Tillich's Ethics," 203.

35. I am indebted to Mark Taylor for this particular understanding of the political.

36. On this point, see William T. Cavanaugh, *Torture and Eucharist: Theology, Politics, and the Body of Christ* (Oxford: Blackwell, 1998).

TEN

What Have Pentecostals to Do with "The Religion of the Concrete Spirit"? Tillich's Theology of Religions in Twenty-First Century Global Renewal Context

TONY RICHIE

Paul Tillich's last public lecture, published posthumously, sets forth his most mature, and probably most provocative, ideas regarding Christian theology and non-Christian religions.[1] Herein he posits, as stated in the lecture's title, "The Religion of the Concrete Spirit" as his highest hope for the future of Christian theology. Tillich's attention to pneumatology with christological criteria and to the development of religion/s as a universal and particular reality holds potential for pentecostal theology of religions. After a brief survey of Tillich's "dynamic-typological" theology of religions, this chapter provides critical mutual engagement of Tillich's theology of the religion of the concrete Spirit and twenty-first century pentecostal/charismatic theology of religions. A discerning pentecostal appropriation of Tillich's "religions of the Spirit" involves a retrieval of Tillichian notions of spiritual presence and ecclesial mission. The result is suggestive for contemporary theology of religions as it prunes potentially problematic elements of Tillich's thought while adapting and translating valuable kernels of his theological legacy into the current body of pentecostal *theologia religionum*.

What Are the Broad Contours of Tillich's Theology of Religions?

Tillich's thought on culture and religion, including Christianity as the fulfillment of paganism and his dynamic typology of religion, was developed throughout his life. Tillich's visit to Japan late in life further impacted his views, giving him opportunity to explore firsthand Shintoism, Buddhism, Japanese Christianity, Confucianism, and the so-called New Religions.[2] Among other things, Tillich's Japan lectures emphasized the spiritual foundation of democracy, implying Christianity rather than Buddhism or Islam is a better fit because of its emphasis on creativity, individuality, and liberty.[3] Furthermore, he told Japanese Christian leaders that "the Christian faith should present itself as a message over against all religions, Christianity included," in language understandable and acceptable to highly civilized people.[4] Of course, Tillich's agonizing experience with Nazism had demonstrated to him that the Christian religion could be co-opted and corrupted (ST 3.176).

Tillich's idea of a latent and manifest church helped him approach world religions positively. For Tillich, world religions, at least in part through the Spiritual Presence, have a dynamic mix of actuality (manifest) and potentiality (latent) that may become more fully realized through Jesus the Christ (ST 3.149–152; 3.152–155). Put another way, an "anticipation" of the New Being in the religions that are open to fuller realization implies "a certain amount of existential participation" (ST 3.141–144, esp.141). For Tillich, Jesus of Nazareth is "the Christ, the final manifestation of the New Being in history" (ST 3.364).[5] True to Tillich's Platonist philosophical roots, one can observe a complex participation of the historical particular in the universal, which itself transcends the particular but nonetheless enters it and transforms it.[6] Indeed, for Tillich salvation can be described as transformation of the old into the new, or a renewal; and it is therapeutic—that is, salvation is healing (ST 3.377–382).[7]

Tillich's preferred term for the church was "the Spiritual Community," described as, "an unambiguous, though fragmentary, creation of the divine Spirit . . . appearing under the conditions of finitude but conquering both estrangement and ambiguity" (ST 3.150). However, the Spiritual Community exceeds the visible, institutional church, or any specific religion for that matter, its "latent" and "manifest" stages implying a participation in the unity of religion, culture, and morality as dimensions of the spirit (ST 3.152; 157).[8] Accordingly, Tillich did not understand conversion and ecclesial mission in absolute terms but as transition into ontological actualization through Jesus Christ as the New Being.[9] He saw "a fundamental a priori kinship between the finite and the infinite without which religious response would be impossible."[10] Thus, in some sense the world's religions would appear to include legitimate responses to God. Yet Tillich stressed the finality and universality of Christianity even as he assumed its continuity with other religions. Significantly, he saw elements of religious responses even in apparently nonreligious or "quasi-religious" groups, including secularism and atheistic Hinayana Buddhism.[11] Nevertheless, neither Mohammed nor Buddha nor any other religious figure or founder are of central significance for history; for Tillich, only Jesus Christ holds that solitary place of universal centrality (ST 3.368–369).

Tillich argued that Christian theology must enter into creative dialogue with other religions to avoid becoming provincial and also in order not to miss a great historical opportunity for progress. It would thus run the risk of becoming a-*kairos* rather than *kairos*. This warning may imply more than merely becoming irrelevant regarding a critical need of the time. Simply put, Tillich understands that *kairos* "describes the moment when the eternal breaks into the temporal, and the temporal is prepared to receive it."[12] Accordingly, the risk is more than missing an opportune moment; it is in resisting the eternal. No wonder Tillich said if could he do his *Systematic Theology* over again he would give more attention to dialogue with the religions and non-Western religious perspectives (*ST* 3.6).[13]

Tillich rejected religious exclusiveness and humanist secularism as ways of relating to the religions.[14] For him, a proper approach to religions included five presuppositions:[15] (1) Divine revelation exists in all religions; (2) Revelation is received by estranged humans in a limited and distorted way; (3) The revelatory process includes mystical, prophetic, and secular critique of the history of religions; (4) There may be a central event in the history of religions with universal significance (Jesus Christ); and (5) Religion and secularism are tools of mutual self-criticism (*ST* 1.110–113; 1.132–135).[16] Tillich's dynamic-typological approach understands all the religions to have sacramental (presence of the Holy), mystical (direct union with the divine), and prophetic (ethical, what "ought to be") elements, and suggests that uniting and integrating these various elements properly is their chief challenge, a task accomplished in the Religion of the Concrete Spirit.[17]

For Tillich, the Religion of the Concrete Spirit unites and integrates the sacramental, mystical, and prophetic elements of the religions. The history of religions reveals an ongoing struggle to achieve a balanced unity. This effort is often frustrated by overemphasis on one or the other elements and can be accomplished only by emphasizing in turn that which has been diminished through under-realization. The inner aim of the history of religions is the Religion of the Concrete Spirit, which is present in them in fragmentary form throughout history but fulfilled in Jesus Christ, who transcends bondage to a particular religion and provides criteria for Christianity to judge itself and also judge others.[18] Notably, the criterion of the New Being in Jesus as the Christ "elevates the churches above any other religious group, not because they are 'better' than others, but because they have a better criterion *against themselves* and, implicitly, also against other groups"—which suggests that the New Being in Jesus Christ is first and foremost directed toward the church, and only secondarily against other faiths (*ST* 3.381, italics added).[19]

Tillich thought early Christianity was not "a radical-exclusive religion" but "the all-inclusive religion" (*ST* 3.205–206). Tillich argued that inclusive inclinations were demonstrated by early Christians laying claim to or borrowing truth from eclectic philosophical and religious sources in the ancient Hellenistic world

(*ST* 3.171).[20] Thus, the early Christian Logos teaching on the universal presence and divine self-manifestation can inform contemporary dialogue. Accordingly, Tillich observes that there has been mutual impact between Buddhism and Christianity, providing a background for Buddhist-Christian dialogue. Such a dialogue might proceed along the principles of (a) comparison of intrinsic aims, (b) relation of humans to humans and of humans to society, (c) the problem of history, and (d) the problem of democracy.[21]

Tillich faults Christianity for a tendency to become a "religion" instead of staying centered in Jesus Christ (*ST* 3.104). Christianity should judge itself and other religions in the light of criteria established by Jesus as the Christ, thus opening up possibilities for change on both sides of the dialogue. Such a self-critical attitude based on Jesus Christ might enhance dialogue with secularism as well. Yet "Tillich does not call for a synthesis of the religions, the end of religion, or the victory of one religion if it remains a 'religion.'"[22] Synthesis would be destructive of the concreteness and dynamic power of each religion, while religion cannot end so long as humans have ultimate questions. Rather, he suggests, "A particular religion will be lasting to the degree it negates itself as a religion."[23] Indeed, for Tillich Spiritual Presence conquers religion as such—that which is prone to demonization and profanation (*ST* 3.243–245).[24] Not Christianity as a religion, but the incomparable revelatory event upon which it is based—the historical manifestation in Jesus as Christ of the eternal New Being—is absolute (*ST* 3.338). So then, we might ask, what is the rhyme and reason for specifically Christian or ecclesial mission? For Tillich, the "purpose of mission is the actualization of the Spiritual Community within concrete churches all over the world" (*ST* 3.193). Moving from latency to manifest actuality in the New Being is at the heart of Christian mission, and includes the Christian church's need to sustain its own life (education) and bear witness to others (evangelism) (*ST* 3.194–196).

Arguably, Tillich's christology tended to emphasize the abstract ontological principle over the concrete existence of Christ, thus potentially weakening his christological doctrine.[25] Nevertheless, Tillich's language, which admittedly at times appeared vacillating, might be explained better according to audience, context, and topic during a particular lecture. Furthermore, the majority of Tillich's work, including his most important work, emphasizes the finality of Jesus as the Christ (e.g., *ST* 2.150–152; 3.148).[26] Yet, if I might put it so, for Tillich Christ is not confined to Christianity, although Tillich contends for the Christian message and mission. In short, Tillich's doctrine of the latent versus the manifest church critiques both Christianity and other religions in light of Jesus as the Christ. Tillich affirms that "Christ is universal and valid for *all* cultures and religions" not on the basis of theoretical proof but on the event-versus-law nature of Christianity, on Christ's sacrifice of the finite for the infinite, and, most of all, on missiological grounds. The daily advance of Christian missions "gives the pragmatic and continuous proof of power and Spirit" that shows Jesus as the Christ has "the power to conquer the world and its ambiguities."[27] Tillich is in no way a "closet pentecostal," but his choice of language here provides some possibilities for pentecostal engagement, especially in christology, pneumatology, and missiology.

As John R. Newport notes, for Tillich "only missions can prove that the church is the agent through which the kingdom of God actualizes itself in history."[28] However, Tillich insists that what Christianity really has to contribute to the world of religions is not simply another religious system (i.e., Western Christianity). As Newport puts it, "The goal of missions is the mediation of the reality of Jesus as the Christ," and this stands as "the criterion for *all* human history."[29] Accordingly, Western Christianity is not the end in itself, but rather a preliminary and transitory expression of the reality of Christ. Thus, the creation of independent churches in different cultures may be Christianity's "greatest triumph," providing "another great proof that Jesus is the center of history."[30]

For personal as well as for theological reasons, including his acquaintance with many Jews, his German background and battle against Nazi anti-Semitism, and his conviction of Christianity's authentic and essential Jewish roots, Tillich was especially interested in Judaism. He wrestled with Jews' rightful place in their ancient homeland and with their special relationship with Christians.[31] Although certainly significant in its own respect, Tillich's intricate engagement with Israel and the Jews is beyond the pale of the present chapter. Suffice it to say that Tillich convincingly argued that the Jews have a continuing and crucial place in God's providence.[32] Yet he always still asserted Christ's centrality and Christianity's significance.

Does Tillich Speak of Theology of Religions with a Pneumatological Accent?

Part IV of Tillich's third volume of *Systematic Theology* most thoroughly elucidates his concept of "Spiritual Presence" (*ST* 3.311–361).[33] Later, he investigates at length its applications to the "ambiguities" of religion, culture, morality, and, finally, to life in general (*ST* 3.162–182). Briefly, Tillich adopts three main symbols for the "unambiguous life," which for him defines or directs the self-transcendent religious quest: Spirit of God, Kingdom of God, and Eternal Life. In this chapter, I'm interested only in the first one. Tillich explains: "The Spirit of God is the presence of Divine Life within creaturely life. The Divine Spirit is 'God present.'" Furthermore, "The Spirit of God is not a separated being. Therefore one can speak of 'Spiritual Presence' in order to give the symbol its full meaning" (*ST* 3.107).[34] For him, Spiritual Presence expresses "unambiguous life" in correlation to "the ambiguities of life under the dimension of spirit although, because of the multidimensional unity of life, it refers indirectly to all realms" (ST 3.107–108). Spiritual Presence, the immanent presence of the transcendent God amid history, represents Tillich's pneumatology. Thus, his doctrine of Spiritual Presence potentially provides a helpful perspective for Pentecostals developing a pneumatological theology of religions.

Tillich recognized that no theological system could do justice to the universal manifestations of Spiritual Presence among the world's religions (ST 3.141). However, he noted that whether in primitive forms, in mythological stages, and especially in mysticism (both Asian and European), and in biblical monotheism, manifestations of Spiritual Presence may be discerned (ST 3.141–143). For him, biblical religion's attitude toward personality and community, especially its emphasis on human dignity and justice, are critical for avoiding the profanization and demonization that can occur when universal religion above religion appears in concrete religions (ST 3.143–144). This insight illustrates Tillich's attempt to be faithful to the Christian tradition while vigorously engaging others.

As for pentecostal theology of religions, it is certainly developing in pneumatological directions. In other words, there is an accent on the agency of the Holy Spirit.[35] There has been some small but significant interaction with Tillich, noting the pneumatological turn of his theology of religions. Amos Yong classifies Tillich's theology of religions as pneumatological and describes Paul Tillich as a potential resource for a pneumatological approach to the religions.[36] He suggests that while not unproblematic, the emphasis of Tillich's pneumatology on "the almost interchangeable confluence of the Spiritual Presence and the New Being as *manifested* in Jesus as the Christ" may hold potential, especially if developed in the context of economic trinitarianism.[37] A little later, I will suggest that a pentecostal theology of religions model obviously christocentric in its appearance may also be robustly pneumatological and relatable to Tillich's "pneumatology" through his Religion of the Concrete Spirit.

Veli-Matti Kärkkäinen classifies Tillich's "dynamic-typological" theology of religions as essentially christocentric, but contends that it "betrays a definite pneumatological orientation."[38] Tillich's pneumatological accent is evident in "The Religion of the Concrete Spirit" as the key to the history of the religions and as the inner aim of the religions.[39] Of course, as Kärkkäinen and Yong observe, Tillich was interested in the "religions of the Spirit" as expressions of mystic and prophetic freedom in contrast to institutionalism and legalism.[40] However, Jesus the Christ is the decisive revelation of the divine, so that "for Tillich both christology (Christ as criterion) and pneumatology (the universal Spirit) are needed for a healthy theology of religions."[41] Arguably, implications for a pentecostal theology of religions desiring to develop bidirectional commitments to christology and pneumatology may be immense.

In his last lecture, Tillich's dynamic-typological approach begins with "the experience of the Holy within the finite" as "the universal religious basis."[42] As noted above, Tillich identifies three major elements within this experiential process. The *sacramental* experiences the Holy within the finite and the particular, that is, within the concrete, in a special way. The *mystical* critically challenges the demonization of the sacramental by moving beyond concrete expressions to reach the Ultimate itself. The *prophetical* religious experience is concerned with ethics and centers on humanity and justice. Tillich suggests not progression or separation between these elements but unity in the Religion of the Concrete Spirit. The *telos*, or inner aim, of religions throughout history is to become a Religion of the Concrete Spirit. However, and this point is important, Tillich does not identify *any* particular religion as *the* Religion of the Concrete Spirit.[43]

Nevertheless, Tillich clearly considers Apostle Paul's doctrine of the Spirit, uniting as it does the ecstatic and rational elements necessary for *agape* and *gnosis*, or love and knowledge, and the order they bring, as the highest expression of the synthesis he envisions in the Religion of the Concrete Spirit.[44] This is a significant confession. First, it explicitly connects Tillich's understanding of biblical (Pauline) pneumatology with his pneumatological theology of religions, especially his teaching on the Religion of the Concrete Spirit. Further, it reveals that the integrative pattern Tillich unpacked in his description of the Religion of the Concrete Spirit may be purposely informed by, as well as expressed in, Tillich's interpretation of Pauline pneumatology. Both possibilities are congruent with Tillich's common method of translating his interpretations of biblical ideas into philosophical language.

Pentecostals might challenge Tillich's critique of "Spirit-theologies" (*ST* 3.144–149, esp. 148). He appears to assume, in spite of indebtedness to and a defense of Spirit-movements (*ST* 3.126, 118), that Spirit-theologies by definition undermine the primacy of Jesus' ultimacy as the manifestation of the Spiritual Presence. If so, this is an error. Tillich argues that Christian relations with world religions must carefully guard the unique "Christ-character of Jesus" (*ST* 3.148). There can be only one ultimate manifestation of the Spiritual Presence, and that is Jesus as the Christ. Pentecostals agree. However, it simply isn't the case that pneumatological theology inevitably implies that the work of Spirit "qualitatively transcends" that of the Christ (*ST* 3.148) and thereby undermines Christ's ultimate uniqueness. The persons of the Trinity aren't competitive but cooperative. For Pentecostals, their Spirit-theology (as Tillich calls it) as a correction of an absence of attention to the Spirit in no way detracts from Christ; rather, it is a restoration of a robust trinitarian theology with important implications for Christian theology of religions.[45] Admittedly, Tillich is concerned about those hijacking religious experience to bring about "an amalgamation of the world religions," but clearer distinctions could be drawn (*ST* 3.148).

Tillich explains that the "dynamic character" of his approach stems from the positive and negative interaction of three elements striving to achieve their inner *telos* of becoming the Religion of the Concrete Spirit within fragmentary and finite history.[46] He graphically describes this "fight of God against religion within religion" as key to understanding "the otherwise extremely chaotic, or at least seemingly chaotic, history of religions." *Christus Victor* symbolizes this struggle and its christological and cruciform criteria for the "critical moments in history, moments of *kairoi,* in which the Religion of the Concrete Spirit is actualized fragmentarily" and "can happen here and there."[47] Nevertheless, the Holy also relates to the secular and even to "quasi-religions" through "theonomy" as the sacred depth of the arts and sciences of secular culture also seek fulfilling direction and find fragmentary actualization in what is really nothing other than the Religion of the Concrete Spirit.[48]

Late in life, Tillich's "hope for the future of theology" was that "the structure of religious thought might develop in connection with another or different fragmentary manifestation of theonomy or of the Religion of the Concrete Spirit."[49] This "interpenetration" would allow the systematic theologian to look more into the particular aspects of the religions, negating extremes of supranatural and natural theology, learning from history of religions methodology in identifying and relating religious phenomena. This avenue requires efforts at understanding religious symbolism in relation to the social matrix and to anthropology.[50] Yet Tillich's "last word" expressing commitment to his own Christian religion remains constant, because without this foundation "no theology at all is possible."[51] Arguably, Tillich increasingly speaks of Christian theology of religions with a pneumatological accent—providing, in my opinion, a substantive starting point for pentecostal engagement.

Can a Pentecostal Profitably Engage Tillich's Theology of Religions?

Some evangelicals have charged Tillich with compromising the uniqueness of Christ in advocating religious pluralism.[52] Yet Tillich is complex and resists facile classification. Perhaps at least in part, Tillich's philosophical methodology is as much or more at issue as anything else.[53] Certainly his philosophical language (or unknown tongue!) can sound very foreign to evangelical (and pentecostal) ears.

I'm reminded of polarization among early Christians over the use of philosophy. Recall Tertullian's famous dictum, "What has Jerusalem to do with Athens?" Yet even Tertullian was not above borrowing Stoic insights when it suited his purposes—although Tillich obviously overstated his case in calling Tertullian "a Stoic philosopher."[54] Neither have Christians through the centuries been able to escape philosophy completely; some have embraced it unabashedly. Enter Tillich. Philosophical theology was his "bread and butter." He concerned himself primarily with ontological questions from an existentialist perspective. At times it is difficult to determine if objections to Tillich are a matter of content or of misgivings over his highly conceptualized philosophical categories and terminology.[55]

My own assumption is that profitable application of Tillichian concepts may be mostly a matter of management. Herein I attempt to work with Tillich's insights in a manner hermeneutically consistent with the pentecostal heritage. Biblical inspiration and authority, high christology, soteriological clarity, and missional ecclesiology—all in a context of robust pneumatology—are my guiding presuppositions.[56] And I can discern a consistently Christian tone throughout Tillich's intuitions on theology of religions.[57] I engage Tillich accordingly. Nevertheless, I do not suggest traditionally conservative Pentecostals should suspend their suspicions of Tillich's oft-touted liberalism.[58] When eating fish, I have to guard against swallowing a bone; but I don't give up eating fish because of it. Why not? Fish is worth the risk! So is it with reading Tillich.

Out of the nearly myriad possibilities, I will select only one implication of Tillich's pneumatological theology of religions for development from a pentecostal perspective: the issue of universality versus particularity. If I am reading Tillich right, he sees the Spiritual Presence issuing forth in the Religion of the Concrete Spirit as linking and uniting these apparent polarities.[59] Accordingly, the Holy Spirit, in preferred pentecostal terminology, would be present and active in the world of religions in a both/and mode rather than either/or. Faithfulness to the christological criterion and the values and vitality of the Religion of the Concrete Spirit determines the extent, although admittedly always fragmentary and finite (that is, incomplete or imperfect), to which a religion authentically participates in and transmits divine life and truth or ultimate meaning and purpose. Christianity, not as a religion per se but because of the universal significance of the Spirit-anointed Christ, is indeed unique; however, not even Christianity can claim for itself ultimate status apart from Jesus Christ. To the extent that another religion may participate in or transmit the Religion of the Concrete Spirit, it is also, though differently, in some sense, involved with Christ through the mysterious workings of the Spirit of God and of Christ.

Extremely important to remember is that the Religion of the Concrete Spirit is not identifiable with any institutional religion or religious system in or of itself, but rather distinctly permeates and progresses it toward God's purposeful goal. (Tillich's teleology will probably sound like eschatology to Pentecostals.) Indeed, as Pentecostals well know, *religion* can be stifling of the Spirit's freshness and free blowing. Accordingly, non-Christian religions, or for that matter even the Christian religion, are not salvific but may serve at best only as particular aids imbibing in and ever moving toward universal reality.[60] Even more important, for Christians in general and for Pentecostals in particular, the universal and ultimate significance of Jesus Christ is uniquely necessary (as in John 14:6 and Acts 4:12). Christ constitutes the core reality of the concrete Spirit. Here can be a consistent approach to pneumatological theology of religions—that is, a theological model interpreted and applied without doing Christian pneumatology grievous injustice.

My own research into early pentecostal theology of religions has discovered positions that resist an all-too-common tendency in contemporary theology of religions to overly identify Jesus Christ with the particular and the Holy Spirit with the universal. Kärkkäinen is agreeing with me when he says, "Christ and the Spirit represent both particularity and universality."[61] I now posit the possibility of what some have called "the religion of Christ," that is, "religion rooted in the person of Christ himself rather than any specific religious system," which "may be made actually present and potentially salvific in the midst of non-Christian religions through the mysterious operation of the omnipresent and ever-active Spirit of Christ (cf. Romans 8:9)."[62] This model assumes a complex but complementary christology and pneumatology. Jürgen Moltmann has agreed that through the religion of Christ, in believers' response to God's Spirit, God's universal relationship to humans and humans' particular relationship to God can come together.[63]

In this context, therefore, I suggest that Tillich's emphasis on Spiritual Presence, Religions of the Spirit, and, most of all, the Religion of the Concrete Spirit potentially provides Pentecostals with a surprisingly familiar and friendly face in which pneumatology can link and unite God's absolute and ultimate being and purpose with God's presence and action in the world of religions, without disconnecting from the uniqueness and necessity of the truth of the good news of salvation in Jesus Christ as proclaimed by Christian churches. Might not the religion of Christ and the Religion of the Concrete Spirit be different ways of trying to say something similar? Might not one argue that, through the Holy Spirit, Christ is present and active beyond the church (i.e., universally) while nonetheless most copiously indwelling her as the one unique institution founded upon the Incarnation event and Pentecost experience (i.e., particularly)? If so, doesn't it challenge pentecostal Christians, as well as others, to strive energetically to actualize more fully what has hitherto been all too fragmentary? Being fully Christian could thus involve authentic relations with those *on the way* even if we don't see them as yet *in the Way*.[64] Thus I must admit with the Psalmist that in describing God's salvation, "I know not its measure" (71:15 NIV)!

For Pentecostals, one advantage of this approach to Tillich is its expansive view of the Holy Spirit. The Holy Spirit is distinctively present and active in the church but is not restricted to it. The Holy Spirit is always the Spirit of Christ, but the Spirit's wide reach stretches beyond institutional Christianity into the world's religions. The Holy Spirit is God's Spirit but is able to dwell among (and in!) human beings. The Holy Spirit indwells human hearts but still fills the entire cosmos. The Holy Spirit, and the "religion," or better, the faith and life the Spirit fosters, is both universal and particular! No wonder the Psalmist rhetorically asked, "Where can I go from your Spirit? Where can I flee from your presence?" (139:7 NIV) No wonder Moses and Aaron called on "the God of the spirits of all flesh" (Numbers 16:22; 27:16 NASB). The universal and the particular join and unite in Christ through God's Spirit. To this extent, I can travel with Tillich.

A pneumatological theology of religions connecting and integrating the universal and the particular enables Christian churches to engage in full-fledged ecclesial mission, including evangelism and discipleship, social and ecological justice, and interreligious dialogue and cooperation, because these represent realms graced with Spiritual Presence calling for the Religion of the Concrete Spirit. Tillich's latent and manifest ecclesiology melds well with his pneumatology at this point. And yet, his warning about demonization of religion calls us to discernment. Acknowledging the reality of demonized religion reassures Pentecostals that they're not being led blindly into a dangerously naïve stance, gullibly susceptible to the devil's wiles. Pentecostals open to God's Spirit's wider work in the world nonetheless oppose Satan's work in the world as well. Evil is real and must be confronted and overcome in Christ by the Holy Spirit's power (1 John 4:4). With Tillich, we enter the struggle assured Christ is victor. Nevertheless, the reality of religious evil ought never to obscure the good and godly reality all around us.

While in this section I mostly tried to show how Pentecostals can learn from Tillich on this topic, Tillich's legacy can also be enriched by pentecostal theology. For example, Yong's work is a striking example of engagement in full-fledged ecclesial mission including evangelism and discipleship, social and ecological justice, and interreligious dialogue and cooperation.[65] His pneumatological integration of Christian beliefs and practices provides robust justification for a Tillichian assumption that diverse aspects of culture represent realms graced with Spiritual Presence calling for the Religion of the Concrete Spirit. Furthermore, our common work on spiritual discernment[66] suggests that while Pentecostals can learn from Tillich about the christological criterion in ways that undermine any absolutist claims to truth, so might Tillich's christological criterion be enriched by pentecostal "this is that" hermeneutics, which locates the living Christ in the present horizon.[67] In which case, demonic claims to absoluteness are ousted by the charismatic signs of the kingdom wrought by the Spirit of the New Being in healing, exorcisms, and other charismata.

What does my conversation with Tillich mean for me as a Pentecostal attempting to develop and articulate our distinctive approach to Christian theology of religions? First of all, Pentecostals can discerningly and discriminatingly partner with major theologians beyond their own tradition with considerable profit, in the process adding to their own repertoire on the one hand, and establishing their credibility with the wider Christian tradition on the other hand. Second, pneumatology is critical to Christian theology of religions, and not exclusively to its pentecostal varieties, providing ways around traditional blockades hitherto untapped or insufficiently tapped. However, third, the only pneumatological theologies of religions palatable for Pentecostals will be those that whole heartedly affirm Christ's utter uniqueness and the church's missional mandate to the world for God's glory. Fourth, radical religious pluralism—any "all ways are equally right" or "all roads lead to God" approach—will not work for Pentecostals, and pentecostal theology of religions will likely always be challenged to set itself over against a politically correct pluralism so endemic in much of today's society. Finally, an informed pentecostal theology of religions, and perhaps also a Tillichian approach renewed by pentecostal thought, will aim at empowering comprehensive Christian mission including evangelism, social responsibility, and interfaith dialogue, along with defending biblical and historic Christian faith and countering destructive religious beliefs and practices (i.e., demonization and profanation) wherever they are found.

Notes

1. Paul Tillich, "The Significance of the History of Religions for the Systematic Theologian," in *The Future of Religions*, ed. Jerald C. Brauer (New York: Harper and Row, 1966), 80–94.

2. Ronald H. Stone, *Paul Tillich's Radical Social Thought* (Atlanta: John Knox Press, 1980), 151. Terence Thomas, the editor of Tillich's *The Encounter of Religions and Quasi-Religions* (Ontario: Edwin Mellen, 1989), xi-xii, argues that Tillich's trip to Japan was a culmination of longstanding interreligious interests. Still, in his last years Tillich addressed the religions in a new way; see John R. Newport, *Paul Tillich: Makers of the Modern Theological Mind*, ed. Bob E. Patterson (Waco, TX: Word, 1984), 56–57 and 89.

3. Recent scholarship finds support for democracy in Buddhism unknown to Tillich (see Stone, *Radical*, 151–152 and 171).

4. This alludes to Tillich's basic argument in *The Protestant Era* (Chicago: University of Chicago Press, 1957) about the Protestant Principle. See also Newport, *Tillich*, 52, and Hannah Tillich, *From Place to Place* (New York: Stein and Day, 1976), 99–106.

5. Christianity's "absoluteness" comes from Christ rather than the Christian religion (*ST* 3.336–338).

6. On Tillich's Platonism, see Adrian Thatcher, *The Ontology of Paul Tillich* (Oxford: Oxford University Press, 1978), 28, 45, 100. Tillich described Protestantism as "a special historical embodiment of a universally significant principle," which he called the Protestant Principle; Tillich also applies the Protestant Principle to the Spiritual Presence and Spiritual Community that combine as "a manifestation of the prophetic Spirit." See *The Essential Tillich: An Anthology of the Writings of Paul Tillich*, ed. F. Forrester Church (Chicago: University of Chicago, 1987, 1999), 69 and 89.

7. Pentecostals might note Tillich's discussion of "faith healing" (*ST* 3.377–378). On transformation as salvific renewal of creation, see *Essential Tillich*, 94. On salvation as participation (regeneration), acceptance (justification), and transformation (sanctification), see *ST* 2.176–182. Please remember Tillich's doctrine of sin as estrangement and its effects (*ST* 2.44–58).

8. Frank Macchia, *Baptized in the Spirit: A Global Pentecostal Theology* (Grand Rapids, MI: Zondervan, 2006), 198–199, suggests paradoxical tensions in Tillich's ecclesiology, especially in distinguishing the visible, historical church in finitude from the Kingdom of God.

9. Thomas, *Religions and Quasi-Religions*, xx–xxi.

10. Newport, *Tillich,* 216.

11. Ibid.

12. *Essential Tillich,* 76.

13. See also Newport, *Tillich,* 176. Tillich certainly did not "disown his life's work" but expressed "regret that he did not do more concerning the encounter of religions" (Thomas, *Religions and Quasi-Religions,* xiv). Tillich likely intended his Religion of the Concrete Spirit to provide theological thrust for the pragmatic need for interreligious dialogue; see Terrance Thomas, *Paul Tillich and World Religions* (Cardiff, UK: Cardiff Academic Press, 1999), 169.

14. Newport, *Tillich,* 176–177.

15. Tillich spoke of sects without defining religions as such (e.g., *ST* 1.141 and *Essential Tillich,* 76).

16. Also see *ST* 2.120; 3.144, 364, 367ff., and Tillich's *Christianity and the Encounter of the World Religions* (New York: Columbia University Press, 1963), 12–13.

17. Tillich, *Encounter,* 45–46. Thomas, *Religions and Quasi-Religions,* xxvi–xxvii, suggests Tillich's dynamic typology is a mixed bag, accurate to an extent, and helpful but imperfect. Notably, Tillich recognized the shortcomings of any typology compared to actual participation in a particular religion (*ST* 3.141).

18. See Tillich, "Significance," 87–89, and *Encounter,* 81–82. Also Newport, *Tillich,* 176–177, and Carl Braaten, *The Flaming Center: A Theology of the Christian Mission* (Philadelphia: Fortress Press, 1977), 11.

19. Thomas, *World Religions,* 158–159, suggests Tillich's Religion of the Concrete Spirit synthesizes themes from earlier writings such as "the religion of paradox" or "the religion of grace."

20. Nevertheless, Christianity needs to maintain a distinctive, and therefore exclusive, center (*ST* 3.79–80), and struggles to prevent adaptation from becoming accommodation (*ST* 3.185–186; cf. *ST* 3.407).

21. Newport, *Tillich,* 179–81; cf. *ST* 3.380.

22. Newport, *Tillich,* 181.

23. Ibid., 182. Also Tillich, *Encounter,* 94–97, 81 and 84. Tillich sounds quite Barthian here. Cf. Karl Barth, "The Revelation of God as the Abolition of Religion," *Church Dogmatics (CD),* trans. and ed. G. W. Bromiley, T. F. Torrence, A. T. Mackay, et al. (Edinburgh: T and T Clark, 1961), I/2:280, and I/2:299–230.

24. For Tillich, conflict between the divine and demonic exists in every religion (*ST* 3.337). However, Tillich understands the demonic against the Hellenistic background of the New Testament not necessarily as personified evil, or even as evil per se, but as ambiguity tending toward distorting the distinction between the finite and the infinite (*ST* 3.102–106). See also Nimi Wariboko, *God and Money: A Theology of Money in a Globalizing World* (Lanham, MD: Lexington Books, 2008), esp. chap. 5.

25. Newport, *Tillich,* 182. See Robert Young, *Encounter with World Religions* (Philadelphia: Westminster Press, 1970), 142.

26. Newport, *Tillich,* 182.

27. Ibid., 183.

28. Ibid.; see also Tillich's "Missions and World History," in *The Theology of Christian Mission,* ed. Gerald H. Anderson (New York: McGraw and Hill, 1961), 282–289.

29. Newport, *Tillich,* 183; orig. italics.

30. Ibid.

31. Tillich, "The Jewish Question: Christian and German Problem," *Jewish Social Studies* 33 (1971) and "Nation of Time, Nation of Space," *Land Reborn* 8 (April-May, 1957), 5. Cf. Glen Earley, "Tillich and Judaism: An Analysis of the 'Jewish Question,'" in *Theonomy and Autonomy: Studies in Paul Tillich's Engagements with Modern Culture,* ed. John Carey (Macon, GA: Mercer University Press, 1984), 213–241.

32. Stone, *Radical,* 148 and 101–102. Cf. Newport, *Tillich,* 184–185.

33. Ironically, Alexander J. McKelway, *The Systematic Theology of Paul Tillich: A Review and Analysis* (Richmond, VA: John Knox Press, 1964), 216, criticizes Tillich's doctrine of the Trinity because he thinks the Spirit dominates christology in this section.

34. Wilhelm Pauck, "To Be or Not to Be: Tillich on the Meaning of Life," in *The Thought of Paul Tillich,* ed. James Luther Adams, Wilhelm Pauck, and Roger Lincoln Shinn (New York: Harper and Row, 1985), 29–43, says Tillich "spoke of faith as ultimate concern; of God as being itself . . . of sin as estrangement and of grace as acceptance; of the Holy Spirit as spiritual presence"; adding that "In explaining the meaning of these terms, he endeavored on the one hand to be as true and profound a diagnostician of the human situation as possible and, on the other hand, to be a clear and truly radical spokesman of the ultimate" (41–42).

35. Veli-Matti Kärkkäinen, "Toward a Pneumatological Theology of Religions: A Pentecostal-Charismatic Inquiry," *International Review of Mission* 91:361 (2002): 187–198, and "How to Speak of the Spirit among Religions: Trinitarian 'Rules' for a Pneumatological Theology of Religions," *International Bulletin of Missionary Research* 30:3 (2006): 121–127; and Amos Yong, *Discerning the Spirit(s): A Pentecostal-Charismatic Contribution to Christian Theology of Religions* (Sheffield, UK: Sheffield Academic, 2000), and *Beyond the Impasse: Toward a Pneumatological Theology of Religions* (Grand Rapids, MI: Baker Academic, 2003).

36. Yong, *Discerning*, 71, 77–85.

37. Ibid., 85. Italics are original. Pan-Chiu Lai, *Towards a Trinitarian Theology of Religions: A Study in Paul Tillich's Thought* (Kampen, NL: Kok, 1994), 115, argues that the third volume of Tillich's *Systematic Theology* and his late-developing theology of religions signal a transformative turn to pneumatology.

38. See Veli-Matti Kärkkäinen, *An Introduction to the Theology of Religions: Biblical, Historical, and Contemporary Perspectives* (Downer's Grove, IL: InterVarsity Press, 2003), 224–234 (231).

39. Kärkkäinen, *Introduction*, 231. Cf. Yong, *Discerning*, 77.

40. Kärkkäinen, *Introduction*, 231, and Yong, *Discerning*, 78.

41. Kärkkäinen, *Introduction*, 232.

42. Tillich, "Significance," 86. Here Tillich draws on Rudolf Otto, *The Idea of the Holy*, trans. John W. Harvey (London: 1923).

43. Tillich, "Significance," 87–88. Cf. Kärkkäinen, *Introduction*, 231–232, and Yong, *Discerning*, 77–78.

44. Tillich, "Significance," 88.

45. See Tony Richie, "The Sevenfold Spirit: A Pentecostal Approach to Christian Theology of Religions," in *Pentecostal Mission and Global Christianity*, Regnum Edinburgh Centenary Series 20, ed. Wonsuk Ma, Kwabena Asamoah-Gyadu, and Veli-Matti Kärkkäinen (London: Regnum, 2014), 224–240.

46. *Pneuma* editorials by Frank Macchia, 29:2 (2007): 185–187, and Dale Coulter, 33:1 (2011): 1–4, suggest Pentecostals are exploring *finitum capax infiniti* (the capacity of the finite for the infinite) regarding "the relationship of the Holy Spirit and the human spirit and the mechanics of such a relationship" (Coulter, 4). See especially Terry Cross, "Divine-Human Encounter: Towards a Pentecostal Theology of Experience," *Pneuma* 31:1 (2009): 3–34 (10–20). Perhaps Tillich is an appropriate partner for that conversation?

47. Tillich, "Significance," 88–89.

48. Ibid., 89–91. Criticized for possibly distorting "the concreteness and historicity of biblical faith" and for questionable implications of his ontological language, Tillich remains acclaimed for his amazing ability to analyze the human spiritual condition in engagement with secular culture. James C. Livingston, *Modern Christian Thought: From the Enlightenment to Vatican II* (New York: Macmillan, 1971, 1989), 370.

49. Tillich, "Significance," 91.

50. Ibid., 91–93.

51. Ibid., 94.

52. Norman Anderson, *Christianity and World Religions: The Challenge of Pluralism* (1970; repr., Downers Grove: InterVarsity Press, 1984), 46–48, 50–51, criticizes Tillich for negating Christ's uniqueness in terms of its particularity and historicity.

53. Thatcher, *Ontology*, 148–153.

54. Paul Tillich, *A History of Christian Thought* (New York: Harper and Row, 1968), 98.

55. Livingston, *Modern Christian Thought*, 356–370. Thomas, *World Religions*, 167, argues incessantly with Tillich's methodology but insists it is to clarify rather than to refute.

56. Tony Richie, *Speaking by the Spirit: A Pentecostal Model for Interreligious Dialogue* (Lexington, KY: Emeth Press, 2011), 26–29, and 62–64. J. Rodman Williams, *Renewal The-*

ology: Systematic Theology from a Charismatic Perspective, 3 vols. in one (Grand Rapids, MI: Zondervan, 1996), 1:18, 27, 52, 99, 170–171, 222, 263, and 383, criticized Tillich yet occasionally quoted him positively.

57. I don't mean to make Tillich sound "evangelical," which would be misleading. Truly his system was resolutely christological but only in terms of "New Being present in Jesus as the Christ" (*ST* 1.50).

58. Pentecostals have had a long but lopsided relationship with fundamentalism that has tended to make many of them suspicious of anything they consider liberal or modernist. Yet overall Pentecostalism is more diverse and less rigid than has often been thought (even by some Pentecostals themselves). Frustration with fundamentalism has been an ongoing feature of pentecostal theology—as has been some friendliness to other (i.e., less restrictive) views. Nevertheless, it would certainly be amiss to assume that Pentecostalism as a whole is anything other than what might be described as conservative or traditional (see Richie, *Speaking by the Spirit*, 300–303). This background suggests to me that any pentecostal appropriation of Tillich, who certainly would never be labeled fundamentalist—or even conservative or traditional—will need to proceed cautiously. Yet, I argue, mature pentecostal theology must wrestle with thinkers like Tillich, whether they agree or not—or perhaps a bit of both.

59. Frederick J. Parrella, "Tillich's Theology of the Concrete Spirit," in *The Cambridge Companion to Paul Tillich*, Russell Re Manning, ed. (Cambridge: Cambridge University Press, 2008), 74–90, esp. 84 and 86, thinks that in Tillich the Spirit transcends historical expression but is present in it, implying, in a carefully qualified sense, both concreteness and/or particularity and abstractness and/or universality.

60. Strictly speaking, only Christ, not our Christian religion, is our Savior. Only Christ qualifies for that glorious title (1 Corinthians 1:10–17).

61. Veli-Matti Kärkkäinen, "A Response to Tony Richie's 'Azusa-era Optimism: Bishop J. H. King's Pentecostal Theology of Religions as a Possible Paradigm for Today,'" *Journal of Pentecostal Theology* 15:2 (2007): 263–268 (267). As implied above, for Tillich Christ is always particular and universal, but the Holy Spirit without concreteness is always universal. Yet the Religion of the Concrete Spirit unites concreteness and particularity with universality.

62. Richie, "Azusa-era Optimism: Bishop J. H. King's Pentecostal Theology of Religions as a Possible Paradigm for Today," in *The Spirit in the World: Emerging Pentecostal Theologies in Global Context*, ed. Veli-Matti Kärkkäinen (Grand Rapids, MI: Eerdmans, 2009), 227–244, esp. 235–240.

63. Jürgen Moltmann, "Preface," in Kärkkäinen, *Spirit in the World*, xi.

64. See also Jewish theologian Abraham Joshua Heschel, "No Religion is an Island," in *Christianity through Non-Christian Eyes*, ed. Paul J. Griffiths (Maryknoll: Orbis, 1990, 2004), 26–40 (35). This challenges soteriological exclusivism (none can be saved apart from the church) and encourages inclusivism (some may be saved through Christ apart from the church) but does not necessarily endorse or promote religious pluralism (all religions are salvific) or universalism (everyone will eventually be saved).

65. Amos Yong, *Hospitality and the Other: Pentecost, Christian Practices, and the Neighbor* (Maryknoll: Orbis, 2008).

66. Amos Yong and Tony Richie, "Missiology and the Interreligious Encounter," in *Studying Global Pentecostalism: Theories and Methods,* ed. Allan Anderson, Michael Bergunder, André Droogers, and Cornelis van der Laan (Berkeley: University of California Press, 2010), 245–267, esp. 260.

67. Amos Yong, *In the Days of Caesar: Pentecostalism and Political Theology* (Grand Rapids, MI: Eerdmans, 2010), 92. See Aimee Semple McPherson, *This Is That: Personal Experiences, Sermons, and Writings of Aimee Semple McPhearson* (Los Angeles: Echo Park Evangelistic Association, 1923).

ELEVEN

The Demonic from the Protestant Era to the Pentecostal Era

An Intersection of Tillichian and Pentecostal Demonologies and Its Implications

DAVID BRADNICK

Paul Tillich's renowned essay titled "The Demonic" played a crucial role in the resurgence of demonology in the twentieth century, and Tillich himself acknowledged the significant manner in which his theology was indebted to his understanding of the demonic.[1] Likewise, pentecostal theology routinely dedicates significant attention to demonology. Yet little dialogue has occurred between Tillichian and pentecostal theologians.[2] In this chapter I aim to initiate the conversation through a pentecostal reflection on Tillich's theology of the demonic. I will begin by summarizing Tillich's position, followed by a synopsis of traditional pentecostal demonology. Next, I will propose a pentecostal-emergentist theology of the demonic and suggest why it may be a productive approach for entering into dialogue with Tillich. Finally, drawing from the psychological and anthropological sciences, I will interact with Tillich's theology of the demonic, proposing possible convergences with a pentecostal-emergentist approach.

Tillich's Theology of the Demonic

Following the Enlightenment, many theologians intentionally avoided the term *demonic* because of its antiquarian connotations. Tillich, however, saw the importance of retaining this language because a total demythologization of symbols establishes a dangerous precedent. "Scientific substitutes" cannot fully exhaust the depth and dimensions or religious language, and so a place must be secured for theological interpretation of symbols, including the demonic.[3] Thus, reductionistic tendencies of the liberal tradition were untenable for Tillich.[4] Yet he also rejected traditional metaphysical views of demons as conscious, autonomous beings. He remarks: "The demonic is fulfilled in the spirit, not in 'spirits,' i.e., beings which are defined only through being demons. Even 'spirits'—if this concept has an objective meaning—are first living forms, that is, 'natures,' in which demonic phenomena, ecstasies and frenzies, can appear or not appear. The affirmation of the demonic has nothing to do with a mythological or metaphysical affirmation of a world of spirits."[5] Instead, for Tillich, the phenomenon of the demonic has always existed and will persist throughout history.[6] It simply cannot be ignored. Consequently, a reconsideration of the demonic is necessary to understand its true nature and enable appropriate engagement with and resistance to it.[7]

Tillich's theology of the demonic must be understood in light of his theology of life. He proposes that life is composed of two dynamics: the essential (pure potentiality) and the existential (actuality). Life is a continuous interaction between the inherent possibilities of creation and their tangible fulfillment. It is the "mixture" of these two elements that allows self-transcendence whereby creation and its creatures move toward newness and fulfillment (*ST* 3.12, 170). Life contains an element of creativity and freedom, which draws every part of creation toward a realization of fresh possibilities inherent within their forms.[8] Tillich calls this "the actualization of potential being" (*ST* 3.30). These potentialities are determined by each form's organic, inorganic, psychological, historical, and spiritual characteristics (or "dynamics").[9] These dynamics provide innovative avenues of development so that creation never remains stagnant.

A form's potentiality, however, is not exclusively virtuous. A form contains the possibility of actualizing existentially, not only in sacred functions, but in evil ones as well. Life has an "ambiguous character" whereby it is capable of expressing both divine and demonic forces. Existential realities, then, may operate as "structures of evil" that can "rule individual souls, nations, and even nature" (*ST* 2.27).[10] For instance, economic systems, such as capitalism, can become demonic.[11] Within individuals it "drives man to confuse natural self-affirmation with destructive self-elevation" (*ST* 2.51).[12] Existential realities become destructive structures that prevent reconciliation, reunion, creativity, meaning, and hope (*ST* 1.49).[13] Hence, the demonic does not exist as a distinct form, a nebulous spiritual substance, or a conscious entity, but it develops within and feeds off of existential actualities.[14]

Demonic manifestations arise as a negation of a form's essential nature. In other words, the form abandons its character as it declares itself to be the ultimate purpose that all other realities must fulfill.[15] Tillich writes, "Anything that claims to be sacred and that does not recognize the demand of the Unconditional is demonic."[16] This occurs when the finite is elevated above the infinite, causing rejection of divine purposes within the form (ST 3.102).[17] Accordingly, the form's existential reality merely becomes a pawn; the form is stripped of freedom and creativity. In other words, its actualized potentiality is bound, replaced by a superficial structure that declares its own autonomy and grandeur (ST 1.222).[18] The demonic merely masquerades behind existential realities in order to exploit and deceive. Like a bottomless "abyss," the insatiable appetite of the demonic renders the form meaningless and void of divine purpose.[19]

This illusion of self-transcendence creates a counterfeit reality.[20] The demonic is not simply destructive; it also includes a creative aspect.[21] Tillich writes, "[These powers] are always at work in every moment of our lives . . . they have a double face. They are the powers that rule the world, and they rule it for good and for evil. They grasp us by the good they bring and they destroy us by the evil they contain."[22] The creative aspect of the demonic attracts and captivates people through the good that is flaunted and fraudulently promised, but, meanwhile, its destructive nature clandestinely wreaks havoc. This dual creative and destructive dynamic devastates the essential nature of the form from which it emerges, while generating a false hope.

The existential nature of life means that creation is always exposed to finitude, estrangement, conflict, distortion, and death (ST 3.12). This also includes susceptibility to the demonic, making no form immune to the parasitic nature of the demonic, including and especially religion. Throughout history, religion has been co-opted by the demonic, and Tillich references examples such as the Inquisition, fundamentalism, and papal infallibility, to demonstrate his point (ST 3.381).

Despite the constant threat of the demonic, Tillich maintained that it can be overcome. But this requires more than human action alone. Divine grace must be appropriated through the Spiritual Community by the New Being and the Spiritual Presence (ST 3.103, 173). This need for divine intervention is expressed by the Protestant principle, whereby only God can bring us into relation with him. Tillich states, "God alone can act and . . . no human claim, especially no religious claim, no intellectual or moral or devotional 'work,' can reunite us with him" (ST 3.224). The Protestant principle reminds us that victory over the demonic can only come through God's work in the Word and the Spirit (ST 3.245).

Triumph over the demonic, however, is never final amid the ambiguities of historical life. Since the demonic is always a possibility, it will never be completely eradicated. Life is always vulnerable to manifestations of the demonic. The demonic can be overcome in specific situations but never permanently, since when one evil is overcome another potentially arises in a different form (ST 2.163, 3.373).[23] Therefore, the church should be consistently vigilant against irruptions of the demonic.

Pentecostal Theologies of the Demonic:
Traditional and Emergentist Approaches

Generally speaking, Pentecostals have been reluctant to engage Tillich's theology of the demonic.[24] This is due, primarily, to differences in their ontology of demons.[25] Most traditional Pentecostals hold to traditional beliefs in demons as conscious, independent spiritual entities—a belief that Tillich rejects. However, several Pentecostals, including myself, are questioning these traditional views. Critical readings of biblical and theological texts, coupled with inter-disciplinary studies, are spawning new perspectives. The following section summarizes traditional pentecostal demonology and highlights its considerable incongruity with Tillich's theology of the demonic. Afterward, I present a pentecostal-emergentist theology of the demonic as an alternative to traditional pentecostal demonology and explore its potential for entering into a critical conversation with Tillich's views.

From the outset of their movement Pentecostals have devoted significant attention to demonology, and William Hamner Piper (1868–1911) and Donald Gee (1891–1966) were two of the most outspoken pentecostal evangelists in this regard.[26] Essentially, they asserted that demons are conscious, metaphysical beings with ontological substance. In so doing, they took a stand against liberalism, whose adherents viewed demons merely as symbols functioning to describe evil political and social realities.[27] Summarizing this position, Gee states:

> We are all impressed, I believe, with the reality of Satan. It is not popular today to believe in a personal devil, but people who are baptized in the Holy Ghost know that he has not gone out of business. The most of us here [sic] know very well there is a real, personal devil, and we know his power to tempt. He was very real to our Lord, and however much we may sneer at such an idea today, to the Lord Jesus, Satan was a terrible reality. I am glad that he has also become a reality to us. I can fight the foe better when I know he is there.[28]

Piper adds, "I have no sympathy with the foolishness, as it appears to me, both from experience and from the Word of God, of the idea that Satan is simply a principle and not a personality."[29] These early Pentecostals maintained a traditional view from their Wesleyan-Holiness roots, concluding that demons are former angels who fell from grace upon joining Satan's rebellion against God. Consequently, early Pentecostals saw no reason to deal with the ontology of demons any further and tended to focus their teachings on spiritual discernment and exorcism.[30]

Early Pentecostals, like Gee and Hamner, set the stage for subsequent views. John Wimber (1934–1998), who is often recognized as an authority on demons within the charismatic renewal movement, also maintained that demons are fallen angels.[31] Similarly, he appealed to scripture, church history, and experience to support their metaphysical existence.[32] Traditional beliefs in demons are also maintained by the majority of contemporary Pentecostals, especially those in the global South, who resist secularism's disenchantment and retain a keen awareness that the world is full of spirits. This ability to synthesize pentecostal beliefs with indigenous perspectives is a major reason that Pentecostalism has grown significantly in the past century.[33]

Thus, most Pentecostals identify any demythologization of the demonic as untenable because it conflicts with their understanding of scripture, tradition, and experience. Consequently, traditional pentecostal demonology has undergone little change since the early years of the movement. Pentecostals may disagree about the tactics used by demons and who can be possessed, but they are consistent in affirming the ontological status of demons as individual, personal, conscious, substantive, and spiritual beings.

Traditional pentecostal demonology, however, confronts a number of biblical, theological and philosophical challenges. Biblical evidence suggesting an angelical fall is tentative. Theologically, should personhood be ascribed to demons?[34] And, philosophically, substance dualism presents the challenge of rationalizing a causal link between spiritual and physical substances.[35] Criticisms of traditional demonology offered by demythologization theologians, in addition to Tillich, also pertain to traditional pentecostal demonology. This is precisely why some Pentecostals suggest that an alternative view is needed to undertake these issues. I propose that a pentecostal-emergentist theology of the demonic may be a promising theological approach.[36]

Emergence theory provides a foundation for an alternative theology of the demonic. *Emergence* is a philosophical interpretation of evolutionary thought that suggests the world is composed of many emergent ontological levels whereby the higher levels derive from increasingly complex systems and patterns. These emergent realities are irreducible to their constituent levels and potentially enact top-down causal agency.[37] In short, emergent realities are dependent upon, yet greater than, the sum of their constituent parts. Thus, an emergentist ontology provides an alternate philosophical framework to the inherent problems within substance dualism.[38]

Given this framework, it is feasible to conceive of the demonic in emergentist terms. In this case, the demonic is not a distinct spiritual substance but a product of evolutionary processes.[39] This allows the demonic to supervene and exert its influence upon the created order. And rather than fallen angels, the demonic comprises a derivative phenomenon that emerges subsequently from living creatures. Furthermore, in regard to human beings, the demonic, as emergent, cannot be reduced to human agency alone. The human condition participates in giving rise to the demonic, but the demonic is not confined to humanity. Once the demonic emerges, it subsists independently from the particular conditions from which it derives. Thus, an emergentist approach reaffirms the destructive character of the demonic without succumbing to the reductionism of demythologization and allows for recognition of the demonic as more than a symbol without subscribing to traditional pentecostal demonology.[40]

In relation to Tillich, a pentecostal-emergentist theology of the demonic provides points of contact for a critical conversation that could not be offered by traditional pentecostal demonology. Accordingly, the next two sections open up a discussion with Tillich from a pentecostal-emergentist perspective, suggesting how these two theologies may stimulate each other.

The Convergence of Tillich and a Pentecostal-Emergentist Theology of the Demonic

Considering the preceding, Tillich's theology of the demonic is markedly incompatible with traditional pentecostal demonology. By looking at his criticism of traditional Christian demonology, we can extrapolate Tillich's disapproval of traditional pentecostal convictions regarding the ontology of demons. However, a pentecostal-emergentist theology of the demonic may not be at odds with Tillich's view. Both express concern with the theological underpinnings of traditional pentecostal demonology and deny personalist conceptions of the demonic. This agreement serves as an obvious point for initiating dialogue between pentecostal-emergentist and Tillichian theologies of the demonic, and the following section explores additional commonalities.

First, Tillich's theology and a pentecostal-emergentist position jointly recognize the shortcomings of demythologization and avoid reducing the demonic to human agency alone. This is exemplified in Tillich's description of the demonic as an abyss and his insistence that human efforts, apart from grace, are futile in overcoming it. Concurrently, a pentecostal-emergentist theology views the demonic as a higher ontological reality that cannot be completely encompassed by its lower constituent levels. Both suggest a type of transcendence whereby the demonic rises to a level of power and cannot be restrained. Although they presume different metaphysical and conceptual frameworks, both agree that the demonic is more than a simple metaphor for human-willed evil.

Second, Tillich agrees with a pentecostal-emergentist theology that systemic evils are a major component of the demonic. Human structures and systems are realities in which the demonic may manifest, although not exclusively, and exert oppressive powers. Thus the demonic is not an independent spiritual substance, but rather a phenomenon that is recurrently connected with these existential realities. A pentecostal-emergentist theology of the demonic differs from Tillich on how the demonic surfaces within these structures, but it is difficult to overstate the role that systems play in both theologies.[41]

Finally, if my reading of Tillich is correct, then the demonic primarily manifests in conjunction with human consciousness. If the demonic manifests by the finite and conditional, claiming the status of the infinite and unconditional and asserting its own ultimacy amid human socialities, then the demonic comes subsequently from the evolution of human beings. Hence, Tillich's timetable for the appearance of the demonic is remarkably consistent with the presumptions of a pentecostal-emergentist framework, wherein the demonic does not originate before the creation of the material world and its various levels of complexity but in conjunction with them. So, both theologies view the demonic as dependent upon the advent of the created order.[42]

These points of agreement should be significant enough to attract the attention of Tillichian and pentecostal theologians. Unlike previous generations, neither can arbitrarily dismiss the other in light of these commonalities. Thus, a pentecostal-emergentist theology of the demonic may indeed serve as a promising gateway for bringing Tillich and Pentecostals into a more constructive dialogue with one another. A full-blown discussion of Tillichian and pentecostal-emergentist intersections goes beyond the scope of this chapter, but these commonalities should serve as important points for further conversations.

Heretofore, I have primarily examined similarities between the Tillichian and pentecostal-emergentist approaches, but their positions are not entirely congruent. There are several divergences that may concern Pentecostals, and the next section examines one of these and suggests how a pentecostal appropriation of emergentist theology of the demonic may "thicken" Tillich's understanding.

A Critical Conversation with Tillich: Pentecostal and Interdisciplinary Perspectives

As a pentecostal, I am not satisfied by an exclusive focus on the ontology of the demonic. I also want to pay attention to the phenomenological manifestations of the demonic that I accept as legitimate, specifically extraordinary demonic manifestations within individuals. Traditionally, Christians, including Pentecostals, have recognized erratic behavior, including unnatural contortions of the body, changes in personality, voice modulations, psychic knowledge, and the ability to speak in other languages, among other expressions, as signs of the demonic.[43] Modern theologies of the demonic tend to ignore or downplay these phenomena, but they do not need to be neglected or ignored within the framework of a pentecostal-emergentist theology of the demonic. Given that the demonic enacts top-down causation upon its constituent components, I postulate that these extraordinary manifestations are the result of this downward action. But the question remains: Can an emergentist construction comprehend these manifestations without resorting to traditional demonological conceptions?

These presumptions have implications for evaluating Tillich's theology of the demonic, primarily because of his evasiveness regarding enthusiastic phenomena often associated with demonic possession. Tillich's understanding of demonic possession alone is quite ambiguous, partly because he focuses mainly upon manifestations of the demonic within political, economic, and religious structures. When Tillich does address demonic possession, he contrasts it with divine ecstasy, but it is unclear if Tillich intends to imply the presence of enthusiastic phenomena traditionally associated with demonic possession (*ST* 1.113–14). Bearing in mind his interaction with Freud, Tillich may view these manifestations as neurotic episodes. He never explicitly makes this connection, but, if this is Tillich's position, then it must be reconsidered in light of post-Freudian psychology.

Freud reduced demonic possession to neurotic episodes or "derivatives of instinctual impulses that have been repudiated and repressed."[44] These impulses normally stem from childhood and are usually rooted in human sexual development. Similarly, Jung attributed claims of demonic possession to *the shadow*—complexes or "personal tendencies, motives, and characteristics that we have barred from consciousness, whether deliberately or not."[45] Jung, however, differs from Freud by downplaying the role of sexuality in repression and also by recognizing the presence of inherited archetypes in the human collective consciousness.[46] Regardless, both viewed possession as a type of psychosis.

For most of the twentieth century Freudian and Jungian explanations dominated the field of psychology; but many contemporary psychologists see problems with universalizing these theories, because they cannot address nonpathological cases of possession. For example, some studies indicate that people who undergo possession may exhibit more stability in their mental health than those who do not. Thus, many instances of possession may not be psychotic in nature.[47] Consequently, psychologists have developed the category of dissociation, which includes nonpathological possession/trance phenomena (PTP).[48] Pathological diagnoses of PTP do not apply to cases in which trance is voluntarily entered and culturally accepted, meaning that possession is multifaceted and must be understood within the context of cultural worldviews.[49] This has implications for Tillich's theology of the demonic. If he understands the traditional signs associated with demonic possession as psychotic episodes, much like Freud, then Tillich's theology also fails to assimilate nonpathological cases of possession and lacks some explanatory power.

Another reading of Tillich, however, is possible. He typically discusses neurosis in the context of despair and limited self-affirmation, but this contradicts his view of demonization as self-aggrandizement.[50] He asserts that all demonic manifestations occur when entities, including individuals, make their own selves the ultimate purpose for which others exist. He writes, "A demonic structure drives man to confuse natural self-affirmation with destructive self-elevation" (*ST* 2.51). However, if despair-based neurosis is the result of oppression caused by demonic systems and structures, then Tillich's understanding may be tenable in light of modern psychological anthropology.

Anthropologist I. M. Lewis's "conflict theory" maintains that possession phenomena result from a social power struggle between those in the elite class and those of a subordinate position.[51] In his study of numerous deprivation cults, particularly the Somali of northeast Africa, Lewis routinely observed and interpreted spirit-possession as a subconscious attempt by women to gain an amplified voice in society. Finding themselves subjugated within a hierarchical system, women "resort to spirit possession as a means both of airing their grievances obliquely and of gaining some satisfaction."[52] He classifies these social dynamics as a sex-war in which the men and women, although interdependent, compete for power. Women use possession as a means to manipulate their spouses when conventional interactions are impotent.[53]

Lewis recognizes this sex-war as indicative of a larger trend. Some societies display shifts in possession demographics, suggesting that tensions between economic classes are related to the lower strata being the primary candidates for possession.[54] Ex-slaves and those occupying servile positions sometimes become the principal mediums for spirit activity. Lewis indicates that he is "concerned here with a widespread use of spirit-possession, by means of which women and other depressed categories exert mystical pressures upon their superiors in circumstances of deprivation and frustration when few other sanctions are available to them."[55] Ultimately, Lewis observes possession as a subconscious means for the voiceless to gain a public hearing.[56] While individuals would typically be punished for this type of protest, spirit-possession provides protection from disciplinary action. Possession frees individuals to voice their disgruntlement because they are not perceived to be acting out of their own volition; rather it is the spirits who operate through them.[57]

Lewis's theory provides key insights for the pentecostal-emergentist and Tillichian theologies of the demonic. First, possession phenomena may be fundamentally linked to systemic evil. From a theological standpoint, the systems and structures observed by Lewis correspond with the manner in which demonic systems act within the pentecostal-emergentist and Tillichian frameworks. Both may agree that these systems are oppressive, denigrating, and domineering. Thus, if we identify these structures as demonic, then enthusiastic possession phenomena may be integrally connected to systemic manifestations of the demonic.[58] Furthermore, this connection is amenable to Tillich's theology of the demonic, if my proposed reading of Tillich is correct. However, Tillich himself was unable to make this connection due to the limited scope of psychology during his time. A pentecostal-emergentist theology of the demonic, however, is able to make this explicit connection. Thus, enthusiastic manifestations associated with possession should not be reduced to derivatives of the human psyche, but they are integrally connected as reactions to demonic systems.

Second, a pentecostal-emergentist position allows acceptance of demonic possession without subscribing to traditional demonology. In traditional demonology, possession typically denotes the infiltration of demons into the human body. This presumes a substance ontology (i.e., dualism), but, as I have mentioned above, this is problematic in considering a causal link. However, a pentecostal-emergentist theology of the demonic is capable of affirming possession without accepting the premises of substance dualism. While the demonic may not be physically or spiritually present within a demoniac's body, the demonic can be understood as supervening upon the human level, resulting in enthusiastic manifestations indicative of the demonic. This is simply a different way of thinking about possession. Therefore, a pentecostal-emergentist position preserves the category of possession and the extraordinary manifestations that signal them without sacrificing theological and philosophical cogency.[59]

Thus, a pentecostal-emergentist and multidisciplinary perspective may provide a theological assist to Tillich's theology of the demonic regarding enthusiastic phenomena that are typically connected to demonic possession. Such an evaluation of Tillich's thought suggests that the phenomenon of demonic possession is much more complex than he could have anticipated. However, as I have demonstrated, a pentecostal-emergentist theology of the demonic may provide insights to develop a more robust theology of the demonic. In relation to social psychology and cultural anthropology, a pentecostal-emergentist approach can accept pathological and nonpathological dimensions of possession phenomena while also maintaining beliefs in the reality of the demonic. In other words, a pentecostal-emergentist theology of the demonic avoids dismissing every alleged instance of spirit-possession as pathological, while also avoiding the other extreme of "seeing a devil behind every bush."

Interestingly, while some Pentecostals have seized opportunities to dialogue with such notable nonpentecostal theologians as Karl Barth and Walter Wink, with regard to the demonic, Tillich has not been embraced as a primary conversation partner.[60] This may be understandable, considering the lack of common ground that traditional pentecostal demonology shares with Tillich's position, but a pentecostal-emergentist theology of the demonic offers the prospect for reciprocity. Tillich may illuminate and stretch pentecostal theologies of the demonic in constructive ways not yet explored, while pentecostal perspectives also may push back on the Tillichian legacy.

While the purpose of this chapter is to initiate a deeper dialogue with Tillich, I have only been able to consider limited aspects of his theology of the demonic. I conclude by suggesting a few areas in which more exploration needs to take place. The first deals with eschatology. As noted above, Tillich argues that the demonic always has the potential to actualize, and new manifestations arise as old ones are eradicated. Thus, Tillich does not recognize a decisive and permanent triumph over the demonic. This may be problematic for most Pentecostals, who advocate a total and definitive defeat of demonic powers upon the parousia.[61] For most Pentecostals the coming eschaton is more than simply a reoccurring ideal; it is rather an impending, yet absolute, victory over the demonic. Thus, Pentecostals and Tillichians need further conversations on how eschatology relates to a theology of the demonic.

Second, Pentecostals and Tillichians need more dialogue on the creative or noncreative dynamic of the demonic.[62] Tillich thinks the demonic fundamentally contains creative and destructive dynamics. He notes, "The Satanic is the negative, destructive principle, inimical to meaning, which is effective in the demonic, in connection with the positive, creative meaningful principle."[63] For Tillich the demonic has a dialectical structure comprising both destructive and creative capacities. The destructive side is represented by the symbol of Satan, but this cannot exist independently from the creative aspect of the demonic. [64] On the other hand, some Pentecostals advocate a privative view of the demonic, whereby it lacks creativity and value and merely hijacks the good.[65] Here, Tillich's theology challenges Pentecostals to think of the demonic from a different angle. If pentecostal theologians choose to reject Tillich's creative dynamic of the demonic, then they must elaborate upon how demonic realities emerge.

In closing, a pentecostal-emergentist theology of the demonic assists in closing the gap between Tillich and Pentecostals. It would be naïve to think all Pentecostals will accept a pentecostal-emergentist position, but for those who are open to its potential, new avenues of thinking may open up. It is impossible to predict what may come out of these conversations, but, if this chapter provides a glimpse, Tillichian and Pentecostal engagements may prove to be quite fruitful.

Notes

1. Paul Tillich, "The Demonic," in *The Interpretation of History*, trans. N. A. Rasetzki and Elsa L. Talmey (New York: C. Scribner's Sons, 1936), 77–122; Paul Tillich, *The Protestant Era* (Chicago: University of Chicago Press, 1948), xx.

2. See Amos Yong, *Discerning the Spirit(s): A Pentecostal-Charismatic Contribution to Christian Theology of Religions* (Sheffield: Sheffield Academic, 2000), 237n19.

3. Paul Tillich, *Dynamics of Faith* (New York: Harper and Row, 1958), 50–52.

4. Tillich, *The Interpretation of History*, 85.

5. Ibid.

6. Tillich, *The Protestant Era*, xx.

7. Tillich, *The Interpretation of History*, 122.

8. Tillich, *The Interpretation of History*, 88. For more on Tillich's understanding of "form" see *ST* 2.178–180.

9. The point of intersection between these dynamics is where Tillich locates the nature of an entity's spirit. Consequently, Tillich's demonology cannot be understood apart from his pneumatology. They are integrally connected. Tillich's pneumatology is another point that needs further dialogue from pentecostal theologians, precisely the purpose of this volume.

10. Tillich also refers to it as "psychical and corporate demonry." See Tillich, *The Interpretation of History*, 90.

11. See Paul Tillich, *Political Expectation* (Macon, GA: Mercer University Press, 1971), 50.

12. Ibid.

13. Ibid., 63–64.

14. Tillich, *Political Expectation*, 66; Paul Tillich, *Advanced Problems in Systematic Theology: Lectures Delivered by Paul Tillich*, ed. Peter H. John (1952), 224. The publisher of this volume is unknown.

15. Tillich, *The Interpretation of History*, 79, 82; Tillich, *Advanced Problems in Systematic Theology*, 221; *ST* 3.344.

16. Tillich, *Political Expectation*, 31.

17. Paul Tillich, "Freedom in the Period of Transformation," in *Freedom: Its Meaning*, ed. Ruth Nanda Anshen (New York: Harcourt Brace, 1940), 143.

18. Tillich, *Political Expectation*, 31.

19. Tillich, *The Interpretation of History*, 84, 88. Although Tillich employs the metaphor of an abyss, I do not read him as advocating a privative understanding of the demonic (i.e., Barth's application of "nothingness"). Vernon R. Mallow uses the term "parasitic" to describe Tillich's view of demonic activity. See his book *The Demonic: A Selected Theological Study—An Examination into the Theology of Edwin Lewis, Karl Barth, and Paul Tillich* (Lanham, MD: University Press of America, 1983), 116.

20. Tillich, *The Interpretation of History*, 122.

21. Ibid., 80–82.

22. Paul Tillich, "Principalities and Powers," in *The New Being* (New York: Charles Scribner's Sons, 1955), 54.

23. Paul Tillich, *A History of Christian Thought: From Its Judaic and Hellenistic Origins to Existentialism,* ed. Carl E. Braaten (New York: Simon and Schuster, 1968), 534; Paul Tillich, "The Right to Hope," *The Christian Century* 107:33 (1990): 1065.

24. For the purposes of this chapter I will use the term "pentecostal" to refer to the Pentecostal-Charismatic movement as a whole.

25. Some exceptions include Nimi Wariboko, *God and Money: A Theology of Money in a Globalizing World* (Plymouth, UK: Lexington Books, 2008); *The Pentecostal Principle: Ethical Methodology in New Spirit* (Grand Rapids, MI: Eerdmans, 2012) and Amos Yong, *In the Days of Caesar: Pentecostalism and Political Theology* (Grand Rapids, MI: Eerdmans, 2010), ch. 4; Yong, *Discerning the Spirit(s),* ch. 3–4.

26. Piper and Gee express an early version of what becomes the prevailing pentecostal position, but early Pentecostals expressed a variety of views regarding demonology. See Nimi Wariboko's discussion of Nigerian Pentecostal Garrick Braide in *Ethics and Time: Ethos of Temporal Orientation in Politics and Religion of the Niger Delta* (Plymouth, UK: Lexington Books, 2010), 91–101.

27. See Walter Rauschenbusch, *Christianity and the Social Crisis* (Norwood, MA: Norwood Press, 1907; repr., 2007).

28. Donald Gee, "Faith—The Christian's Star in the Night: The Subtle Power of the Unseen Foe," *The Latter Rain Evangel,* October 1, 1929, 6.

29. William Hamner Piper, "Power Over All the Power of the Enemy: In My Name They Shall Cast Out Demons," *The Latter Rain Evangel,* May 1, 1910, 15.

30. For more on this topic see James M. Collins, *Exorcism and Deliverance Ministry in the Twentieth Century: An Analysis of the Practice and Theology of Exorcism in Modern Western Christianity* (London: Paternoster, 2009); Grant Wacker, *Heaven Below: Early Pentecostals and American Culture* (Cambridge, MA: Harvard University Press, 2003).

31. John Wimber, *Power Healing* (San Francisco: HarperCollins, 1991), 37, 104–106.

32. Ibid., 100.

33. See Allen Anderson, "Deliverance and Exorcism in Majority World Pentecostalism," in *Exorcism & Deliverance: Multi-Disciplinary Studies,* ed. William K. Kay and Robin Parry (London: Paternoster, 2011), 101–119.

34. For more on this see Nigel G. Wright "Deliverance and Exorcism in Theological Perspective 1: Is There Any Substance to Evil," in Kay and Parry, *Exorcism & Deliverance: Multi-Disciplinary Studies,* 204–206.

35. The implications here apply not only to the demonic but also to pneumatology as a whole, including the work of the Holy Spirit.

36. Pentecostal theologian Amos Yong appropriates emergence philosophy and sketches an emergentist theology of the demonic in his book *Spirit of Creation: Modern Science and Divine Action in the Pentecostal-Charismatic Imagination* (Grand Rapids, MI; Eerdmans, 2011), 173–225.

37. For more on emergence see Philip Clayton, "Neuroscience, the Person, and God: An Emergentist Account," *Zygon: Journal of Religion and Science* 35 (2000): 613–652; Philip Clayton, *Mind and Emergence: From Quantum to Consciousness* (Oxford: Oxford University Press 2006); Timothy O'Connor, "Emergent Properties," *American Philosophical Quarterly* 31 (1994): 91–104.

38. For more on the theological and philosophical issues with substance dualism, see David Bradnick, "A Pentecostal Perspective on Entropy, Emergent Systems, and Eschatology," *Zygon* 43:4 (2008): 925–942.

39. This also has implications for angels and other spiritual entities addressed in my essay "Spirits and the Star: A Spirit-Filled Cosmology," in *Interdisciplinary and Religio-Cultural Discourses on a Spirit-Filled World: Loosing the Spirits,* ed. Kirsteen Kim, Veli-Matti Kärkkäinen, and Amos Yong (New York: Palgrave Macmillan, 2013), 213–226.

40. I elaborate upon an emergentist proposal in my forthcoming PhD dissertation titled "Loosing and Binding the Spirits: Towards an Emergentist Theology of the Demonic" (Regent University School of Divinity, 2015).

41. Yong has initiated dialogue with Tillich on these points and suggests that further engagement needs to occur from Pentecostals. See his book *In the Days of Caesar: Pentecostalism and Political Theology* (Grand Rapids, MI: Eerdmans, 2010), ch. 4.

42. This also has implications for how angelic beings are understood and will need to be considered in future projects.

43. See Moshe Sluhovsky, *Believe Not Every Spirit: Possession, Mysticism, and Discernment in Early Modern Catholicism* (Chicago: University of Chicago Press, 2007), 81, 151, 193.

44. See Sigmund Freud, "A Seventeenth-Century Demonological Neurosis," in *The Standard Edition of the Complete Psychological Works of Sigmund Freud,* ed. James Strachey, vol. 19 (London: Hogarth Press, 1999), 72.

45. David L. Hart, "The Classical Jungian School," in *The Cambridge Companion to Jung,* ed. Polly Young-Eisendrath and Terence Dawson (Cambridge: Cambridge University Press, 2008), 98.

46. See Carl G. Jung, *The Archetypes and the Collective Unconscious* (Princeton, NJ: Princeton University Press, 1990), 285; Renos K. Papadopoulos, "Multiple Personality Dissociation, and C. G. Jung's Complex Theory," *Journal of Analytical Psychology* 34:4 (1989): 365.

47. See Amaro J. Laria, "Dissociative Experiences Among Cuban Mental Health Patients Spiritist Mediums" (PhD diss., University of Massachusetts, 1998); Paul F. Dell and John A. O'Neil, eds., *Dissociation and the Dissociative Disorders: DSM-V and Beyond* (New York: Routledge, 2009), 175.

48. Dell and O'Neil, 174–178.

49. See Stefano Ferracuti, Roberto Sacco, and Renato Lazzari, "Dissociative Trance Disorder: Clinical and Rorschach Findings in Ten Persons Reporting Demonic Possession and Treated by Exorcism," *Journal of Personality Assessment* 66:3 (1996): 525–539.

50. Tillich, *The Courage to Be,* 2nd ed. (New Haven, CT: Yale University Press, 2000), 66.

51. Anthropologists typically do not differentiate between spirit possession and demonic possession. Spirit possession may encompass demonic possession (as labeled by theologians) but is not limited to this phenomenon. Spirit possession involves the spirits of ancestors, spirits from other religions, or, in the case of Christianity, possession by the Holy Spirit. The term "demonic" imposes an etic theological category upon spirit-possession, and anthropologists tend to avoid making theological assessments, moral evaluations, or value judgments. Therefore, this chapter will broadly interact with anthropological investigations of spirit-possession, making correlations as appropriate from a theological perspective.

52. I. M. Lewis, "Spirit Possession and Deprivation Cults," *Man* 13 (1966): 314. See also I. M. Lewis, *Ecstatic Religion: A Study of Shamanism and Spirit Possession* (New York: Routledge, 2003), 68.

53. Interestingly, Lewis notes that spirit-possession becomes relatively rare within egalitarian societies, thus providing quantitative evidence to bolster his views. See Lewis, "Spirit Possession and Deprivation Cults," 320.

54. Ibid., 322.

55. Ibid., 318.

56. While Lewis's theory has received notable and widespread recognition among anthropologists, it is not without its criticisms. Some caution against universalizing Lewis's theory and suggest that alternative theories may coexist alongside his. See Janice Boddy, "Spirit Possession Revisited: Beyond Instrumentality," *Annual Review of Anthropology* 23 (1994): 414; Emma Cohen, *The Mind Possessed: The Cognition of Spirit Possession in an Afro-Brazilian Religious Tradition* (Oxford: Oxford University Press, 2007), 93; Janet McIntosh, "Reluctant Muslims: Embodied Hegemony and Moral Resistance in a Giriama Spirit Possession Complex," *Journal of the Royal Anthropological Institute* 10 (2004): 91–112.

57. See also Aihwa Ong, "The Production of Possession: Spirits and the Multinational Corporation in Malaysia," *American Ethnologist* 15:1 (1988): 28–42. Ong analyzes spirit-possession in a Malay factory where women "seized by vengeful spirits explode into demonic screaming and rage on the shop floor" (28). Ong perceives these episodes as retaliatory actions against the factory's management.

58. "Legion" in Mark 5:1–20 may be a reference to Roman imperialism. See Paul W. Hollenbach, "Jesus, Demoniacs, and Public Authorities: A Socio-Historical Study," *JAAR* 49:4 (1981): 567–588.

59. This has implications for the manner in which exorcisms are performed, lending to the need for further theological reflection.

60. See Frank Macchia, "Created Spirit Beings" in *Systematic Theology: A Pentecostal Perspective*, ed. Stanley M. Horton (Springfield, MO: Logion Press, 1994), 194–213; Yong, *Discerning the Spirit(s)*, 128–132.

61. The centrality of eschatology for Pentecostals is explored by Donald Dayton in *Theological Roots of Pentecostalism* (Peabody, MA: Hendrickson, 1987).

62. Nimi Wariboko has initiated this conversation in his book *God and Money*.

63. See Tillich, *The Interpretation of History*, 80–81.

64. Ibid., 82.

65. See Yong, *The Spirit of Creation*, 216.

TWELVE

Eschatology in the Theology of Paul Tillich and the Toronto Blessing

The Ontological and Relational Implications of Love

PETER ALTHOUSE

Pentecostal theologians seldom select Paul Tillich as a dialogue partner in their discussions of eschatology. Tillich's eschatology is an ontological theology in which the rhythm of life passes from essence through estranged existence to essentialization in New Being (ST 3.421).[1] Spiritual Presence, Kingdom of God, and Eternal Life are symbolic indicators that point to possibilities for essential fulfillment as the *kairos* moments of eternity impinge on the historical process. Alternatively, pentecostalism is a multidimensional movement that has a variety of eschatological positions, including latter rain eschatology, dispensational millennialism, as well as different kinds of inaugural and realized eschatologies. In this chapter, I will discuss the stream of pentecostalism known as the Toronto Blessing, recently branded Catch the Fire, in relation to Tillich's kairos eschatology. Specifically, Tillich's eschatological symbols of Spiritual Presence, Kingdom of God, and Eternal Life offer a theological framework for understanding the eschatological developments in Catch the Fire. Conversely, Catch the Fire's emphasis on relational love as the sign of the manifestation of the kingdom of God in ecstatic "signs and wonders" suggests avenues for the realization of divine presence in the concreteness of human existence.

Paul Tillich's Eschatology

Tillich's eschatology is rooted in an ontological theology that has been influenced by existentialism. Tillich's emphasis is on the exploration of human finitude and the threat of nonbeing, existential estrangement, or the ambiguity of life.[2] In existence, life is estranged from created essence in which ontological disintegration continuously threatens human life.[3] However, "existence" and "essence" are abstractions that designate two poles in the qualifications of being. Tillich uses the term *actuality* to explain the uniting of essence and existence in concrete life as the process of actualizing the potentiality of essence.[4]

For Tillich, the unity of life is a process found in circular, horizontal, and vertical dimensions that seeks self-integration, self-creation, and self-transcendence. However, existential estrangement threatens this unity by disrupting life's processes and driving the self in sundry directions, from which the ambiguities of life emerge (*ST* 3.30–31).

Yet human life yearns for unambiguous life, and this is found in the breaking in of New Being, albeit in a fragmentary and momentary manner. New Being is described as the creative and redeeming power of reality that overcomes estrangement. It is the power of new creation that reunites essence and existence.[5] New Being is realized most profoundly in Jesus Christ, who is the quintessential symbol of New Being. Jesus of Nazareth becomes the Christ through his sacrifice on the cross, revealing the process for what human beings ought to be. He reveals that essential humanity is possible while living under the conditions of existence. Through the surrender of his finitude at every moment in total transparency and unbroken relationship to the Father, Jesus reveals the path for all human beings in their concrete existence to realize their essential potentiality.[6]

Against this backdrop, Tillich's eschatology is defined in relation to the kairos of time breaking in from the eternal into the temporal—yet with the double movement of the temporal in the process of being prepared to receive the eternal.[7] Eschatological time has a double meaning: both finish and end. Human history, biological life, and the cosmos will at some point come to an end. However, the end can also mean the completion or fulfillment of historical life as the *telos* of history (*ST* 3.394–395). Tillich advances kairos time as the qualitative reality of the Kingdom of God that is pregnant in the fullness of time. The kairos of the Kingdom of God is "at hand" and is uniquely found in the mission of Christ in history, as the center of history, as the "great kairos." However, Tillich makes a distinction between kairos and kairoi (plural). The incarnation of Christ in history is the unique kairos of history, but the re-experience of the great kairos in particular experiences (kairoi), through which the Kingdom of God breaks into history and manifests itself in history, are decisive moments. These kairoi occur in penultimate movements of the church as prophetically latent or manifest instances of the coming kingdom (*ST* 3.370). Tillich warns, however, that when the particular historical claims are made absolute and displace the centrality of the Christ event, these kairoi can become demonic (*ST* 3.380).

Spiritual Presence, Kingdom of God, and Eternal Life are eschatological symbols that point to the conscious quest for unambiguous life as the fulfillment of essential possibilities (*ST* 3.108). Spiritual Presence symbolizes both human spirit and the divine Spirit that is present in all life. Kingdom of God is a social symbol that is actualized in eschatological expectation as the double movement of yearning for self-transcendence and the divine goal for history that is both internal to history and trans-historical (*ST* 3.109). Eternal Life is the symbol for unambiguous life in that it addresses the spatial and temporal ambiguities of finitude. All three symbols interact; but they are differentiated in that Spiritual Presence seeks to overcome the ambiguities of life, Kingdom of God seeks to overcome the ambiguities of history, and Eternal Life seeks to overcome the ambiguities of life beyond history (*ST* 3.109).

The symbol of Spiritual Presence creates ecstasy, which drives the human spirit beyond itself while preserving the structures of the human self. This ecstatic character cannot be grasped by the person yearning for it, but instead the Spirit grasps the person (*ST* 3.112). Spiritual Presence interacts with the human spirit in a mystical sense through "inspiration" and "infusion" (metaphorically, "breathing" and "pouring"), which implies the reception of something that enters a person who receives the Spirit (*ST* 3.115–116). The dual process is, for Tillich, the eternal kairos breaking into the finite, though the temporal is prepared to receive the eternal in the concreteness of history.[8] On the other hand, Tillich borrows from Plato (*Symposium*) to argue that love is the movement toward another being in order to overcome existential separation (*ST* 3.136).[9] Where "faith is the state of being grasped by the transcendent unity of unambiguous life—it embodies love as a state of being *taken into* the transcendent unity" (*ST* 3.129). Love has an existential or mystical character. Tillich praises the silence advocated in the mystical tendencies of the Quakers, who saw experience as decisive (*ST* 3.127), and through mysticism Spiritual Presence is experienced when the mind is grasped by ecstasy; however, transcending concrete realities brings the risk of losing the self (*ST* 3.143). The mystical is suggestive of the journey of faith towards union with the depths of life in order to transcend estranged objectivity and meaningless subjectivity.[10]

The place of love as mediated by Spiritual Presence defines love ontologically as the being of life in its movement from separation to (re)union.[11] Love for the other is participating knowledge that changes both the lover and the loved. Love infuses the totality of the human subject. The various kinds of love, such as *agape, eros, philia, epithymia* (or *libido*), as well as emotional and ethical love, derive from love's ontology as qualities that in their spheres of meaning connote the movement from separation to reunion. Agape, for instance, is defined as the depth or ground of life that transforms life and love.[12] Agape characterizes divine life as the love of God toward the creature, and through the creature toward the divine. The infusion of love is expressed toward other creatures (*ST* 3.136–138). Drawing on Plato and Aristotle, Tillich argues that eros is love's power, pushing toward union with the Good as the power of being and the drive toward the highest form that moves the world as the object of love; yet without eros, love for God is not possible.[13] Philia is that which unites the personal and the communal, but only in relation to other qualities of love such as eros. Epithymia, or its Latin cognate libido, is defined as desire for sensual self-fulfillment, but not in a Freudian sense of pleasure to cope with internal tensions.[14] "Love reunites that which is self-centered and individual. The power of love is not something which is added to an otherwise finished process, but life has love in itself as one of its constitutive elements. It is the fulfillment and the triumph of love that is able to reunite the most radically separated beings, namely individual persons."[15] Prayer and worship are rituals through which the reception of, and the response of, love move life toward its fulfillment, though in a fragmentary way. Prayers of contemplation are creaturely participation in the transcendence of finite reality that bypass the ambiguity of finite language through silence (*ST* 1.267, 3.191–192).[16]

The symbol of the Kingdom of God is the realization of the living tension between the presence and not-yet presence of Spiritual Presence in the inner working of history as well as its transcendent reality that lies beyond history (*ST* 3.390–391).[17] Tillich's early work in *The Socialist Decision* explicates the inherent eschatological and prophetic character of social transformation. He argues that the socialist principle accents the symbol of "expectation" as prophetic in character. Its fulfillment is not in its origin, but in a promised future.[18] Prophecy is understood not as predictive of future events, but as the promise of the new and our concrete reorientation toward it.[19] Forward-looking expectation is a living tension between that which is not yet and that which is hoped for; and yet this is an active tension in that humanity is expected to strive for that which is hoped.[20] However, the existential emphasis in Tillich's theology means that the eschaton breaks through from eternity into the present at any and every given moment, confronting ambiguous life with unambiguous or essential reality. Tillich does not abandon future expectation in the eschatology of his earlier work; instead he contextualizes its meaning.[21] In *Systematic Theology*, Tillich argues: "Therefore man's historical consciousness has always looked ahead beyond any particular new to the absolutely new, symbolized as 'New Creation'" (*ST* 3.326). Nevertheless, Tillich takes on an increasingly existential position.[22] He argues that "the eschaton becomes a matter of present experience without losing its futuristic dimensions: we stand now in the face of the eternal, but we do so looking ahead toward the end of history, and the end of all which is temporal in the eternal" (*ST* 3.396). The eschatological is not focused on a cataclysmic future in time and space; rather it is existential in that we come face to face with the eternal in any moment in history (*ST* 3.395).

The symbol of Eternal Life is the transcendent side of the Kingdom of God in which all the potentialities of history are fulfilled, though liberated from ambiguous distortions. The temporal transition into the eternal is not a temporal event because time itself is created, but a transcendent event in which the finite is taken up into eternity. However, the eternal is not timelessness or endless time. The eternal is not a future state, but ever present in finite humanity as well as the whole of life; in relation to time, the eternal has both a forward and an upward movement. Eternal Life is the permanent final fulfillment and complete unity of all life in participation with the divine. The eternal is the transcendent unity of time—past, present, and future together (*ST* 3.399–400). The symbol of the resurrection points to Eternal Life in which the Kingdom of God incorporates all dimensions of being (*ST* 3.413). The resurrection points to Eternal Life as the transformation of old being into New Being, the transformation of created reality into new reality, and is thus the universal symbol for eschatological hope (*ST* 3.414). However, Eternal Life is conceived of not as particular moments in time in the past or the future, but as a process occurring in every moment in time, so that creation and consummation or beginning and end are always grasped in the eternal (*ST* 3.420).

The Kingdom is at Hand: The Eschatology of Catch the Fire

In the 1990s a charismatic revival broke out in a small Vineyard church at the west end of Toronto, Canada, led by John and Carol Arnott. The revival, dubbed the Toronto Blessing and now known as Catch the Fire (CTF), drew pilgrims from all over the world to experience this new wave of the Spirit. Ecstatic manifestations such as laughing, weeping, bodily spasms and jerks, spontaneous falling, incomprehensible utterances, speaking in tongues, prophecies, words of knowledge, and healings of all kinds came to define the renewal. John Wimber and other Vineyard leaders quickly severed ties with the Toronto church, specifically over the more controversial manifestations of animal noises. The press as well as scholars were fascinated with the charismatic nature of the renewal. Sociologist Margaret Poloma conducted extensive research, consisting of observations, interviews, and surveys, that was published as *Main Street Mystics*.[23] Michael Wilkinson and Peter Althouse have conducted field research on recent developments in the renewal and have discovered that despite assumptions of the renewal's demise,[24] CTF is currently going through rapid institutionalization in a way that supports its mission, but still attracts large crowds to its conferences and seminars, where bodily charismatic manifestations such as laughing, ecstatic groans, and jerks are still observed.[25]

Although charismatic manifestations, or "signs and wonders," are the more prominent aspects of Toronto's renewal, CTF leaders advocate an experience of divine love as more fundamental to its mission, and this is specifically cultivated through soaking prayer. Soaking prayer is an innovation in CTF that is

meditative in form and captures all sorts of pentecostal and charismatic practices. It began in the ecstatic experience of falling to the ground during charismatic worship and prayer (known as being "slain in the Spirit," "resting in the
Spirit," or playfully as "carpet time"), but has been routinized in the deliberate
act of lying on the floor with pillows and blankets and opening one's self up to
the presence of what participants claim to be "the Father's love." Soaking prayer
occurs in large renewal services where people lie down at the front, sides, and
back of the auditorium, but it is also practiced by individuals or small groups in
churches and homes. Christian music that is soft and spa-like is played, lights are
dimmed and sometimes candles are lit while participants soak in prayer for an
hour or more. Through soaking prayer, charismatics report an experience of a
profound sense of divine love; they are transformed through the healing of emotional wounds, feel a sense of forgiveness, and are able to forgive those who
have hurt them in some way. Having experienced such a profound, even mystical sense of love, these charismatics then express this love to others in compas-
sionate and benevolent ways.[26] In other words, love is at the root of the charismatic's experience of God, and signs and wonders are indicators of the presence
of the Father in love.

The theological justification for charismatic manifestations, signs and wonders, and healing in CTF is a kairos eschatology that is proleptic in orientation.
This new wave of charismatic renewal was influenced by Fuller Theological
Seminary Professor George Ladd's inaugural view that emphasized the *prolep-
sis* of the kingdom already present but not yet in its fullness. Vineyard leader
John Wimber appropriated Ladd's theology to argue that the kingdom of God
will fully come in the final second coming of Jesus Christ, but that charismatic
manifestations break into the present in kingdom power. Signs and wonders are
indicators that the power of the kingdom has come. Spiritual warfare was often
a result of the inbreaking of kingdom power, in what is claimed to be an ongoing battle to overcome the forces of darkness in the world. Kingdom theology
emphasizes the proclamation of the kingdom, healing the sick, casting out demons, and performing miracles.[27] Wimber's eschatology has greatly influenced
John Arnott's theology and teaching, though without the more extreme aspects
of spiritual warfare.

Arnott is often heard announcing that the kingdom is present in CTF meetings. While in an ecstatic state of worship he will pronounce "the kingdom
of God is at hand," "thy kingdom come, thy will be done," or that we must "press
into the kingdom." Charismatic manifestations are "realized" in the present
as the "inbreaking" of the kingdom through the Spirit in which God comes in
love and power, but at the same time charismatics are encouraged to press in
or enter into the kingdom. At one renewal event, Arnott encouraged people to

raise their hands as high as they could into the air to press into the glory of the Lord, to reach their hands into the heavens. He said, "Let my hands be an extension of Jesus." As the congregation received the "anointing" in their hands, he then had them touch areas of their bodies that were in need of healing. A number of participants claim to be healed of emotional and/ or physical ailments after having experienced a profound sense of love that urged them to forgive God and others for past hurts. The charismatic leaders in the movement are bearers of the kingdom and disclose it through the impartation of spiritual gifts to participants, though they teach that anyone can be a bearer of the kingdom and impart the charismatic gifts. An impartation is normally passed on through touch or the laying on of hands, but playful innovations such as blowing from the mouth or pretending to "shoot" the person with the power of the Spirit can be seen. Soaking prayer facilitates the experience of the inbreaking kingdom through which prophecies, revelations, visions (mental images), healing, weeping, and laughter are mediated in the body as divine communication. Charismatics experience God as if the kingdom has already arrived, but with awareness that there is a discrepancy between what is and what is to come. The emphasis is on the demonstration of the kingdom in the present, through which divine love is experienced in signs and wonders, healing, or physical or bodily manifestations.

Eschatological Comparisons between Tillich and Catch the Fire

Although the context of Tillich's theology and the charismatic renewal has cultural, historical, and theological differences, a number of similarities can be observed between the eschatologies of Tillich and CTF. The most prominent similarity is the emphasis on the kingdom of God that is defined by kairos time and the ecstasy of Spiritual Presence as the work of love. As well, both Tillich and CTF accent the yearning for reunion from existential estrangement. For Tillich this reunion is defined theologically as the concrete actualization of essential possibilities of unambiguous life, while for CTF this reunion is experiential and couched in the language of renewal, in which the existential estrangement of broken relationships with God and others is overcome through the overwhelming presence of the Father's love as mediated through the Spirit.

Tillich espoused an eschatology that attempts to maintain the tension between the presence and not-yet presence of the kingdom. Expectation plays a part in Tillich's understanding of the not-yet aspects of the future, and expectation is prophetic in nature. Yet past, present, and future collapse into the eternal now, where every moment is pregnant with essential potentiality. However, it can also be argued that the inverse is true in that no moment is eschatologically transcendent, so that the eschaton collapses into the historical process.[28] Nevertheless, the eschaton is definitely *not* a future cataclysmic end in time and space, though all life will at some point come to an end, because such a view would undermine the meaning of creation and history.

CTF proclaims an eschatology that accents the realization of the kingdom in signs and wonders, which connects to the lived experience of the presence of God in love. The expectation and subsequent demonstration of signs and wonders form (a) powerful sign(s) that point to the presence of the kingdom in the world at any given moment. However, in a more primary sense the presence of the kingdom is experienced as the gracious love of the Father, to which other charismatic manifestations point. This love is symbolized in various metaphors such as "liquid love," "compelled by love," intensive love," or "love revolution." CTF makes a distinction between the sin that is generated by "performance," i.e., the busy-ness of life and ministry, and the reception of divine love as a moment of grace that reveals to the recipient his or her true being as a son or daughter of the Father.

Kairos time is an important element of the kingdom for both Tillich and CTF. Tillich rejects both chronological time as the basis for the kingdom's realization as well as the notion that the prophetic is predictive of the future in a linear sense. Rather kairos is the realization of the kingdom as the fullness of time. The unique kairos is found in Jesus Christ and his sacrifice in obedience to the Father. Other kairoi (plural) all flow from the great kairos of Christ in history. These kairoi are moments when the kingdom of God breaks into history. They are prophetically latent in history but emerge at given moments as instances of the kingdom's manifestation. However, if these kairoi are used by church or secular authorities as totalizing claims that displace the centrality of the gospel of Jesus Christ, then they can become demonic distortions in ambiguous life.[29]

CTF also advocates the kairos of the kingdom in its belief that when the kingdom is at hand, God's presence is revealed in charismatic manifestations. The manifestations, though, are not an end in themselves; rather they are entry points for God to work in love and power in the lives of Christians and, through them, to the lost and despairing peoples of the world. The emphasis is on human wholeness, where love and forgiveness are "poured" into human lives to transform them into children of God; and through the experience of the love of the Father, charismatics passionately share this love with others. Such sharing is a realization of the Great Commandment to love God and love neighbor, but in a reciprocal love between God and the believer rather than a duty performed by a penitent. Soaking prayer is both a ritual and an image of being filled with divine love regularly in order to love others compassionately.[30] Both Til-

lich and CTF have an ontological foundation of love that is framed eschatologically as "reunion" or "renewal" with the source of love. For Tillich the kingdom
breaks in as a kairos event from the essence or ground of life, while at the same
time the historical context is prepared for the reception of the eternal. Likewise,
for CTF the kingdom breaks into the present from the heavenly realm, while at
the same time believers can "press into" the kingdom through praise and worship. However, CTF leaders would not engage in an existentialist philosophy to
articulate their theology, though the experiential emphasis is contextually existential, even mystical.[31]

Spiritual Presence is an important aspect of the kingdom's presence for both
Tillich and CTF, though with major differences. For Tillich, Spiritual Presence
is a symbolic expression of the work of the Spirit in estranged existence. Spiritual Presence is ecstatic in character, both in yearning for transcendence and in
being grasped by it, though Tillich is clear that ecstasy is structured rather than
chaotic. In fact, Tillich makes reference to some ecstatic pentecostal practices,
but cautions that they cannot be the "cause" of Spiritual Presence (ST 3.115, 275).
For a Protestant theologian, Tillich is also positive about the "infusion of love."
He connects infusion to the biblical narrative of Pentecost, which highlights
"breathing" and "pouring," but also to the existential (even mystical) experience
in the believer's journey through estranged existence in the hope for union with
God. Prayer and contemplation are important practices in the believer's journey
toward unambiguous existence.

CTF also emphasizes the work of the Spirit in mediating the presence of the
Father's love to the heart of the believer. Many of the ecstatic experiences about
which Tillich is ambivalent are commonly observed in CTF meetings. In fact,
CTF worship is described as carnivalesque, though there is still a ritual structure.[32] Charismatic rituals allow participants to enter liminal space where they
experience the existential crisis of lived life and yearn to grasp the potentialities
of an alternate reality; that reality is mediated to them through the Father's lov-
ing presence, but it is fragmentary, and the moment one begins to reflect on the
experience it has collapsed into the mundane. CTF draws upon the mystical tradition for its theological understanding of the presence of the Spirit and recom-
mends classic texts by the mystics. CTF also draws on the narrative of Pentecost
to support its charismatic practices. The themes of being filled with the Spirit,
sons and daughters that prophesy, speaking in tongues, healing, etc., are seen
as correlates between the book of Acts and charismatic practices. Most important, however, is that the mediation of the love of God in the believer is claimed
to be profound and life-changing. The "infusion" of love is fundamental to the
way CTF envisions itself and its relationship with other churches and the secular
world. The manifestation of the kingdom is the manifestation of God's love. All

other signs, manifestations, impartations, and healings point to the presence of the Spirit in love.

The eschatological framework for both Tillich and CTF is *proleptic* as they navigate the tension between the already and the not yet. For Tillich, the existential conditions of life and history are pregnant with the essential potentialities, defined as the kairos inbreaking of Eternal Life that creates the possibilities of the Kingdom of God in history through Spiritual Presence to receive the eternal. However, these kairotic moments are fragmentary and fleeting. For CTF, the emphasis is on the present manifestations of the kingdom in charismatic signs and wonders breaking in from the heavens as worshippers press into the heavens from their own existential brokenness. Tillich develops an eschatological framework that proposes an ontological foundation of love and its yearning for essential reunion in existentially estranged conditions. While the ontology of love is implicit, CTF focuses on the relationality of love, in which charismatics see themselves as accepted, which then energizes them to express this love benevolently to others. The ritual practices of CTF contextualize Tillich's abstract philosophical theories to provide lived praxis in the experience of divine love and its implications for the eschatological journeys of people in real-life situations—people who are beginning to grasp, and be grasped, by a love that flows into them, enabling them to forgive and love others.

Notes

1. Russell McConnell, "The Eschatology of Paul Tillich," *Southwestern Journal of Theology* 36.2 (Spring 1994): 23; Raymond Bulman, "Tillich's Eschatology of the Later American Period (1945–1965)," in *New Creation, or Eternal Now: Is There an Eschatology in Paul Tillich's Work?* ed. Gert Hummel (New York: Walter De Gruyter, 1991), 145.

2. David H. Kelsey, "Paul Tillich," in *The Modern Theologians: An Introduction to Christian Theology in the Twentieth Century,* ed. David F. Ford, 2nd ed. (Malden, MA: Blackwell, 1997), 90.

3. See especially Tillich, *ST* 2, throughout. Also Kelsey, "Tillich," 93.

4. Kelsey, "Tillich," 95.

5. Walter Leibrecht, "The Life and Mind of Paul Tillich," in *Religion and Culture: Essays in Honor of Paul Tillich,* ed. Walter Leibrecht (New York: Harper and Row, 1972 [1959]), 21.

6. Nimi Wariboko, *The Principle of Excellence: A Framework for Social Ethics* (New York: Rowman and Littlefield, 2009), 89–91; Kelsey, "Tillich," 94.

7. Nimi Wariboko, *The Pentecostal Principle: Ethical Methodology in New Spirit* (Grand Rapids, MI: Eerdmans, 2012), 10.

8. Nimi Wariboko, *The Pentecostal Principle,* 10.

9. Kelsey, "Tillich," 92.

10. Paul Tillich, *Theology of Culture*, ed. Robert C. Kimball (New York: Oxford University Press, 1959), 107.

11. Paul Tillich, *Love, Power, and Justice: Ontological Analyses and Ethical Applications* (New York: Oxford University Press, 1954), 25.

12. Tillich, *Love, Power, and Justice*, 33.

13. Ibid., 21–22, 31.

14. Ibid., 28

15. Ibid., 26.

16. In a way similar to silence, glossolalia bypasses the ambiguity of finite language by voicing its finite in the breakdown of language to represent the divine. See Richard A. Baer, "Quaker Silence, Catholic Liturgy, and Pentecostal Glossolalia—Some Functional Similarities," in *Perspectives on the New Pentecostalism*, ed. Russell P. Spittler (Grand Rapids, MI: Baker Book House, 1976), 150–164.

17. See Kelsey, "Tillich," 97.

18. Paul Tillich, *The Socialist Decision*, trans. Franklin Sherman (New York: Harper and Row, 1977 [1933]), 101.

19. Ibid., 103.

20. Ibid., 102. See also Paul Tillich, *The Eternal Now* (New York: Charles Scribner's Sons, 1963), 123–124.

21. Bulman, "Tillich's Eschatology," 139.

22. See for instance, Paul Tillich, *The Courage to Be* (New Haven: Yale University Press, 1952).

23. Margaret Poloma, *Main Street Mystics: The Toronto Blessing and Reviving Pentecostalism* (New York: Altamira Press, 2003).

24. For instance, Stephen Hunt, "The 'Toronto Blessing'—A Lesson in Globalized Religion?" in *Canadian Pentecostalism: Transition and Transformation*, ed. Michael Wilkinson (Montreal: McGill-Queens Press, 2009), 233–248.

25. Michael Wilkinson and Peter Althouse have conducted two years of field research that includes 25 observations, 126 interviews, and a survey instrument. The research was generously funded by the Flame of Love Project and the John Templeton Foundation. Observations made in the chapter are based on this fieldwork. See Michael Wilkinson and Peter Althouse, *Catch the Fire: Soaking Prayer and Charismatic Renewal* (DeKalb, IL: Northern Illinois University Press, 2014).

26. Wilkinson and Althouse have identified three cases where rituals of soaking prayer and charismatic renewal expand benevolence as an expression of love: CTF Montreal, Tierra Nueva, and River City Church Jacksonville. Leaders of CTF Montreal claim that experiences of the Father's love have cultivated a greater love for reaching out to French-speaking Africans and its own congregational mix of French-speaking Haitians, Africans, and Caucasians, to seek forgiveness through public apology in the hope of racial reconciliation. Tierra Nueva is active in social justice issues, advocating for immigrants working in prisons and developing sustainable farming in Honduras. River City Church Jacksonville works with a low-income housing complex for poor African Americans, where it not only provides for basic necessities and life-skills training but wants to be a re-

deeming presence in the community. In all three cases, a profound experience of the Father's love through soaking prayer and charismatic worship is claimed to be the motivation behind these benevolent activities. Wilkinson and Althouse, *Catch the Fire,* 140–155.

27. Stephen Hunt, "'Doing the Stuff': The Vineyard Connection," in *Charismatic Christianity: Sociological Perspectives,* ed. Stephen Hunt, Malcolm Hamilton, and Tony Walter (New York: St. Martin's Press, 1997), 84–85.

28. Jürgen Moltmann makes this argument of Barth and Bultmann's crisis eschatologies, but it could also be made of Tillich's kairos eschatology. See Jürgen Moltmann, *The Coming of God: Christian Eschatology,* trans. Margaret Kohl (Minneapolis: Fortress Press, 1996), 13–22.

29. See Jean Richard, "The Roots of Tillich's Eschatology in his Religious-Socialist Philosophy of History," in Hummel, *New Creation or the Eternal Now,* 34–40.

30. See Michael Wilkinson and Peter Althouse, "Apology and Forgiveness as an Expression of Love in a Charismatic Congregation," *PentecoStudies* 11.1 (2012): 87–102; and Peter Althouse and Michael Wilkinson, "Playing in the Father's Love: The Eschatological Implications of Charismatic Ritual and the Kingdom of God in Catch the Fire," *ARC: The Journal for the Faculty of Religious Studies, McGill University* 39 (2012): 93–116.

31. See Poloma, *Main Street Mystics,* 24–33.

32. Poloma, *Main Street Mystics,* 2. Also see Victor Turner, *From Ritual to Theatre: The Human Seriousness of Play* (New York: Performing Arts Journal Publications, 1982), 84–85.

THIRTEEN

Paul Tillich, Pentecostalism, and the Early Frankfurt School

A Critical Constellation

PAMELA HOLMES

Paul Tillich, early classical Pentecostals, and the Early Frankfurt School of critical theory have important insights that deserve examination in light of the economic woes of the contemporary Western world.[1] Therefore, this chapter begins such an exploration by, first, situating the three conversation members before uncovering the early twentieth-century problem these three discern. Second, the conversation that emerges from our triad of interlocutors will be presented before, third, refocusing the issues in the contemporary period and, fourth, proposing a way forward for both contemporary Pentecostals and Tillichians.

The Problem

Tillich

Shaken to the core of his being as a result of the horrors he witnessed and experienced as a chaplain during World War I, Tillich concludes that his Lutheran theology is no longer sufficient for the problems plaguing modern life. Recognizing that he himself is enmeshed in both modernity and Christianity and thus could only comment from within them, he nevertheless insists that Christianity must do something similar.[2] Realizing that it reflects some aspects of modernity, Christianity must simultaneously live with modernity while at the same time mounting protests against its abuses. As far as Tillich is concerned, the Protestant churches had already attempted this in various ways. Lutherans had engaged the relationships between the churches and modernity using philosophical and literary questions. Calvinists had focused on social and political matters. Americans had banished God from philosophical and scientific considerations, and even its ethics, which contains a residue of Christian foundations, had become utilitarian, altruistic, and wedded to a legitimation of late capitalism.[3] As Tillich explains it,

> In the name of Christianity the English revolution created a capi-
> talist society as a realization of the rule of God . . . The Bible be-
> came the law book of the people . . . Then it becomes custom and
> law . . . The religious background was preserved . . . And with secu-
> larization the shaping of Christianity falls into the hands of the sup-
> porting forces of capitalist society—the economic and the political.
> Assimilation into the forms of life of the economically dominant
> bourgeoisie, and subordination to the political unity of the domi-
> nant Anglo-Saxon capitalist state became equated with assimilation
> into theocracy.[4]

As a result, Tillich concludes, Protestant Christianity is no longer able to critique
modernity and its problems.

Early Pentecostalism in Canada and the United States

At the beginning of the twentieth century, some early Pentecostals in Canada
and the United States held the view that contemporary churches were infested
with sinful modern ways of thinking and living. For example, the Azusa Street
newspaper *The Apostolic Faith* proclaims "We are not fighting men or churches,
but seeking to displace dead forms and creeds and wild fanaticisms with living,
practical Christianity."[5] Similarly, Carl Brumback, one of the first official histo-
rians of the Assemblies of God in the United States, describes "American Protestantism" at the time as "wealthy, cultured, and influential, but, with the exception of a few conservative groups, its spiritual state was at a low ebb" due to
the influence of modern thinking, including "Darwinism and Biblical Higher
Criticism."[6] Worship was formalized and "nonexperiential," reflecting the tastes
of the "intelligentsia," who had little patience for "primitive displays" of emotion or conversion experiences. Brumback insists that, with the exception of the
Holiness Movement, the churches were worldly and allowed "card-playing, the-
atre-going, and dancing." The clergy were professional, thereby widening the
gulf between clergy and laity. Churches were "class conscious," with denominations that had once welcomed the poor now moving up the economic social lad-
der. No longer did the poor feel at home in worship. By embracing the modern
world, the churches had become "spiritually cold."

Similarly, Thomas Miller writes in his book *Canadian Pentecostals: A History
of the Pentecostal Assemblies of Canada*, "the Pentecostals were, in fact, disturbers
of the old order in the church. It always has been a fact of revivalism that it breaks
with hoary old methods, superficial sanctity, and ecclesiastical formalism. Early
Pentecostal leaders were frowned upon, or entirely rejected. Their new-found
convictions of conversion and Baptism in the Spirit were condemned. Thousands
of believers became, as it was so quaintly put at the time, 'come-outers.'"[7] Miller

claims, "It was neither 'social protest' nor 'economic deprivation' that motivated the early-century believers to carry out a worldwide program of evangelization. It was their strong conviction that God was reviving His Church in 'the last days' in preparation for the 'soon return of Jesus.'"[8] Their protests were against denominations and churches that succumbed to the prevailing theological liberalism and modernism. They decried the "higher criticism" that invaded the seminaries and robbed Christianity of all relevance for modern man. Particular Pentecostals denounced the then-popular view of churchmen that "education" and "social reform" would improve society and transform human nature. These attitudes and concerns, connected with the fundamentalist/liberal controversy earlier in the twentieth century, led to the establishment of separate Pentecostal Assemblies of Canada Bible Colleges.

For both Brumback and Miller, modernity and its way of thinking and believing seeped into the established churches, and this was part of the problem leading to the eventual establishment of Pentecostal churches within Canada and the United States.

Early Frankfurt School

Critical theory is historically associated with the *Institut für Sozialforschung* (Institute for Social Research) established in 1923 in affiliation with the Goethe University in Frankfurt, Germany, during the early years of the Weimar Republic. Particularly under the tutelage of Max Horkheimer, who became the institute's director in 1930, the Frankfurt School, as it eventually became known, was a radical, multidisciplinary school of social and cultural criticism, social research, and philosophy, which at first drew heavily upon Hegel and Marx. Eventually it moved beyond this reliance to formulate its own seminal approaches and insights.[9] According to Horkheimer, in the modern period humanity overlooks the provisional and contextual nature of knowledge,[10] and thus promotes a closed, value-laden process that reifies ideas in such a manner as to both mirror and provide an ideological legitimation for elites and their concerns within society. Modern enlightenment rationality, enamored as it was with the abstract methodology of mathematics and formal logic and the reproducible, empirical evidences of the sciences, claims to yield hard evidence that can be universalized. However, Horkheimer insists that such knowledge is not at all objective, but is instead pragmatic and instrumental, even though it claims to be absolute and ahistorical, scientific and systematic.[11] An illusionary disconnect between theorizing and its results is created and maintained.[12] Any concerns regarding freedom or justice is hived off from this instrumental rationality and relegated to the arena of ethics. Therefore, Horkheimer, along with his colleague Theodor Adorno, insists that abstraction had become a tool of totalitarian domination serving the interests of the status quo.[13] Rather than civilizing humanity and allowing for a "truly human condition" to emerge, the modern enlightenment has led to self-destruction and disaster as humanity sinks "into a new kind of barbarism."[14]

Unfortunately, Horkheimer accuses, Christianity's institutionalized churches are too enmeshed in culture to pick up the struggle for social justice that modern, instrumental rationality has abandoned. In fact he soundly criticizes "bourgeois morality and religion" as being "nowhere as tolerant as when they judge the life of the rich, and nowhere as strict as toward those that want to eliminate poverty."[15] As a result, "true discipleship" in the form of an "image of perfect justice" often leads many people away from religion.[16]

Summary

All three of the constellated conversation members are in agreement that there is something wrong with our world. All three, in various ways, agree that modernity and its way of thinking and style of life constitute a serious problem. All three agree that Western Christianity is both enmeshed in and complicit in modernity's problem. While early twentieth-century Pentecostalism's evaluation of the problem may not have been as theoretical as the Early Frankfurt School's or Tillich's, the denouncing and leaving was certainly as radical.

The Solution

Tillich

The solution to the ills of modernity for Tillich during his pre-American years includes the utilization of a blended rational and prophetic criticism. Rational criticism included the many ways in which various disciplines rationally, critically analyzed the different aspects of reality using concepts and ideals. Given this approach, rational criticism is bound by and restricted to reason. In comparison, prophetic criticism includes the "boundless," to move beyond what is rational in order to question reason itself and its all forms.[17] While prophetic criticism requires rational criticism in order to be concrete, rational criticism needs prophetic criticism in order to be inevitable and unconditional. Used alone, either legitimates rather than challenges the status quo. When combined, rational, prophetic criticism, echoing the "protest" commended by the Hebrew prophets,[18] demands a "religious regeneration of a Christian society."[19]

This *Protestant principle*, as Tillich later labels the rational, prophetic criticism, involves "what theology calls 'faith,' namely, that state of mind in which we are grasped by the power of something unconditional which manifests itself to us as the ground and judge of our existence."[20] However, it also concerns itself with the real life situations of humanity, including that of workers who have been deprived of the surplus benefits of their labor, resulting in a "contradiction between the Protestant principle and Protestantism as it actually is."[21] Therefore, during the 1920s Tillich advocates for a type of "religious socialism" that went beyond the Marxian and strictly secular versions to embrace a "depth dimension," including God's involvement within the world of humanity in the hope of transforming culture.[22] By the time of his writing of *The Socialist Decision* in 1933, Tillich is convinced that only the prophetic impulse coupled with the principles undergirding the Enlightenment could save Germany from Nazism and humanity from itself. As he explains, "Religious socialism is the attempt to bring into awareness the element of faith at work in socialism, to reveal socialism's inner conflict, and to lead it to a solution that has symbolic power."[23]

Due to the criticisms received from both religious folks and socialists, Tillich revises his earlier expression, religious socialism in *The Socialist Decision*. However, he retains his theological approach—even although some of the language changes to terms such as "believing realism," that is, a "realism of expectation" that arises from religious subsoil.[24] Explicitly denouncing Nazism and anti-Semitism as well as particular forms of socialism, he advocates for the socialist principle and for a grasp of what a solid socialism could be within contemporary culture. And such a solid socialism includes the spiritual. In fact, as Tillich explains, it is the prophetic principle that turns socialism into an ethical demand. Extrapolating from the myth of origin common to various systems, Tillich argues that any longing for some golden age in the past could become an eschatological hope of an expected future consummation. Tillich admits that thinking in terms of origin, particularly when these are viewed simply as a finite historical event, can become a stagnant and even possibly limiting process that dictates what one can and must be. However, there are other ways of utilizing such a myth. Part of the ambiguity of a myth of origin is its potential to be progressive, to place a demand on the present to be all that was hoped for in that original event of happening. The key is to recognize and act upon the foundation established by the "Whence" of the myth of origin while at the same time focusing on its "forward motion toward the new" represented by the question of "Whither."[25] While all groups are in some sense "bound" to a myth of origin, if only to define and explain themselves as they carve out and maintain space for themselves within a plurality of other groups, it takes the prophetic to move them beyond this bondage.

While this prophetic principle is important to Christianity, it is not assured. As Tillich pronounces, "A Christianity that abandons its prophetic foundation by allying itself with political romanticism has lost its own identity."[26] Nevertheless, in autobiographical musings written shortly before his death in 1965, Tillich states, "If the prophetic message is true there is nothing 'beyond religious socialism.'"[27]

Pentecostalism

While Brumback, as noted, denounces the modern practices and thinking noticeable within traditional churches, as far as he is concerned, all is not lost because all have not "bowed the knee to Baal" and apostatized.[28] In describing the Azusa Street Revival, Brumback claims that the word *Azusa* is a misspelling of the third person singular of the Spanish verb *azuzar,* meaning "to provoke, to irritate, to stimulate, to incite, to stir up, to put one against another, to cause conflict."[29] He then goes on to explain that, misspelled or not, the word is significant because the Pentecostal movement since Azusa Street has "provoked, irritated, stimulated, incited, stirred up, put one against another, and caused conflict"—that "Azusa (or Azuza) sparked a twentieth-century reformation against formalized religion."[30] Clearly Brumback views the fledging Pentecostal movement in its very existence as a prophetic and radical critique of churches and culture in the United States.

For Thomas Miller, within Canada the "concept of themselves as being divinely enlightened, filled with God's Spirit and sanctified to God's use" set the early Pentecostal people apart.[31] Modern, secular enlightenment wasn't sufficient. Neither were the teachings of "the so-called 'social theologians' of the time" that "rejected any supernaturalism in the Bible" and "taught that mankind would create its own 'heaven' on earth.'"[32] Miller claims that "the horror of the First World War helped to dispel these mistaken philosophies."[33] As a result, the Canadian Pentecostal people made a radical break with churches that aligned themselves with known modern teachings of the early twentieth century. They became "come-outers."[34]

Early Frankfurt School

For the critical theorists of the Early Frankfurt School, both a critical way of thinking and a prophetic type of Christianity, which opposed the dominating effects of instrumental, technical rationality within capitalist cultures, were necessary if humanity was to be free. Therefore, these theorists argued against versions of modern thinking that they viewed as inhumane or unjust. For example, Horkheimer argues against Hegel's idealist system whereby the objective, absolute World Spirit realizes itself in history by subsuming the particular to the universal.[35] While Horkheimer considers particular, concrete disciplines, such as art, philosophy, and religion, and particular values of individuals, including their passions, interest, and drives, he accuses Hegel of cunningly using the particular creations and values of human beings by forcing them to participate in and to be subsumed by the universal life of the Spirit for the Spirit's realization. In response to such instrumental use of human beings, Horkheimer insists that all human knowledge be viewed as historical products that can only be understood contextually. As historical products, human knowledge is subject to change and thus must be recognized as provisional.[36] Suspicious of any claims to be progressive, and opposing positivism in any form, Horkheimer posits a "critical" rather than "traditional theory," which took seriously the assumption that people are not mere instruments but are active agents and must be dealt with accordingly.[37] Horkheimer's open-ended, historical, and socially grounded critical theory includes within it an emancipatory concern for the "reasonable conditions of life."[38] Critical theory's subject is "a definite individual in his real relation to other individuals and groups, in his conflict with a particular class, and, finally, in the resultant web of relationships with the social totality and with nature."[39] Its method is a sustained, interdisciplinary critique of the status quo with its traditional mode of theorizing.

Theodor Adorno, in building on this early understanding of critical theory, argues that all knowledge must remain particular and provisional in order to avoid conceptual domination through universalization. According to Adorno, while abstract thinking requires the use of universals, reflection on particularities is important if only to deduce that such particularities are not mere chance or accidental. Adorno rejects the tendency of modern rationality to manipulate subject-object processes and interactions in order to obtain conceptual mastery. He insists that recognizing that an object is not the same as the conceptual ideas subjects impose on it has the potential to free objects from any attempt at control by the subjects who are conceptualizing them.[40] The ideas, feelings and values of subjects cannot be understood as truth and imposed on the object. Nor can objects be reduced to the concepts of a subject. Rather through an interdependent process, assumptions and preconceptions about an object are illuminated and corrected.[41] Any remaining aspects of an object that elude categorization and conceptualization by a subject in any thinking or system are not only particular and unique but are also real and may, in fact, possess unrealized possibility.[42] Adorno's version of critical theory demands that particulars, including people, be emancipated rather than remain subjected to or used by universals, including dominant and dominating social systems.

While these dominating systems included Christianity, Horkheimer's work in particular suggests that religions, including Christianity, contain protests against injustices and the status quo by those who have experienced suffering. While on the one hand religion could function as an opiate, drugging the population to the miseries they were experiencing, or even openly acting as an ideological conduit legitimating oppression and injustice in order to buttress the status quo, on the other hand, Christianity was the repository of the ideals, hopes, and longings for a more just and humane life, oftentimes in a utopic form (in its teachings on heaven and an other- worldly existence). While Christianity could and did inhibit justice, it nevertheless, at the very least provided a reservoir for its preservation.[43]

Summary

While all three members of the constellation have agreed that humanity needs to be liberated from the effects of modernity, they have disagreed as to how that could be achieved. The Early Frankfurt School and Tillich turned to theorizing as a means toward that emancipation. The Early Frankfurt School insisted that a radical break from traditional means of theorizing must be made and critical thinking be adopted. Such critical thinking must remain contextual, provisional, and open-ended, even going so far as including a sustained negativity in the case of Adorno. Any religious ideas, including Christian, were to be viewed as ambiguous and suspect. Tillich, in contrast to the Frankfurt School, intellectually and theoretically engaged a radical, new form of prophetic Christianity in his version of socialism. While his thinking was more positive than the Early Frankfurt School's, it also was contextual and interdisciplinary. While the Early Frankfurt School began to despair that human beings would ever be free from domination,[44] both Tillich and Pentecostalism maintained the hope that freedom was possible. Pentecostals, while rejecting the intelligentsia and their types of theorizing, nevertheless acted in radical ways by turning their backs on the Christian churches that had embraced modern ways of thinking. Unfortunately, in-depth theorizing was missing from their radical behavior.

One of the areas in which all three were in agreement was the *radical* nature of the critique and changes that were required in order for hope to be regained and sustained. This radical nature involved getting at the deep root and source of what was going wrong in order to assess and correct it. It also involved making a break from the status quo in its various manifestations. How successful these three participants were in acting upon their solutions is the focus of the next section.

The Contemporary Situation

Tillich

In later years, sensitive to the prejudices of his American audience, Tillich carefully insists that religious socialism is interested not simply in the economic sphere but in life as a whole. As he states:

> We understood socialism as a problem not of wages but of a new theonomy in which the question or wages, or social security, is treated in unity with the question of truth, of spiritual security. On

the other hand, we realized more than most Christian theologians ever did that there are social structures that unavoidably frustrate any spiritual appeal to the people subjected to them. Religious socialism is not a political party but a spiritual power trying to be effective in as many parties as possible. It had and has sympathizers and goes on the Left as well as on the Right.[45]

Nevertheless, while distancing himself from both "scientific" and "political" Marxism, particularly as they were revised into various forms of communism, Tillich readily admits that he "found in Marx an understanding of human nature and history which is much nearer to the classical Christian doctrine of man with its empirical pessimism and its eschatological hope than is the picture of man in idealistic theology."[46] Eventually Tillich moves away from his blatantly prophetic, socialist path toward the construction of a systematic theology that was no real threat to the capitalism of his adopted homeland.

Pentecostalism

Pentecostalism in the United States and Canada has lost its earlier radical behavior and become part and parcel of the religious and economic landscape of its contexts. While these changes in behavior from the radical to the domesticated may have allowed Pentecostalism to survive if not thrive, it has also involved some significant compromises. Where once Pentecostalism criticized the churches, it has become part of the larger evangelical community. Many American Pentecostals are part of the National Association of Evangelicals, and many Canadian Pentecostals are part of the Evangelical Fellowship of Canada. Pentecostals have even become such an integral part of the ecumenical movement that they were included in Edinburgh 2010, a celebration of Edinburgh 1910, from which the World Council of Churches evolved.

Beyond the churches, Pentecostalism is quite at home within the context of capitalism. One of its subsections, the Word of Faith movement, even goes so far as to teach that financial prosperity it a gift promised by God in the Scriptures. In the process, Canadian and American Pentecostalism have embraced a theology that not only is universal and idealist but at the very least is no threat to and even legitimates the late capitalist cultures within which it is enmeshed. Consequently this segment of Pentecostalism has almost completely lost its ability to advocate for people who are suffering under the weight of global capitalism's abuses. Rather a significant amount of time is spent on protecting its own newly achieved power as a religious force with which to be reckoned. As Tillich discovered, it's difficult to critique capitalism when you are benefitting from it, including its abuses. Perhaps this is an area where both Tillich and Pentecostalism can heed the warnings of the Early Frankfurt School.

The Early Frankfurt School

Walter Benjamin, in his densely written and somewhat controversial "Theses on the Philosophy [Concept] of History," outlines in fragmentary form his view of the relationship between philosophy and theology[47] and raises the question of the present's responsibility to the dead, particularly those who have been the victims of injustice. Benjamin insists that human history has been a riotous and stormy catastrophe rather than progressive.[48] History is not simply a series of events that the elite deemed useful but rather an arena full of atrocities demanding redeeming. Human history was not simply the product of powerful forces and peoples; it was a graveyard of grievous wrongs to be righted. At the same time, historical materialism brought theology down to earth where it belonged, among people, rather than projecting humanity's ideals out there onto some future state or God.

Adorno picks up on some of Benjamin's insights and translates them into his own work.[49] For example, Adorno adapts Benjamin's understanding of reality as a universe of disparate elements that humanity, as subjects, constellates together and interprets in order to form a meaningful picture, oftentimes assumed to be actual and true. Nevertheless, reality as thus perceived is not an orderly totality. Constellating different subjects allows for perceptions and experiences to be reordered in a conscious and determined manner in order to expose the erroneous nature of the current state of affairs and reason.[50] Due to what he perceives to be the all-pervasiveness of domination, Adorno insists that the only type of intellectual activity sufficient to the task of paying the dues of the past, or of freeing humankind from modern, instrumental rationality, is that of a sustained negative dialectic.[51] Thinking against thought by allowing contradictions to be recognized and included is what is required in order to avoid any sort of "spiritualized coercion."[52]

Summary

Pentecostalism in the United States and Canada has lost its earlier radical orientation and has become part of its religious and capitalist culture. Tillich has set aside his earlier radical theorizing regarding religious socialism in order to function as a theologian within the capitalist United States. As a result, rather than resolving the problems of modernity in the radical fashion they deemed necessary, Pentecostalism and Tillich failed by capitulating to the Western status quo. In contrast, the members of the Early Frankfurt School, even after their time in the United States and their return to Germany, continued their critical theorizing by insisting that all such work remain provisional, ongoing, incomplete, always negating—or, in a term familiar to both Tillich and Pentecostalism, eschatological. In this sense, within a Western context that encourages complete, systematic, technical rationality, their approach remains radical. The most that can be said about their work is that it is unfilled.

A Provisional Way Forward

One way for Pentecostalism and Tillichians to move forward is to regain their radical tendencies and shake off their entanglements with the status quo of Western capitalist societies. Part of this disentanglement involves recognizing that all theological statements are ongoing discussions, and therefore must remain provisional and not ossified and restricted to any statements of faith (various Western Pentecostal denominations and fellowships) or systems of theology (Tillich). The emphasis on experience found in all three of the constellated participants above may assist with this disentanglement. All three agree that experience is a legitimate and neglected aspect of thinking, whether philosophical or theological, that needs to be engaged in order to avoid an idealist collapse of the particular into the universal. For Tillich and Pentecostalism, by focusing on both the subjective experience and some supposedly objective ideal, a balance may be found. Similar to Tillich, Pentecostalism, with its emphasis on the transcendent Holy Spirit immanently at work within the world, counters a strictly thisworldly approach that could lead to despair by insisting on the recognition of an otherworldly ideal. While Pentecostalism in Canada and the United States has tended toward individualism in its experiential expressions, the Pentecostalism of Majority World has discerned the communal and environmental aspects.[53]

One of the experiences Tillich deems important is what he calls *ecstasy* (*ST* 1.113, 3.112–114). Ecstasy involves a means of transcending the limits of one's own mind without negating the rational, thereby moving thinking beyond the subject–object dualistic structure that concerns Adorno and his negative dialectic (*ST* 1.112–114). While acknowledging that they possess similar qualities, Tillich distinguishes *ecstasy* from *enthusiasm,* which only claims that God is within oneself or one is within God, whereas ecstasy involves transcending oneself (*ST* 1.111–112). According to Tillich it is the Spiritual Presence that creates this ecstasy in such a manner as to do no harm to those who experience it, or to their ability to reason (*ST* 3.112). Similarly Pentecostals agree that any experience of the Spirit is always with the person's permission and submission to the Spirit, and always remaining within the person's control.[54] For both Tillich and Pentecostals it is the divine that initiates this encounter; one cannot bring it on oneself. Tillich views the Spiritual Presence as a symbol indicating that the divine Spirit is immanently moving in and with humanity (*ST* 3.157–161). While Pentecostals may agree with the relational nature of the Holy Spirit's immanent involvement with individuals, broader implications beyond the local church have been somewhat ignored, as have fuller explanations for what is occurring in these events.[55]

Tillich's metaphorical categories could provide an impetus for further reflection that moves beyond the Christian churches and prophetically engages this world, with all its complex challenges, toward a deeper form of reconciliation and healing. In the process, Pentecostals would be well advised to consider Tillich's statement regarding the risks involved in "confusing the Spiritual Presence's impact with that of a psychologically determined overexcitement" (ST 3.118). Instead, due to the "multidimensional unity of life," including those aspects within which humankind is involved, all are included in the "Spirit-created ecstasy" (ST 3.118). To ignore this, in Tillich's opinion, is to become involved in a profane reductionism that ignores the witness of the New Testament.

Additionally, while Tillich dismisses Spirit Movements that equate ecstasy with some sort of psychological or emotional experience (ST 3.115–118) or attempt to limit the functioning of the Spirit by a literal interpretation of the Scriptures, a conversation with Pentecostalism may have assisted him with linking the prophetic portions of the Hebrew Scriptures with the instructions attributed to the Apostle Paul in the Christian Scriptures.[56] While Tillich discusses the Pentecost event in his work on the Divine Presence, he does not seem to recognize the potential that such a link provides (ST 3.150–152). In contrast, early Western Pentecostalism accessed Lucan texts to do just that, by cross-referencing the passages in the early chapters of Acts with passages from Joel.[57] As a result, the prophetic nature of Pentecost was reinforced so that Spirit-filled Christians could be empowered to witness in word and deed to the gospel. While some later Pentecostals have assumed a more Fundamentalist approach to the interpretation of the Scriptures, Tillich's concern regarding a literal reading was avoided by Western Pentecostalism in the early years and continues to this day in many segments of the global movement, by locating authority in the Spirit which moves among the Spirit-inspired Scriptures, the Spirit-birthed-and-gifted community,[58] and the experiences deemed to be of the Spirit.[59] In this hermeneutical approach, "Only Spirit discerns Spirit," to quote Tillich (ST 3.161). While an article of this size precludes it, an exploration of the potential of such a discussion between Tillich and nonFundamentalist Pentecostal is warranted. In the process, values, principles and norms beyond Tillich's "religious, cultural and moral dimensions" ones (ST 3.266–75) may be illuminated which remain eschatological and thus provisional thereby undermining any attempt on the part of humanity to succumb the Holy Spirit to any concretized religious form manifesting the human spirit rather than God's.

One aspect of using that Lucan lens to link the prophetic impulse to the present could include an exploration of the more socialist nature of the Spirit filled community mentioned at the end of the second chapter of the Acts account. Such an aspect could bring Tillich's earlier religious socialism, which he insists he never rejected in the opening pages of Volume Three of his Systematic Theology, overtly back into the discussion. To not do so, using Tillich's term, may be "a-kairos" in its "missing the demand of the historical moment" which includes serious economic problems (*ST* 3.6–7). Reclaiming this prophetic impulse might assist in moderating the tendency and temptation to legitimate the excesses of late capitalism while responding in a timely fashion to the contemporary concerns of humanity.

Both Tillichians and Pentecostalism have something of value to offer to the contemporary Western world with all its economic woes. This article has argued that potential exists in a conversation between Pentecostalism and Tillichians particularly within their prophetic and socialist impulses. However, in order to move forward, both will find it necessary to embrace the insights of the Early Frankfurt School that thinking, in order to be positive and productive, must remain critical and provisional in order to avoid being co-opted by the technical rationality of late capitalism.

Notes

1. I have chosen select members of the Early Frankfurt School because later members of the school, such as Jürgen Habermas, present contextual revisions of this early work. The Early Frankfurt School included such members as Max Horkheimer, Theodor Adorno, and Walter Benjamin, among others. In my ongoing work, I am creating my own contextual revision in conversation with Pentecostalism.

2. Paul Tillich, "Christianity and Modern Society," in *Political Expectation,* ed. James Luther Adams (New York: Harper and Row, 1971, 1981), 1–2.

3. Tillich, "Christianity and Modern Society," 6–8.

4. Ibid., 4–6.

5. *The Apostolic Faith* 1 (1906):1, 2.

6. Carl Brumback, *A Sound from Heaven: The Dramatic Beginning of the 20th Century Pentecostal Revival* (Springfield, MO: 1961, 1977), 2–6. All other quotations in this paragraph are from these pages.

7. Thomas Miller, *Canadian Pentecostals: A History of the Pentecostal Assemblies of Canada,* ed. William A. Griffin (Mississauga, ON: Full Gospel Publishing House, 1994), 101.

8. Miller, *Canadian Pentecostals,* 103.

9. Eduardo Mendieta, "Introduction: Religion as Critique," in *The Frankfurt School on Religion: Key Writings by the Major Thinkers,* ed. Eduardo Mendieta (New York: Routledge, 2005), 7.

10. Martin Jay, *The Dialectical Imagination: A History of the Frankfurt School and the Institute of Social Research, 1923–1950* (Berkeley: University of California Press, 1996), 360. John McCole, Seyla Benhabib, and Wolfgang Bonb, "Introduction—Max Horkheimer: Between Philosophy and Social Science," in *On Max Horkheimer: New Perspectives,* ed. John McCole, Seyla Benhabib, and Wolfgang Bonb (Cambridge, MA: MIT Press, 1993), 13.

11. Max Horkheimer, *Critical Theory: Selected Essays,* trans. Matthew J. O'Connell et al. (New York: Continuum, 1972), 6–10, 25, 27, 102, 188–243, 358–359.

12. Horkheimer, *Critical Theory,* 197.

13. Max Horkheimer and Theodor Adorno, *Dialectic of Enlightenment,* trans. John Cummings (New York: Continuum, 1944, 1998) xi, 3, 6, 9, 11–13, 26–32. See also Horkheimer, "The Revolt of Nature," in *Eclipse of Reason* (New York: Continuum, 1947, 1997), 93–94.

14. Horkheimer and Adorno, *Dialectic of Enlightenment,* xi.

15. Max Horkheimer, *Dawn and Decline* (New York: Seabury Press, 1978), 54.

16. Horkheimer and Adorno, *Dialectic of Enlightenment,* 131.

17. Tillich, "Protestantism as a Critical and Creative Principle," in *Political Expectation,* 10–11.

18. Ibid., 11n2, 11–12, 15, 17.

19. Ibid., 16–17n8.

20. Paul Tillich, *The Protestant Era* (Chicago: University of Chicago Press, 1948; Phoenix Books, 1957), 235, 163.

21. Ibid., 164.

22. Paul Tillich, *The Socialist Decision,* trans. Franklin Sherman (New York: Harper and Row, 1977), 23–26. Tillich credits the Blumhardts with the religious transformation of socialism from its strictly idealist and materialist focus to a recognition that God could work through it.

23. Tillich, *The Socialist Decision,* 71.

24. Ibid., xxxvi–xxxvii.

25. Ibid., 25–26.

26. Ibid., 22.

27. Paul Tillich, *My Search for Absolutes* (New York: Simon and Schuster, 1967), 40.

28. Brumback, *A Sound from Heaven,* 6.

29. Ibid., 39.

30. Ibid., 39–40.

31. Miller, *Canadian Pentecostals,* 101.

32. Ibid., 102.

33. Ibid., 104.

34. Ibid., 101.

35. Max Horkheimer, *Between Philosophy and Social Science: Selected Early Writings,* trans. G. Frederick Hunter, Matthew S. Kramer, and John Torpey (Cambridge, MA: MIT Press, 1993, 1995), 2–6.

36. Horkheimer, *Between Philosophy and Social Science,* 359–363.

37. Horkheimer, *Critical Theory,* 238.

38. Ibid., 199.

39. Ibid., 200–202, 211, 218.

40. Theodor Adorno, *Negative Dialectics,* trans. E. B. Ashton (New York: Continuum, 1966, 1973), 183.

41. Theodor Adorno, "The Actuality of Philosophy," in *The Adorno Reader,* ed. Brian O'Connor, trans. Benjamin Snow (London: Blackwell, 2000), 24.

42. Horkheimer, *Critical Theory*, 347.

43. Ibid., 129–131.

44. Horkheimer and Adorno, *Dialectic of Enlightenment*, xi.

45. Tillich, *The Protestant Era*, xiv.

46. Ibid.

47. Including "historicism, empathy, bourgeois historiography, the idea of progress" and "universal history." Jasiel Cesar, *Walter Benjamin on Experience and History: Profane Illumination* (San Francisco: Mellen Research University Press, 1992), 7.

48. Cesar, *Walter Benjamin on Experience and History*, 106; Benjamin, "Eduard Fuchs: Collector and Historian," in *The Essential Frankfurt School Reader*, ed. A. Arato and E. Gebhardt, (New York: Continuum, 1982), 226–227.

49. Rolf Wiggershaus, *The Frankfurt School: Its History, Theories, and Political Significance*, trans. Michael Robertson (Cambridge, MA: MIT Press, 1995), 91–92, 94.

50. Theodor Adorno, "The Actuality of Philosophy," in O'Connor, *The Adorno Reader*, 32.

51. Adorno, *Negative Dialectics*, 3–12.

52. Ibid., 141, 145.

53. For example, Jean-Jacques Suurmond, "Christ King: A Charismatic Appeal for an Ecological Lifestyle," *Pneuma: The Journal of the Society for Pentecostal Studies* 10:1 (Spring 1988): 26–35.

54. Based on personal observation in worship and ministry within Canadian Pentecostalism.

55. For examples, the works of Stanley Horton and Myer Pearlman who are among the earlier Pentecostal theologians in the United States and Canada.

56. Tillich does mention Spirit-Christology but nevertheless emphasizes Pauline descriptions. See for examples *ST* 3.139–146, 412 where he specifically states that the Spirit is a central concept of Paul's theology.

57. See Roger Stronstad, *The Charismatic Theology of St. Luke* (Grand Rapids, MI: Baker, 1990) and Martin W. Mittelstadt, *Reading Luke-Acts in the Pentecostal Tradition* (Cleveland, TN: CPT Press, 2010).

58. See Kenneth J. Archer, *A Pentecostal Hermeneutic for the Twenty-First Century: Spirit, Scripture, Community* (London: T and T Clark, 2004) and Amos Yong, *Spirit-Word-Community: Theological Hermeneutics in Trinitarian Perspective* (Eugene, OR: Wipf and Stock, 2002), for examples of a trilectical approach.

59. See Pamela Holmes, "Acts 29 and Authority: Towards a Pentecostal Feminist Hermeneutic of Liberation," in *A Liberating Spirit: Pentecostals and Social Action in North America*, ed. Michael Wilkinson and Steven Studebaker (Eugene, OR: Pickwick Publications, 2010), and Pamela Holmes (mistakenly published under Pamela Johnson), "An Educational Encounter: A Pentecostal Considers the Work of Elisabeth Schüssler Fiorenza," *Refleks—med karismatisk kristendom i focus* 3 (Fall 2003), where I add the fourth element, experience.

Responses

FOURTEEN

Socialist Spirit in Tillich, Pentecostalism, and the Neoliberal Demonic Today

MARK LEWIS TAYLOR

Between the questions "where from" and "where to" lies the whole system of theological questions and answers.

—PAUL TILLICH

The argument of this response essay is that Paul Tillich's notion of Spirit is best interpreted as a complex, prosaic, mundane, and political dynamic of life, and that precisely in this way we best grasp how Tillich's socialist Spirit might engage Pentecostalism in what I take as its world struggle today with the neoliberal global demonic.

The above epigram is taken from the very last part of Paul Tillich's *Systematic Theology,* published in 1963, just two years before his death. In it Tillich sums up his entire system of theological correlation. It is particularly striking because he here situates his system between the same coordinates he used in his 1933 work, *The Socialist Decision.* This is more than accidental. It is evidence of the enduring force of his religious socialism in the view of Spirit he developed in the closing parts of his system. The epigram above strikes the main chords of Tillich's chapter in *The Socialist Decision,* "The Two Roots of Political Thought," where he explores human "consciousness oriented to the 'whence' (*Woher*) and to the 'whither' (*Wozu*)."[1] His magnum opus written in the United States, then, which is usually interpreted as having left behind the religious socialism of his years in Germany, is here positioned by Tillich within the key framework of *The Socialist Decision's* religious socialism.

The persistence of a socialism in his *Systematic Theology* confirms what he said in lectures of 1965, the year of his death, when he challenged an essay title, "Beyond Religious Socialism," which *The Christian Century* gave to his article in the series "How My Mind Changed in the Last Ten Years." At that time, in lectures for the University of Chicago Law School, Tillich wrote, again in language reminiscent of *The Socialist Decision:* "If the prophetic message is true, there is nothing 'beyond religious socialism.'"[2] He admits that after World War II he "felt the tragic more than the activating elements of our historical existences," and that he "lost the inspiration for, and the contact with, active politics" so evident in *The Socialist Decision*.[3] It should be noted, though, that the supposedly more quiescent post-emigration Tillich of the United States nevertheless dared airing critical political views. He interpreted the "world wars" of Europe partly as a result of its own colonialism. He questioned U.S. imperialist and even racist presumptions during World War II—offering up such critiques even at Midwest locations in Indiana, and just six months after Pearl Harbor.[4] Recall that, for his Voice of America addresses into Germany during World War II, he was "blacklisted by the U.S. Army as pro-German."[5] Moreover, while Tillich did fear his socialist writings becoming too public in the United States, he still wrote of U.S. conformism as source of potential fascist trends there.[6] Finally, as I have already intimated and hope to show by my conclusion, Tillich's religious socialism, and hence the political vision of his early work, reached a highly elaborate stage in volume 3 of *Systematic Theology*, in the form of historical, prophetic, even socialist spirit. Tillich's religious socialism did not let go of his late life thinking and theology, even if the immigrant forced to live between worlds after 1933 lost his contacts with and inspiration for activist politics.

Why is this reminder of the continuity of his later theology with the structure of the socialist decision so important for a response to this book on theological conversations between pentecostal theology and Tillich's thought? My answer is that being thus reminded forces us to seek some fresh understandings of Tillich's view of Spirit,[7] thus setting our conversation between his own and pentecostal views of the Spirit into a more fruitful engagement. I say "more fruitful," first, because it gives us a way to provide a clearer understanding of just what Tillich meant by *Spirit* in his work, which seems a fitting way both to conclude this volume and also open it to further conversation. Second, I think that that what I term Tillich's "religious socialist spirit" offers some key perspectives on Pentecostalism's struggle with contemporary neoliberal global politics.

Thus, my response to the chapters in this volume is not a chapter-by-chapter examination, nor do I offer my own comparison of Tillich with pentecostal theology. The pentecostal thinkers here have done that better than can I, and the conversation will no doubt continue among pentecostal thinkers willing to engage Tillich's works. Further, I would like to record here that these pentecostal thinkers here have engaged Paul Tillich with considerable care and insightful analyses—showing generous attentiveness toward the liberal and socialist Tillich that contemporary progressive and radical theologians often fail to give back to pentecostal texts and thinkers.

In what follows I offer two preparatory sections, one on the importance of pentecostal movements and theology today, and another on Tillich's Spirit and the supranatural. In my most important section, "Tracing Spirit in Life," I lay out as concisely as I can how Spirit works in Tillich's system and writings. It is a dauntingly complex working, but that complexity itself is a sign of what Tillich takes Spirit to be. Then, in a final section, "Religious Socialist Spirit and Pentecostalism Today," I will suggest how Tillich's notion of Spirit might engage contemporary pentecostal movements in the current world situation.

Pentecostal Movements and Theology Today

A good argument that theologians should attend to Pentecostalism, today, can be made from Tillich's own sensibility. In one of the essays of *The Protestant Era*, Tillich said the "Those who want to know the power of reality in the depth of their historical existence must be in actual contact with the unrepeatable tensions of the present."[8] This is no simple call for relevance. It is a reminder that as thinkers, especially theologians, their thinking is always already embedded in and engaged with the world. Even the conceptuality by which Tillich derived his ontological concepts was not performed prior to experience. Those concepts are "products of a critical analysis of experience" (*ST* 1.166). I consider the growth of Pentecostalism in the twentieth and early twenty-first century to be one of the major significant transformations in religion and Christianity of our time. We also face something like Tillich's "unrepeatable tension"—better tensions—especially if we consider the various relations possible between this Pentecostalism's global rise and the current neoliberal global order.

First, consider the sheer oft-remarked global rise of Pentecostalism. Writing in the *Journal of Ecumenical Studies,* Simonmary Asese Aihiokhai writes that "Pentecostal affiliation in America today is the only Christian religious affiliation that has consistently grown in its membership for the past nineteen years." In Africa, "Pentecostalism is fast-spreading and is redefining the religious topography of the continent."[9] Thinking about the phenomenon in Africa, but also on nearly every continent, anthropologist Jean Comaroff writes, "As in many other parts of the world, from the US to Ukraine, São Paulo to Seoul, the Pentecostal movements that have waxed most luxuriantly across the continent [Africa] and in recent times promote conceptions of belief, personhood and emotion that contrast markedly with the ontology of mainstream Protestant modernism."[10]

Precisely here, in Pentecostalism's contrasting "markedly with the ontology of mainstream Protestant modernism," we find a tension which should be of interest to Tillich scholars and to any engaged theologians. Tillich, while often associated with "the ontology of mainstream Protestant modernism," was on modernity's "boundary" and was himself also highly critical of "mainstream

Protestant modernism." As one who criticized Protestant modernism and yet found his own way to be in and of it, he makes a ready conversation partner with Pentecostalism today, precisely because Tillich and Pentecostalism—from very different vantage points and histories, to be sure—both exhibit and resist Western modernity's powers.

A second point must be made about this relation to modernity. As Tillich knew well, and emphasized, Western modernity was a colonizing and exploitatively capitalist modernity. He is not alive to describe that modernity today, as he did in his own time, so allow me some brief comments on late modernity's global order today. Crucial to understanding the politics, the way power works internationally, is a theory of the asymmetrical power held by formerly colonizing states and their contemporary, largely Northern-based economic initiatives (in Europe, the United States and North Asia). Since the end of World War II, the predominance of this global North entailed U.S. hegemony, economically and militarily. To be sure, global North groups seek modes of fractioning off groups of corrupt local elites anywhere, especially in poorer countries, for servicing the overall economic domination by the North. What I will call the *neoliberal order* is this North-based geopolitical and economic domination, enforced by U.S. military might, which gives imperial backing to this hegemonic arrangement (usually called "globalization" or "development").

The highly racialized and thereby dehumanized populations of the formerly colonized territories, extending through the largely equatorial regions of the global South, are seen mainly as sites for natural resources and cheap labor, and so constitute a region that is heavily policed. These regions have even been referred to by U.S. Pentagon planners as a kind of "non-integrating gap"[11] in the globalization order, which must be especially subject to surveillance and contained to protect globalization. In these regions, the by-now routine programs mandated and enforced for struggling poorer nations include the maintenance of low wages (and resistance to higher minimum wages), the cutting of state expenditures for social services to pay down the debt to already wealthy countries, the privatization of national industries, and the opening of poorer nations' territories to "free-trade export zones" and resource extraction, made available at the lowest possible costs to outside agents, whose promises of "investment" are usually hard to resist.

In addition—and this is particularly important for understanding Pentecostalism's relation to the neoliberal order—wealth generation/accumulation is an ever-more abstract process, and "quasi-monetary instruments across space and time" form a kind of "electronic economy."[12] Much of the poorer regions of the world know well the human costs of what Naomi Klein has termed "disaster capitalism." Not only have the poorer sections of Africa, Asia, and Latin America felt the sting of neoliberal politics, so too have countries like Russia, especially after the disintegration of the Soviet Union. The disaster forced onto post-Soviet Russia and the cost paid by its civilians was a history quickly researched and confirmed, but also quickly forgotten.[13] Tillich in his day knew the disastrous result of planning reason, whether that of Soviet-styled totalitarianism or of exploitative capitalism (today a kind of "inverted totalitarianism"[14]), and he named them both Leviathan, to highlight these exploitative global systems as an "all embracing portent that, in the interest of the state, swallows all elements of independent existence, political and economic, cultural and religious."[15] The U.S.-armed global neoliberalism, especially as described in the texts I have cited in this paragraph, ably qualifies as Leviathan. Tillich would term it a manifestation of the *demonic,* a concept I will introduce below.

In this context, let me now turn to anthropologist Jean Comaroff's discussion of a twofold relationship between recent, growing Pentecostalism and this neoliberal order. In turning to Comaroff, as I do in this chapter, I am turning to a scholar who is an outsider to Pentecostalism, like myself. Yet, several of her analyses productively engage issues that pentecostal insiders have also raised.[16] Her analyses also resonate with a number of issues and themes I have encountered over the years in interreligious conversations with and about Pentecostalism in Latin America. The first of her analyses is what she terms ontological, in her unique sense of the term; the second sociological.

Comaroff stresses that Pentecostalism's relationships to neoliberal orders are matters neither of simple reaction to, nor of easy affirmation of, those orders. Both reaction and affirmation are "dialectically entailed with the transformations of the current moment. I would say that the crucial point is to understand *how* Pentecostal world growth is both."[17] To anticipate, I put it this way: Pentecostalism may be described today as in a resistance against liberal modernity and its cool rationality and relativizing of meaning, but its mode of countering late modernity can often affirm the postmodern formations of late capitalism, especially its highly electronic, post-Fordist cultivation of earthly desire and entrepreneurial ambition.[18]

Consider what Comaroff terms the *ontological dimension* of the relationship between the neoliberal order and Pentecostalism's rise. This dimension concerns the ways recent pentecostal shifts in worship and self-understanding intensify the sense of revelation, a sense of the divine that constitutes the being of believers. Especially as the church has become a South-to-South—as well as North-to-North (and North-to-South/South-to-North) electronic network, direct intervention of the divine in human affairs takes an especially dramatic role. It is performed with conventions distributed by electronic media and is highly animated in assemblies, producing, writes Comaroff, "a white heat that resets time and re-establishes truth."[19] Anthropologist Comaroff is not, of course, offering up another Western missionary lament about extravagant emotionalism. Her main point is that under current conditions—in the South African megachurches and pentecostal communities that she studies, and elsewhere globally—there has arisen a new "economy of affect," where ritualized demonstration of enthusiasm "becomes evidence of a forthright relation between heart and deed." She is not critical of this. She is, more accurately, seeking to position Pentecostalism in relation to Western late modernity. If modernity, especially as rooted in Enlightenment rationality, was cool, mental, reductive of emotion and affect, the antidote is to cultivate affect with modern technology. In its "white heat" a new place to stand is felt, carrying new senses of certainty, even of moral rectitude. In fact, Comaroff observes how often "passion as incarnate power and potential" can even serve as a force to rival lying and corruption.[20] A political figure, then, who can cultivate and display this economy of affect can be seen as one revealed as righteous and not corrupt.

The interesting point about Comaroff's "ontological dimension"—and here I begin to surface a certain tension—is that this mode of intensified pentecostal being, while functioning as a reaction to the coolness of modernity and its rationality, in fact can work quite nicely to service the latest formation of capital. "Affect is increasingly summoned in the idiom of mass-marketed consumer desire, becoming the prime vehicle of subject-formation everywhere."[21] Of course, we would need to add that Pentecostals' performed affect is not the only site of this mass-marketed desire. We could add global sites of cinema, the circulating affect of the *telenovelas* and more, the selling of fashion and luxury. In all these sites of performance, liberal and many non-Pentecostal Christianities are compromising just as much, if not more, with late modern and neocolonizing capital. But Comaroff's point is that for pentecostal faith the intensity of affect has grounded a new mode of revelational being that aims to be resistant to modernity even if, ultimately, it can play the same game.

Consider, then, her second analysis, in the *sociological dimension*. Here Comaroff sees Pentecostals seeking to restore holiness in the wake of modernity by rebuilding wholeness, i.e., taking the many parts of the national or regional whole, atomized and dispersed by modernity's dominance, and reintegrating them within its own religious vision and organizational structures. One spokesman for Nigerian Pentecostalism has announced a goal for the church in Nigeria as "Total Take-Over of the country."[22] Religion is charged with making, remaking the whole. To be taken in are domains of welfare, education, health provisions, and so on, responsibilities often allotted to the state. The positive way to spin this drive is to call it a comprehensive "faith-based activism." The less savory term, to some, would be "theocracy," a mode of rule that pulls the many spheres of living within the religious purview and structure—a "theocratic impulse," in Comaroff's language.[23] It can be hard to recognize because it is often combined with affirmations by the church of entrepreneurial small business, "multiplex, face to face organizing," and so on. But ultimately—like the U.S. suburban mega-church that issues its own credit cards, has its own bank, its schools and other social services—the aim is to take in all for God and to sanctify it there.

Again, in this move, there is a resistance to Western modernity and the deprivations it allows and fosters in the economic disasters it exploits. Pentecostalism displays a struggle to take back agency, to form counter-communities amid the failure of the state to meet basic communal and social needs. Pentecostalism often provides "alternative economies."[24] And yet, again, often here such churches can run right along in the tracks of late capitalism. Such "born-again" faith's alternative economy actually can lubricate the neoliberal turn, strengthening the neoliberal order, since it the latter is quite content to "out-source" responsibility for meeting human need to local groups, handing them over to underground and alternative economies, so that a largely corrupt nation-state can preoccupy itself with servicing the transnational economy.

Readers may think I have travelled far from the issue of Spirit around which conversation between Tillich and Pentecostals might occur today. This divergence is only apparent, however, and for two reasons. First, Pentecostalism and its spirituality are growing in a period of rapid intensification of the neoliberal order. Second, and perhaps more important to this volume, the Spirit of concern to Paul Tillich is structured precisely to address such a time, when a Leviathan haunts and disorders the well-being of everyday peoples. This is true, especially, if we recall the religious socialist frame for all his work. So I turn in the two next sections to Tillich's notion of Spirit, enabling a final section's treatment of churches' resistance to the Leviathan order, as we shall see, a mode of the demonic today—the neoliberal demon.[25]

Tillich's Spirit and the Supranatural

Many of the contributors to this volume highlight Tillich's openness to the notion of Spirit in his theology, evidenced in his acknowledgement that his "present system is essentially, but indirectly, influenced by the Spirit-movements, both through their impact on Western culture in general . . . and through their criticism of the established forms of religious life" (*ST* 3:126). Several consider whether Tillich could be termed an enthusiastic theologian on the basis of such an acknowledgment. Perhaps this is so, but only if we consider that being enthusiastic is only one example of what he meant by the Spirit's "ecstatic" forms. Moreover, ecstasy, for Tillich, included many processes that are far more prosaic and mundane than what is usually termed enthusiasm. Indeed, Tillich as theologian and person was marked by enthusiasm. He considered indifference in persons intolerable. His philosophical style could never hide a penchant for passion, indeed the passion of inner resources and of interpersonal engagement. But to overstress the notion of enthusiasm would limit the Spirit's work, in Tillich's mind, and also could suggest, misleadingly, that wonders provoking enthusiasm are the major sites of Spirit.

Most of the writers in this book seem comfortable with this reminder about Tillich, provided one guards a pentecostal sense of descending or downward-coming power, and charismata (gifts and wonders). I am not quite sure where Tillich was on the matter of charismata. Several other authors here note that Tillich is unclear. But if one recalls comments given in an interview when asked about faith healing,[26] Tillich was prone to see that kind of charism, or wonder, as a power carried in some people's natural ability to heal through their touch (he even claimed the ability for himself). But for Tillich it was not a supranatural power, above or outside the natural or human spheres. It was part of human interaction and bodily interplay, a kind of touch that amid pain and separation can, at certain times and with the right conjoining of persons, be therapeutic. But this was not the quintessential example of what Spirit was for Tillich, nor were other occasions of "downward" power. So what would Spirit be?

I draw an example from part 5, "History and the Kingdom of God," of *Systematic Theology*. It is a particularly crucial passage. First, Tillich is here considering the basic question of how "the concept of the new" is to be understood, how it emerges. Given the centrality of New Being in his theology, especially in Jesus as the Christ, reflection on the emergence of the new is crucial. Second, Tillich here treats of Spirit in its most constitutive and determinative modality, as the formation of *political* conditions of historical life, with which the symbol the Kingdom of God is primarily concerned (*ST* 3.311). Then third, this passage I select comes at the heart of Tillich's reflection on how the new emerges as causality, as such contained within, constrained by, substance. Here, then, he is writing of causality in all the multiplicity of life's dimensions, and in history where life and spirit attain their most complex relation (*ST* 3.321–326).

Tillich's example here treats the emergence of the "underivably new" in the creation of Shakespeare's *Hamlet*. Granted, this is a literary, and hence, perhaps elitist, example; but think, if you prefer, of the making of a popular film or a song. The same dynamics Tillich treats here would apply, in understanding the emergence of the underivably new. Tillich writes thus: "In the creation of *Hamlet* by Shakespeare the material, particular form, personal presuppositions, occasioning factors, and so on, are derivable. All these elements are effective in the artistic process which created *Hamlet;* but the result is new in the sense of the underivable. It is in this sense that we speak when we say that under the dimension of the spirit, general causality becomes causality as creating the new" (*ST* 3.324). This underivable, as emerging through all these many factors of "conditioning precedent," intensifies respect for both sides of the creative process. On the first side, the side of the emergence's preconditions, there is an astonishing multiplicity of conditions. So much so, it is sheer understatement to say that, for Tillich, the Spirit is mediated. Indeed yes, multiply and complexly so—always! And yet, at the other end of the emergence process, the new is striking. It warrants the name Tillich gives to it, *underivable*. And as he continues to reflect on it, he also describes it as an "unconditional element" (*ST* 3.324).

It is this notion of the unconditional as underivable, from among many preconditions, that keeps Tillich's notion of Spirit distant from any supranaturalism. Any "downward action" of divine initiative, its "inbreaking" as in some Reformed traditions, is, for Tillich, largely a motion of immanence itself—underivable and unconditional, yes, but emergent from within its preconditions. Indeed, several works in pentecostal theology also point to this notion of immanental emergence as congruent with pentecostal vision.[27] As the Tillich/Pentecostal dialogue proceeds on the question of spirit and emergence, however, it is important to recall that Tillich's notion of *Spirit* is much closer to a theory of sacrality, of a carefully defined and circumscribed Spirit at work in life. It is more this than a doctrine of Spirit, or a *loci* concern in systematic theology— orthodox, liberal, modern, neo-orthodox, liberation. In my view, this brings Tillich much closer, I think, to radical, immanence theologies than to theologies of a doctrine of spirit, surely to notions of spirit as "person," or "third article of the creed."[28]

When I say that Tillich's notion of Spirit is prosaic, I do not mean that it has the character or style of prose, even though, as I will note below, he devotes much prose to explain Spirit's unfolding. But I also mean prosaic in the other of its meanings, as common or unromantic. One might say quotidian, undramatic—even if performed with an acute artistic and expressionist symbolic sensibility. Spirit's underivably new emergence, for Tillich, has a life-like flow, a seeping forth from and amid its preconditions. This is Tillich's ecstatic as it works in different ways everywhere, where the new is emergent. Perhaps it is utterly consonant with his view of spirit that his Harvard secretary reported that while Tillich was writing volume 3 of *Systematic Theology*, he listened to Duke Ellington's "Mood Indigo," a musical form of ecstasy, I would say—mellow, subtle, intricate, repetitive, while continually surprising with nuances underivably new.[29]

Consider another example for clarifying Spirit, in Tillich: the action of breathing. It is appropriate to take this as example, with most etymologies relating spirit/Spirit to "breath"—as in *ruach* (Hebrew), *pneuma* (Greek), *spiri-*

tus (Latin), *Geist* (German). To reflect on breath is to think in the very heart and pervasive livingness of nature, maybe of changing matter, too—something that Tillich would invite us to do because for him Spirit in history includes the inorganic realm. But consider breathing, new emergences of the next breaths. It occurs in a way that maintains the continuity of a certain form of life (the breathing being). Both the new breath, inhaling and exhaling, and also the continuing forms and dynamics of the breathing being, are crucial to the new breath. The new breath, the next breath is a function of its preconditions: lungs, heart, blood flow, atmospheric conditions, social practices of exercise, vulnerability to and freedom from disease, and so on. The next breath, amid and because of multiple interplay of its preconditions and mediations, is nevertheless "underivably new." We may not notice this, but we are never precisely the same with the next breath. Moreover the next breath, and many others we often take for granted to be forthcoming, actually cannot be assumed. They are fragile and vulnerable emergences, issuing in various modes of life between stability and radical instability. This is consistent with Tillich's abiding sense that any constitution of being, including New Being animated by Spirit amid life, is always a tensive relation between "ground" and "abyss." This labile tension and fragility is a hallmark of Tillich's sense of Spirit. A blockage, an act of violence, a certain unplanned moment of bodily deterioration interrupting the next breath—these are nearly always at hand. Each breath, common parlance might say, is a miracle. Tillich's language is that it is "underivable new," a case of *ex-stasis* in the dynamic structure of life. All the preconditions have to be there for it to emerge, but the newness of the next breath is underivable from them. Spirit, for Tillich, is like *that*.

Where does this place Tillich concerning miracles, hard-to-explain occurrences attributed to "downward" divine action and intervention? For the most part, for Tillich, they can remain unexplained, even though, with the right research and powers of explanation, they can be subject to psychological, social, or natural explanations. Or, he would appreciate language about such occurrences as figures deploying powers of art and symbol, crucial for theology and for understanding Spirit and New Being. I know of no place where Tillich would receive claimed miracles as just-so-accounts of empirical phenomena, or credit them with supernatural or supranatural reality. Tillich even took his non-supranatural approach to the issue of whether God was miraculously in Jesus, whether Jesus was the "God-Man" walking around in a single body as many believers hold. Clearly, Tillich does not share that belief. I have known many to dismiss him as viable theologian, setting him outside the Christian tradition, on simply this christological perspective, as he aired it in an essay on the incarnation and spoke of the entrance of "mythological and superstitious" notions into understandings of the incarnation.[30] More positively, though, he develops his christology in other directions, seeking to unfold what is for him a deeper, more profound notion of Spirit's creation of New Being in and around the faith and love associated with Jesus' legacy. The superstition of the God-Man is neither a precondition nor a part of Tillich's own understanding of Spirit. New Being in Jesus as the Christ is effected by Spiritual Community and Spiritual Presence in history, and in ways that are *not* supranaturalist. Professor Terry Cross, in this volume, takes up this issue in a section of his chapter, and proposes that Tillich needs a stronger sense of the "inner word" of the present Spirit-grasped life, to "jump the millennia," he writes, in order to stay connected to history.[31] This would hardly be a "jump" that Tillich could make, as Cross also knows. This is not just because Tillich was a liberal modern Protestant, but because he would find such a notion unintelligible. For him the action of Spiritual renewal is, again, more prosaic, more culturally and historically mediated, than it is a work in an "inner word" of individual faith. Interpretations of the history and meaning of incarnation will continue to be one of the debated sites in Tillich-Pentecostal dialogues. Now, we need to journey down some of the major labyrinthine turns of Tillich's view of Spirit breathing, emerging (prosaic and ecstatic), manifesting New Being.

Tracing Spirit in Life

When I write of the "labyrinthine turns" of Spirit in Tillich's system, I have in mind the multiple sites and passageways of Spirit's emergence in volume 3 of *Systematic Theology*. The multiplicity and complexity here can be truly daunting to readers. Sometimes it seems as if Tillich himself is challenged to keep the volume's contents in a presentable form in this, his longest volume, which treats Life and Spirit, and History and the Kingdom of God.

Theorizing Spirit's Multidimensionality

I want to offer two preparatory points about Tillich's theory of this multiplicity, before presenting Spirit's dynamic structure. First, it is perhaps fully appropriate for readers to confront an unwieldy and complex text, given the pervasiveness and elusive ways of Spirit. The unwieldy character of the text and prose is a result not only of Spirit's multiplicity, but also of its complexity. This is spawned, in part, by Tillich's taking the categories (substance, causality, time, space) as organizing rubrics in life's multidimensionality. When turning to history, where Spirit comes to its full concreteness, Tillich keeps it nestled in the matrix of nature, its organic and inorganic dimensions, both on micro- and macro-levels of planetary existence. Thus, to trace Spirit in Tillich is to keep in mind this complexity.

Second, it should be remembered that, for Tillich, this multidimensionality and complexity, which he names *life*, is where we live now, where we have
our actuality. Thus, there is a primacy in his system that he claims for Life and
Spirit (and then for History and the Kingdom of God) over the earlier correlations of Being and God, and Existence and the Christ. When laboring through
volumes 1 and 2, treating of the first two correlations, readers can be led to
think that we humans are really being encouraged by Tillich to live, as explored
in Tillich's volume 1, with the courage provided by God in relation to our ontology of Being, or that, as in volume 2, we are living challenged to accept a salvation provided by Christ for our estranged existential despair amid the "structure of destruction." Years of tracking students reading through the *Systematic
Theology* has revealed this tendency among readers. When, on the last page
of volume 2, Tillich reminds readers that the first two volumes are a set of "abstractions" preparing for the next, third volume (*ST* 2.180), readers can feel a
mild sense of betrayal. Tillich had made this point also in his introduction (*ST*
1.67), but it is easy for readers to forget that note, especially after their hard labor of reading through the first two volumes. "After learning Tillich's ontology
and new ways to think of God," queries the student, "and after embracing existentialism and fresh ways of reimaging Jesus along the way of an expressionist
portrait of the biblical picture of Jesus—now, Tillich tells me, all this has been
abstraction?" Alas, yes. But this does not mean that volumes 1 or 2 were not necessary. They were crucial as abstractions, and they become more meaningful,
now, when we view them from the context of Life and Spirit and especially in
History and the Kingdom of God.

I often explain to students that volumes 1 and 2 provide two dreams or visions, neither of which correspond to how and where we live now, but which
are meant to be instructive for considering "the life" we do now live. We cannot, Tillich suggests, understand the ambiguities of our lived setting without
those abstractions. Volume 1 is a kind of state of dreaming innocence, to use one
of Tillich's own terms for the pre-Fall mythic state. Really the entire correlation
between Being and God in volume 1, wherein a "courage to be," rooted in God
as being-itself, preserves all the tensions of ontology in creative and tensive balance—this is itself a kind of dream of innocence, an ideal projection of "essential being." It is not actualized until wrestled with in life and amid Spirit at play
in life's ambiguities. Similarly, volume 2, on Existence and the Christ, provides a
vision of salvific remedy by the Christ symbol and its corroborating symbols, redressing "the nightmare" of estrangement and alienation. This is another projection, here of "existence" redressed by the Christ. But we do not live there either;
that is, we do not dwell in a space where the nightmare is simply redressed by a
salvific message. No, we live in a place where the state of dreaming innocence

(essence) and estrangement redressed salvifically (existence) are presented to us together, in flux, given to us as two projections often in conflict, two competing dreams, as it were—one of dreaming innocence, one the nightmare and rescue. This is where spirit works, *amid the ambiguities* between these two.

Dynamic Structuring of Spirit in Tillich

In this section, I present *the content* of Tillich's dynamic structure of Spirit. Moreover, I do so in a way that respects the kind of primacy that Tillich gives to Spirit's emergence in history. This is the point at which Spirit's most important feature, its political constitution of ecstatic New Being, is inaugurated, and his religious socialist Spirit might speak to Pentecostalism's world situation today. Tillich makes four key moves in laying out the content of Spirit in volume 3. We must take each in turn.

THE FUNCTIONS OF LIFE AND THEIR PRINCIPLES

First of all, and perhaps most importantly, we must keep to the fore what Tillich terms the *functions of life* and their driving *principles of life*. Several of the chapters mention these as intrinsic to his understanding of life and spirit, and indeed this is right. There are three life-functions: self-integration, wherein Spirit creates centeredness in life; self-creation, wherein Spirit creates growth in life; and then self-transcendence, wherein Spirit creates the sublime in life. But these really lack content, if we do not also see them in relation to the ontological polarities of Tillich's view of "essential being," those polarities that are also broken under the conditions of "existence." Each of the three functions of life are sites at which Spirit goes to work in life bringing healing to the radical brokenness of the corresponding ontological polarity. Here is where we have to recall Tillich's abstractions in volumes 1 and 2.

So, for example, the first function, self-integration, is the way Spirit restores the tensive balance between the poles of *individualization and participation.* In the complexity of biological and social factors that constitute the human dimension, this function of life is called *morality.* As self-integrating, the moral concern is not mainly with law or duty, but with Spirit's creation of centering power and meaning for selves in community. This centering function is what prevents the poles of individualization and participation, or individualized selves and their worlds, from becoming alienated from one another, as they are under conditions of existence. In what Tillich technically terms *life,* we experience sometimes the creative unity of individualization and participation, and oftentimes their pulling apart. And so we often are stranded in loneliness on the individualized side, or, in on the participation side, trapped in collectivization. Both are painful cases of estrangement and alienation. Both deny to the human either genuine solitude for the self or real community in which one becomes a person for and with others. When Spirit emerges, a genuine solitude and community occur together, and the principle of centeredness whirls, as it were, against atomizing individualism *and* bureaucratic or systemic collectivization. For Tillich, and he gives these as examples, "slaves, children and women" have all been denied status as persons, which means they have been denied that union of individualization and participation that makes for full personhood in community (*ST* 1.175). Providing to such as these a restoration of the first polarity's creative tension is precisely what Spirit does through the life-function of self-integration.

The second life-function that Spirit enlivens, that of self-creation, with its principle of growth, also must be understood in relation to its proper ontological polarity—this time, that of *dynamics and form*. All life in its multidimensionality, for Tillich, features a creative tension between these. In humans, these work together, ideally, to produce "culture." But under the conditions of our existence, they pull apart and expose humans in their cultural lives to the twin evils of chaos, on the one side, and rigid formalism, on the other. Spirit through the function of self-creation activates the principle of growth by weaving dynamics and form back into relation. As an example, consider a teen who experiences growth that is life-giving neither by sheer affirmation of his or her vital energies (dynamism alone), nor by the imposition of some guardian's world of tightly binding law and rule (form alone). What fosters growth is both dynamistic affirmation of the youth's vitality, but also with and in relation to form. In life, though, we tend to fluctuate between knowing *both* the creative union of these *and* their being estranged from one another. Spirit's work is to bring forth their creative union by strengthening and shaping the life-function of self-creation.

Finally, the life-function of self-transcendence, with its principle of the sublime, addresses the polarity of being that is both culmination and turning point, namely that of *freedom and destiny*. Among humans this life-function is that of religion. The religion Tillich is after is that which occurs in life and holds freedom and destiny together in creative tension. Achieving this is what Spirit activates as self-transcendence, an experience of "the sublime," the term, for Tillich, meaning the driving of life "*in* itself and *above* itself," which is not "supranatural" (life can be *above* itself without being supranatural). Tillich's philosophical way of explaining self-transcendence is to write that it is a way of "going beyond limits," or moving "toward the great, the solemn, the high" (*ST* 3.31). Without this motion, freedom and destiny pull apart, freedom becoming arbitrariness, and destiny a subjection to fate and necessity. Note that the notion of the sublime as self-transcendence's principle is not just a spatial notion. Tillich, indeed, deploys notions of the "high" and the "beyond" here, but they are ciphers pointing to the solemn and the great, more rare qualities *of* life than they are special spaces *outside* of life. What matters is the content—here, self-transcendence as marked by Spirit's restoration of the tensive and creative relation between freedom and destiny. Examples are difficult here, since Tillich says that empirical descriptions of this life-function, self-transcendence, cannot be given. This is because as Spirit works self-transcendence, it is only human consciousness that knows, and sometimes articulates, its fruit (*ST* 3.87–88). Only in this consciousness, Tillich claims, can humans recognize and experience a congruence of their freedom (as deliberating, deciding, and responsible) with their destiny (that larger field of forces to which they belong and know themselves to be given, formed by nature, history, and themselves) (*ST* 1.185). Nevertheless, when selves are denied self-transcendence, greatness, dignity—all these as a sense of the sublime—people do sometimes articulate their alienation and so provide historical examples. Late twentieth-century indigenous Maya, for example, claimed in the context of Mexican politics and neoliberal markets that they were not simply poor, which indeed they were, but that they also were being denied dignity. This meant, in Tillich's terms, that there was estrangement marked by arbitrariness and necessity, and so a yearning for self-transcendence wherein freedom to deliberate, to decide on possibilities, and to be responsive/responsible, could be integrated with their larger context of belonging to history, land, and culture—to their destiny.[32] Spirit, in activating the principle of the sublime, then, works toward this reintegration of freedom and destiny for human consciousness in the world.

This discussion of the three functions of life and their principles constitutes only what I am terming the first of four key moves in the dynamic structure that makes up the content of Tillich's notion of Spirit. Let me treat more briefly the remaining three. They are also important.

THE AMBIGUITIES OF LIFE

The second aspect of Spirit's content emphasizes the importance of ambiguity as the site of Spirit's most crucial work. When Spirit goes to work redressing the broken ontological polarities by enlivening the life-functions, it does so by addressing our core ambiguity: our fluctuating mode of living, see-sawing between experiencing the union of our essence, on the one hand, and the brokenness of our existence, on the other. We experience in life neither unbroken union of the polarities nor their total brokenness. Take the polarity of individualization and participation. It is not simply that Spirit comes, so to speak, and finds this polarity broken. Instead, it finds humans experiencing both brokenness (their "estranged existence") and also some experience of their unity ("their essential unity"). This "both-and" is the ambiguity that is Life for Tillich. This does not mean, for Tillich, that Spirit emerges simply to increase the already positive domain, making "progress" away from the negative brokenness. The work of Spirit is more radical than that. It redefines entirely humans' reigning understanding of things like morality, culture, and religion in such a way that a truly *un*ambiguous essence can be known even under the conditions of estranged existence. So Tillich dares to propose. But, more cautiously, Spirit in history never works this entirely. The *un*ambiguous experience—say, when you have that deep fusion of essential personhood amid rightly related individualization and participation—can only happen "fragmentarily," writes Tillich. When one reads volume 3, then, tracing Spirit means tracing how Tillich understands Spirit to address the numerous ambiguities in life. Indeed, there are multiple ambiguities for each function of life. There are well over one-hundred pages treating these ambiguities as humans meet them in morality, culture, and religion, and still more when he turns to History. To wrestle with these ambiguities is to move more deeply into the content of what Tillich means by Spirit.

If this were an essay on christology, I would have to say more about how this enlivening by Spirit, restoring tensive balance to the polarities, is related to Jesus as the Christ.[33] Suffice it to express here, as the key christological dynamic, that in communities of faith and love humans see from within those contexts the biblical picture of Jesus, a figure confessed to be the Christ because he is sublime, realizing his essence under conditions of existence. Jesus is thus often described by Tillich as having the traits of "majesty" and "serenity," two features by which Tillich accents the biblical picture's portrait of a sublime Jesus (along with his qualities of "self-surrendering love" and "unbroken unity with God") (*ST* 2.138).[34]

THE TRANSCENDENTAL UNION OF MORALITY, CULTURE AND RELIGION

The third point to be made about the content of Tillich's notion of Spirit concerns its overall aim. As Spirit is at work amid the large number of ambiguities of each of the three life-functions, the aim is a "transcendental union of morality, culture and religion." This is a kind of union of unities, a bringing together in one spiritual whole the functions of human life (morality, culture, and religion), because Spirit has been at work resolving ambiguities and restoring unities within each of the functions of human life, enlivening self-integration, self-creation, and self-transcendence. What ignites the transcendental union is the work of the principle of the sublime in self-transcendence, which then, as a kind of spreading Spirit awakening, activates the growth principle of self-creativity in culture (in both *theoria* and *praxis*), and the centering principle of self-integration in morality. More specifically, under self-transcendence's principle of the sublime, there is an overcoming of *profanization* (Tillich's term for resistance to self-transcending drives) and an overcoming, too, of *demonization* or the demonic (again, not a domain of "demons"), which is Tillich's term for aspects of finite life erupting with divine or quasi-divine force and presumption, evident in forces seeking to rule over, in exploitative and destructive ways, other domains of finite life.

A thoroughgoing secularism would exemplify Tillich's sense of profanization as obstacle to self-transcendence, because it empties out any sense of the sacred moving within finite life. But there are some very religious forms that can be profaning, too. Failures in what Tillich terms *serious prayer*, for example, manipulations of the sacred for one's own finite concerns (say, to win a basketball game, to find a parking space), are departures from Spirit's sublime principle. As to the demonic or the process of demonization, which self-transcending religion must also overcome, examples here would include virulent national chauvinisms—whether U.S. "American exceptionalism" and imperialism, or Israel's contemporary forms of Zionist policy in Palestinian occupation. Since both U.S. and Israeli policies have often taken their collective powers as being quasi-divine, often unquestionable on the basis of grounding religious narratives, they are modes of religious demonization that Tillich's self-transcending Spirit must conquer. Spirit here invokes the great power of the Protestant principle. Tillich summarizes: "The Protestant principle is an expression of the conquest of religion by the Spiritual Presence and consequently an expression of the victory over the ambiguities of religion, its profanization, and its demonization" (*ST* 3.245). This enables the transcendental union to occur. It happens in Spiritual Communities, whether in churches centered on Jesus the Christ (manifest Spiritual Community) or in other groups lacking that particular center but still displaying the Protestant principle (latent Spiritual Community). In these communities, faith and love are at work. *Faith* is not belief, certainly not belief in irrational claims, but a state of being grasped by the ultimate import of this transcendent union of unambiguous life worked by the self-transcending sublime principle of Spirit. Then, *love* is experiencing the process of being "taken into that transcendent unity," almost always worked through the intricacies of dialogical encounter in group life (*ST* 3.129). There is no understanding the real content of Spirit, for Tillich, without recalling Spirit's struggle here to overcome, by the Protestant principle, profanization and demonization, thus effecting the transcendental union of morality, culture, and religion.

SPIRIT'S SOCIAL-HISTORICAL SUBSTANCE

The final point concerning the content of Tillich's Spirit is implied in the previous one, about the importance of Spiritual Community as the context in which Spirit does its work. Here I accent the *social-historical substance* of Spirit's transforming work. Spirit does its salvific, healing work in history-bearing

groups moved by the principle of the sublime known in faith and love. Tillich states this a number of times as he transits from the fourth to the fifth
part of volume 3. "The divine Spirit's invasion of the human spirit does not occur in isolated individuals but in social groups, since all the functions of the
human spirit—moral self-integration, cultural self-creation and religious self-
transcendence—are conditioned by the social context of the ego-thou encounter" (*ST* 3.139). Later, when discussing human historical existence, his argument
confirms that even his section on Life and Spirit was a kind of abstraction—
an abstraction from where Spirit works in ambiguous *historical* life, not just in
ambiguous life in general. "Life processes in a community are immediately determined," writes Tillich, "by the historical dimension in accordance with the
fact that the direct bearers of history are groups rather than individuals, who
are only indirect bearers" (*ST* 3.308). History was at work in all the functions
of life he was describing throughout part 4, and "the processes of life themselves are horizontally directed, actualizing the historical dimension in an an-
ticipatory way" (*ST* 3.297).

So what is at stake in accenting this fourth point at the culmination of Tillich's system? We can begin by recalling how often it is quoted that Tillich's
christology is completed by a Spirit ecclesiology. True enough: "Christ is not
the Christ without those who receive him as the Christ" (*ST* 2.99). But this statement Tillich construed as not only mandating a move conceptually to Spirit and
Spiritual Community, to his pneumatology and ecclesiology, but also to the dimension of history where the symbol, the Kingdom of God, is embraced by the
churches. History and the Kingdom of God are "integral parts of the Christological work," as well as are Life and Spirit (*ST* 2.180).

The Spirit that comes to fruition in history, which then reaches for the symbol of the Kingdom of God, is Spirit where the social, and soon also the political,
are revealed by Tillich as especially crucial. Spirit plays in, and is carried by, history-bearing groups, in their sociality. But Spirit's sociality is most predominantly
constituted by "the political realm." If, then, I speak of Tillich's notion of Spirit
as "Religious Socialist Spirit"—and in spite of the diminished character of his
socialist activism in later life—it is because his understanding of Spirit reaches
its full concreteness in an affirmation of this political sociality. Tillich is socialist in foregrounding the intrinsically social and political character of ultimacy,
of Spirit, at the heart of self-transcending religion. It is, then, no accident that
Tillich's introduction to the final part 5 of *Systematic Theology* includes the summary statement I took as epigram of this chapter, which is also the basic framework of his *The Socialist Decision*. In other words, his mature theological system,
for all its different turns through doctrinal notions and the absence of reference
to contemporary political movements, delivers us back into the world of history-

bearing groups (a term also frequenting *The Socialist Decision*), and of principles that animate those historical groups in all their social and political specificity.

Lest readers sidestep the politics of Spirit in which Tillich's work culminates, or try to depoliticize the notion of the Kingdom of God, Tillich drives his point home at key parts of the discourse on historical existence as site of Spirit: "The political realm is always predominant because it is constitutive of historical existence." Again, "if the cultural or religious historian crosses the political boundaries he is aware that this is an abstraction from actual life, and he does not forget that the *political* unities, whether large or small, remain the conditions of all cultural life" (*ST* 3.311).[35] He notes also that "it is significant that the symbol in which the Bible expresses the meaning of history is political: 'Kingdom of God,' and not 'Life of the Spirit' or 'economic abundance'" (*ST* 3.311). This is not a political reductionism in Tillich. After all, every part of the multidimensional unity of life, for him, also participates in history. This is why he also includes a powerful role for individuals (*ST* 3.346). But this does not disrupt the "predominance of the political function in historical activity," because history-bearing groups are the modes of movement in historical life, structuring the power that any agent has within the internal life of the group and in relation to other groups. Tillich's powerful respect and emphatic claims for the predominance of the political in daily life may grow out of what he witnessed throughout his life: war, at first hand and as a result of European nations' very political brinkmanship; the disintegration of political structures in Germany between the wars that created rampant unemployment and food-shortages for nearly everyone; the rise of Nazism and its comprehensive impact; and also the conformism in the United States that he saw connected to potentially dangerous political consequences.[36] The historical Spirit of *Systematic Theology's* culmination is consonant with much of *The Socialist Decision* (1933), published exactly thirty years prior to the emergence of volume 3 of his system (1963). In the 1933 book, he had been obliged to follow the meandering ways of prophetic spirit through the maze of other principles driving romanticist and liberal bourgeois groups into ambiguous, and often contradictory, relations with prophetic spirit's socialist principle.[37] In the 1963 conclusion to his system, he has followed concrete Spirit into history, this time through an even more intricate maze of diverse principles of Spirit—Spirit which, through its principle of self-transcendence, restores healing amid the various other functions of life and their ambiguities. When in 1965, just months away from death, Tillich said, "There is 'nothing beyond religious socialism,'" this certainly includes his completed system. It lacks abundant references to socialist movements, but it is still animated by religious socialist Spirit. Tillich thus refers unapologetically, in his third volume, to his earlier religious socialism, as what gave him the term "theonomy" for speaking of the impact of Spirit on culture (*ST* 3.249), and what generated a crucial awareness in action—implementing biblical prophetism (*ST* 3.356) and attuning action to a sense of the *Kairos* (*ST* 3.369), the fulfilled time for Spirit's emergence in history.

Religious Socialist Spirit and Pentecostalism Today

Let me return to the issue of Pentecostalism today, facing the Leviathan of neoliberal global orders. How might Tillich's religious socialist Spirit be at work in those churches, if it is, and what challenges might Tillich's theory of Spirit hold for such Pentecostalism, at least as I briefly focused above on some of its current tensions by way of Comaroff's work?[38] Here, in closing, I want to suggest a way to deploy Tillich's discourse of Spirit for interpreting pentecostal churches' success and struggle. The very content of Tillich's notion of Spirit, its historicality and politicality, makes such observations possible, perhaps also necessary.

Let us recall that for Tillich the churches are sites of Spirit's historical self-transcendence, and hence representatives, or embodiments, of the Kingdom of God, insofar as they resist profanization and demonization. Precisely this resistance by the churches is the sign of their enlivening by Spirit in Tillich's sense. The new, powerful ontology opened up by Pentecostalism's "new economy of affect," as Comaroff puts it, is one way that pentecostal churches can be seen as embodying this, resisting late modernity. If one face of Western late modernity and abstract neoliberal economies is an abstraction from the body, and a flattening of affect, then I think we can state that the intensifications at work in the embrace of passion and dramatic performance can be seen as ways in which the church resists modernity's profanization. This can be true no matter how one, intellectually, assesses the truth claims of worshipers articulating their faith and practices. I might not believe the content of a passionate song's reverent lyrics, but I can value the hedge against modernity that such passion inspires, embodies, and so unleashes into society and history. Recall, for Tillich, profanization means the emptying out of bodies and finite life of sacral depth, of ultimate concern(s), and animating modes of self-transcendence. Profanization in the extreme, as reductive of all self-transcendence, is forthrightly resisted by a Pentecostalism achieving what Comaroff terms a new ontological intensification of Pentecostalism's economy of affect.

Even more is there evidence of a resistance to late modernity's neoliberal profanization when pentecostal churches take on social services that have been abandoned by states that are pulled into the global order's corrupt economy of brutality. In this way, the churches embody historical functions of self-transcendence (representing the Kingdom of God) by meeting needs of depersonalized humans in their midst, and often of the violated natural order, too. The neoliberal order is a profanizing order, a profane realm, in Tillich's sense, not simply because it is secular and maybe also atheist (though often it is neither); it is profane because it atomizes and "thing-ifies," and so destroys. The alternative economies of large megachurch pentecostal ecclesial domains, then, whatever others might think of them for a certain "Total Take-Over" ideology or "theocratic" impulse, have the undeniable impact of gathering those broken by neoliberal regimes into some communality, making life where all too often disaster capitalism spreads death and debilitation of body politics. This is a fundamental contribution of tendencies at work in what Comaroff termed contemporary world Pentecostalism's sociological dimension.

Recall, though, that for Tillich, churches of the Spirit guard self-transcendence, and so in history move with powers of expectation under the symbol Kingdom of God when they also struggle against demonization. Here is where there may be some pushback—or at least a helpful reminder—from Tillich's religious socialist Spirit toward pentecostal world formation today. Spirit in the churches, Tillich emphasized, resists not only the emptying out of self-transcendence (profanization), but also the rise to claimed ultimacy of any finite realms and collectives. This is why Tillich named as demonic cases of world imperialism and fascism, especially the Nazism of his 1930s and 1940s Germany. As mentioned above, he also termed them Leviathan. Today's U.S.-armed global capitalism, the neoliberal order, is such a demonic structure, such a Leviathan, especially given the fact that it is so often unquestioned and unchallenged—sometimes not even called out as the brutal system it is. The peoples of the United States, whose government arms and enforces the transnational neoliberal order, make up one of the most religious of nations in the world. They also often sanction the guarding of their nation's prosperity and power with beliefs in the divine mandate of the United States, its sacred manifest destiny, and thus, at least indirectly, affirm the military backing of its economic wealth. As such, U.S. citizens' civil religion is one of the most brutal and powerful cases of the "prosperity gospel." Many liberals who lament the prosperity gospels across poorer regions of the world fail to note that giving military support to, and everyday reverent compliance with, U.S.-armed global capitalism makes of the neoliberal order itself a kind of prosperity gospel. It is a demonic collective with both political and religious dimensions.

To name and resist this form of demonization, neoliberalism today, is a challenge to *all* the churches, or would be, insofar as they are guided by Tillich's notion of the Spirit. But given the dramatic rise of pentecostal churches—often in those regions suffering the low-intensity and high-intensity wars and U.S. covert special operations, and after decades and centuries of ravaging by European colonization—one might ask: what are the best ways to strengthen the necessary work of these churches who might name and resist the neoliberal "demon" there? Over years of work in Latin America, I know well that pentecostal communities working in poor contexts can and do motivate such naming and resistance, especially among Pentecostals in Mexico and Ecuador, both sites of indigenous Pentecostals who proactively work against neoliberal trade agreements.[39] Nevertheless, pentecostal groups over much of the global South, like almost all Christian churches, are divided ideologically on neoliberalism, with many supporting or remaining silent about what I have termed the neoliberal demon. As keen sites of Christian growth in the global South, pentecostal churches find that the question remains: how to strengthen their resistance to ways the neoliberal demon seeks to co-opt all the religious communions.[40] Comaroff highlights how Pentecostalism's economy of affect and the take-over of social service provisioning, while being ways to fight neoliberal modernity today, can also lubricate that modernity. In this way, neoliberalism's demonic power can blunt the political-theological force that the pentecostal churches might mount against late modernity's profane ways. In fact, and Tillich was always aware of this, Spirit in the churches achieves its overcoming of the profane and the demonic within their ecclesial life, through being forged into creative historical assemblages by self-transcending Spirit to rival destructive political and social forces in history.

I stress, again, again, that no matter how dramatic their growth in numbers, it is not the role of pentecostal churches alone to mount this resistance to demonization, any more than it was for them to go up alone against Western modernity's profanizing ways. Other churches, *especially within the United States, and especially those steeped in the intellectual discourse of modernity,* need to achieve their own resistance to demonic neoliberalism. This would be a solidarity with pentecostal churches of the world South being challenged to name and fight U.S.-armed neoliberal orders. The churches in this relation of solidarity will need, Tillich also reminds, the many "latent" Spiritual communities, groups who do not name Jesus the Christ as their center (workers' groups, youth movements, antiracist struggles, emancipatory movements by women and those of alternative sexualities—all these and more, with the churches, constituting a kind of Spirit-expanded proletariat) (*ST* 3.376).[41] In brief, the question would be: where, today, is there at work a counter-imperial faith, in churches ready to take on the demonization at work in U.S.-armed global capitalism? Tillich's religious socialist Spirit points to Spiritual Communities, in history, that would dare challenge precisely such a demonic neoliberalism.

Notes

1. Paul Tillich, *The Socialist Decision*, trans. Franklin Sherman (New York: Harper and Row, 1977), 4.

2. Paul Tillich, *My Search for Absolutes,* with drawings by Saul Steinberg (New York: Simon and Schuster, 1967), 40; compare to *Socialist Decision,* 20–26.

3. Ibid., 50.

4. Paul Tillich, "The Storms of Our Times" (6 May 1941), in Tillich, *The Protestant Era,* trans. James Luther Adams (Chicago: University of Chicago Press, 1948), 251–252.

5. Ronald H. Stone and Matthew Lon Weaver, *Against the Third Reich: Paul Tillich's Wartime Radio Broadcasts into Nazi Germany* (Louisville: Westminster John Knox Press, 1998), 9.

6. Paul Tillich, *The Courage To Be* (New Haven: Yale University Press, 1951), 103–104.

7. By Spirit I mean all the manifestations that Tillich tends to trace and refer to with other capitalized expressions, particularly *Spiritual Presence* and *Spiritual Community.* Tillich also uses the lower-case term *spirit* for referring to a particular dimension of life's multiplicity, particularly *the human dimension,* as distinct from, say, organic and non-organic dimensions, a human dimension that is biological and social, and culminates, for him, in psychological and historical dimensions. Readers should not be confused thinking that Spirit is present only to humans, to human spirit. By no means. It *is,* indeed, related to the spirit, lower case, to humanity, but it is all-pervasive and radically immanent to all other dimensions of the multidimensional unity of life, as well. In all the dimensions—though in different ways—Spirit is ecstatic emergence, coming with an unconditional and underivable mode of "self-transcendence." For the Spirit/spirit distinction, see Tillich, *ST* 3.21–28.

8. Paul Tillich, *The Protestant Era* (Chicago: University of Chicago Press, 1948), 75.

9. Simonmary Asese Aihiokhai, "Pentecostalism and Political Empowerment: The Nigerian Phenomenon," *Journal of Ecumenical Studies* 45:2 (Spring 2010): 249–264; see 249–250.

10. Jean Comaroff, "Pentecostalism, Populism and the New Politics of Affect," in *Pentecostalism and Development: Churches, NGOs and Social Change in Africa,* ed. Dena Freeman (New York: Palgrave Macmillan, 2012), 41–66.

11. Thomas P. M. Barnett, *The Pentagon's New Map: War and Peace in the Twenty-first Century* (New York: G. P. Putnam, 2004).

12. Still one of the best introductions to neoliberal global economics and politics is Alfredo Saad-Filho and Deborah Johnston, eds., *Neoliberalism: A Critical Reader* (Pluto Press, 2005). A very readable, well-researched account is Naomi Klein's *Shock Doctrine: The Rise of Disaster Capitalism* (New York: Picador, 2008). On the nature of U.S. centralizing power in relation to its dominance of global currency exchange and notions of empire, see the chapter "Money and Empire," in Nimi Wariboko, *God and Money: A Theology of Money in a Globalizing World* (Lanham: Lexington Books, 2010), 159–196.

13. For one fine account, see Stephen F. Cohen, *Failed Crusade: America and the Tragedy of Post-Communist Russia,* updated ed. (New York: W. W. Norton, 2001).

14. Sheldon S. Wolin, *Democracy Inc.: Managed Democracy and the Specter of Inverted Totalitarianism* (Princeton: Princeton University Press, 2008).

15. Paul Tillich, *The World Situation,* Social Ethics Series 2, ed. Franklin Sherman (1945; Philadelphia: Fortress Press, 1965), 9.

16. In addition to sources listed in footnote no. 63, below, see also Katherine Attanasi and Amos Yong, *Pentecostalism and Prosperity: The Socio-Economics of the Global Charismatic Movement* (New York: Palgrave Macmillan, 2012).

17. Comaroff, "Pentecostalism, Populism and the New Politics of Affect," 62.

18. On the notion of post-Fordist and "postmodern" capitalist accumulation, see David Harvey, *The Conditions of Postmodernity* (London: Blackwell, 1996).

19. Comaroff, "Pentecostalism, Populism and the New Politics of Affect," 57.

20. Ibid., 59.

21. Ibid.

22. Ibid., 54.

23. Ibid., 53.

24. Amos Yong, *In the Days of Caesar: Pentecostalism and Political Theology* (Grand Rapids, MI: Eerdmans, 2010), 23–26.

25. I clarify below Tillich's senses of the demonic and demonization. Here, I note that *the demonic* names not a realm of demons in any supranatural sense, but more a collective power of destruction and domination, which arises from, and distorts, the vitality of human and created orders. It arises from the depths, or abyss, of human creatureliness. National Socialism, in his Germany (1933–1945), was a case of the demonic.

26. Paul Tillich, "Philosophy of Life," interview video, Pittsburgh Theological Seminary, 1961.

27. See sections on emergence, for example, in Amos Yong, *The Spirit of Creation: Modern Science and Divine Action in the Pentecostal-Charismatic Imagination* (Grand Rapids, MI: Eerdmans, 2011), ch. 5. Along this line of emergence thinking in Tillich and Pentecostal theory, see also Nimi Wariboko, "Emergence and Ethics: From Outline and Interpretation to Prophetic Spirit," *Dharma Deepika* 13:1 (July–December 2010): 50–64, and "Emergence and the 'Science of Ethos': Toward a Tillichian Ethical Framework," *Theology and Science* 7:2 (May 2009): 189–206.

28. For this take on immanence theologies, see Russell Re Manning, ed., *Retrieving the Radical Tillich: His Legacy and Contemporary Importance* (New York: Palgrave Macmillan, 2015).

29. Grace Calí, *Tillich First-Hand: A Memoir of the Harvard Years* (New York: Exploration Press, 1996), 84.

30. Paul Tillich, "A Reinterpretation of the Doctrine of Incarnation," *Church Quarterly Review* 249 (1949): 133–148, at 134–135.

31. See above [text above footnotes 29–35, and text above footnotes 36–39].

32. On the Zapatistas and dignity, see Subcomandante Marcos, *Our Word is Our Weapon: Selected Writings* (New York: Seven Stories Press, 2002), 40, 47–48, 75.

33. For a brief summary of Tillich's christological moves, see my introduction in *Paul Tillich: Theologian of the Boundaries* (Minneapolis: Fortress Press, 1986), 24–28.

34. My own departure from Tillich here is based on a twofold critique of Tillich's christological method. First, Tillich is too content with a largely aesthetic view of the "biblical portrait" for quickening theological interpretations of the meaning of Jesus' life and death (and these *are* always interpretations), and thus Tillich slights historical re-

search into the Jesus movement and the ways this research might also quicken christo-logical imagination. Second, and as a consequence of the first, Tillich misses the impor-tance of the mode of Jesus' death, by crucifixion at the hands of Roman and religious elites protecting imperial religious power. The crucified—executed, even lynched—Jesus could *not* have been "serene and majestic" in this counter-picture. He would have been one who screamed, was tortured, exposed to the threat of dogs and birds of prey—but perhaps buried by sundown, and yet re-membered. In this way, there was a re-constitut-ing of the body and bodies in life-giving communities. See Mark Lewis Taylor, *The Exe-cuted God: The Way of the Cross in Lockdown America* (Minneapolis: Fortress Press, 2001).

35. Italics are Tillich's.

36. Tillich, *The Courage to Be,* 112.

37. Tillich, *Socialist Decision,* 66–93.

38. I am bracketing, for this response, the equally important question of what Til-lich's view of Spirit might mean for other church communions.

39. Mark Lewis Taylor, "Spirit," in *The Blackwell Companion to Political Theology,* ed. Peter Scott and William T. Cavanaugh (Malden, MA: Blackwell, 2004), 377–392, espe-cially 89–90.

40. For additional literature on Pentecostal churches' engagement with neoliberal powers, see the other essays in Dena Freeman (cited above, note 10); cf. Israael Batista, *Iglesias de Jubileo, las iglesias evangélicas en el nuevo milenio* (Quito: Ediciones Consejo Lati-noamericano de iglesias, 2000), and Donald E. Miller and Tetsunao Yamamori, *Global Pentecostalism: The New Face of Christian Social Engagement* (Berkeley: University of Cali-fornia Press, 2007).

41. On the notion of Tillich's expansive proletariat, beyond the scientistic vanguard elite of some Marxisms, see Tillich, *Socialist Decision,* 99–100.

FIFTEEN

A Spirited Encounter

The Promise of Ecstasis and the Constraints of Supranaturalism

JOHN J. THATAMANIL

The winds of the Spirit have, as always, been blowing and will continue to blow throughout the whole of creation, but theology's response to the same has been less than spirited until the final decades of the twentieth century and now the early part of the twenty-first. A variety of factors have played a role in this overdue course correction, but thoughtful observers would do well to list the rise of the pentecostal movement and, to a lesser extent, the contributions of Paul Tillich as important factors in improving Spirit's theological fortunes. It is, therefore, most felicitous to deepen a conversation between these two theological streams, a conversation that has been well inaugurated in the pioneering work of Amos Yong and Nimi Wariboko. This particular volume heralds a substantial broadening and deepening of this conversation, and I am happy to play a part in nurturing the intellectual ties between scholarly communities that will enable the conversation to flourish.

Readers who are uninitiated in this nascent conversation might be forgiven for wondering whether we do not have here a theological odd couple. What does Tillich's sober, modernist anti-supranaturalist theology have to do with the ecstatic, counter-modernist supranaturalism of pentecostal theologies? Are they not inhabitants, to use Steven Studebaker's language, of "incommensurable thought-worlds?"[1] Do we not have here, as Tony Richie briefly wonders, a contemporary instance of the longstanding Tertullian rivalry between a rational Athens and a wild and unpredictable Jerusalem, the scene of the Spirit's polyglossic Pentecost manifestation?[2]

But almost immediately, this dichotomy has to fall away. Tillich himself is through and through a theologian of the Spirit—and indeed, to be more exact, a theologian of the ecstatic Spirit who recognizes and validates the possibility of glossolalia. Tillich is not the theologian that many take him to be, as the authors of this volume rightly recognize. The same call to move beyond stereotypes and partiality must be made for the other side. Pneumatological exuberance has been amply matched by conceptual rigor on the pentecostal side, including now a substantial and growing reflection on the relationship between Pentecostalism and science, nature, economics, and the world's religious traditions.

Indeed, the conversation that takes place within the pages of this book between Tillich and pentecostal theologies bears many of the markers of healthy conversation in interreligious encounter. When interreligious conversation goes wrong, traditions are essentialized into antagonistic camps, and their textured positions are simplified in reductionist fashion. As a consequence, representatives of the traditions find themselves constrained to inhabit inflexible caricatures. Between rigidly essentialized parties no meaningful conversation can take place, only contestation. None of these signs of conversation gone wrong are present in this volume.

Although there is ample contestation and debate herein, within the pages of this book pentecostal theologians read Tillich capaciously and generously. He is permitted to be what he truly is: a pneumatological theologian who stands ready to be captured by the Spirit, a theologian of grace, who longs for the Spirit's gracious coming, a longing that is even recognized as eschatological. Tillich is not reduced to a mere foil or counter to pentecostal positions. Moreover, the book's authors demonstrate that Pentecostalism is a living, vibrant, and even radical intellectual tradition. Readers are blessed to encounter some of the most creative thinkers within pentecostal theology laboring to birth the tradition's own future. That future is shown to be prophetic, even disruptive, and avowedly political rather than merely personal. Still more, a variety of thinkers in this volume seek by way of Tillich's assistance to articulate a holistic account of the Holy Spirit as the Spirit of life itself. Veli-Matti Kärkkäinen, for example, contends that Tillich can assist pentecostal pneumatology precisely because of his appearance as a visionary on this front, anticipating the work of thinkers such as Jürgen Moltmann well before their time. One gathers from Kärkkäinen that pentecostal thinkers have yet to arrive at so robust and encompassing account of the Spirit.

But even after facile essentializations and caricatures that would obstruct dialogue are removed, there remain genuine questions of compatibility between would-be conversation partners. Any dialogue worthy of the name is ventured with the hope of cross-fertilization. We speak *with* each other rather than *at* each other because we hope to learn and be transformed thereby. Does not the capacity to receive from another require sufficient common ground so as to make reception both possible and desirable? Does such common ground exist between Tillichians and Pentecostals? And if common ground is not given, might it be created?

Finally, talk of cross-fertilization suggests that *both* parties in this conversation stand to be enriched. If so, Tillichians must receive as much as they have to give to Pentecostals and vice versa. Where such mutuality is absent, there is reason to believe that conversation has not yet arrived at maturity and balance. If the basic premise of this book is that Tillichians and Pentecostals have much to learn from each other, then we must find evidence of mutual learning and transformation. My reflections here are meant to answer these questions and to offer some provisional judgments about the state of this still emerging conversation.

By way of anticipating my conclusion, I suggest that there is one recurrent obstacle in the conversation between Tillichians and pentecostal theologians: the question of supernaturalism. While virtually every other matter of theological import permits of negotiation and reinterpretation, time and again Tillich's refusal to imagine a superworld of divine beings and an interventionist deity proves to run headlong into pentecostal convictions not about the Spirit so much as about spirits. About Spirit, considerable common ground can be found. About spirits, demonic and otherwise, incommensurability abides.

Writers in this volume are cognizant of this obstacle. Some recognize the obstacle and appear to insist that Pentecostals will, of necessity, find Tillich wanting on this front and will have to part ways. Terry Cross, for example, asserts that at least on this score, Tillichian reservations about the extraordinary and the miraculous indicate that his "modernism speaks louder than this voice of the Spirit."[3] Pamela Holmes observes that the pentecostal movement was born in part as a reaction against mainline acceptance of higher criticism and Darwinian evolution. Tillich, by contrast, accepts both. What does this fact of origins mean for the conversation between Tillich and pentecostal theology?

Still other authors in this multivocal volume move in Tillich's direction and argue that there is nothing in pentecostal experience that requires a commitment to naïve supranaturalism (Kärkkäinen). For example, David Bradnick's pentecostal-emergentist account of the demonic accepts and works from the premise of an evolutionary account of the origins of life. Bradnick's emergentist position seeks to work out an account of spirits and the demonic that he hopes Tillichians might accept because it does not fall prey to supranaturalism.

This tension on the supranaturalism question is internal to pentecostal theology and would be found therein quite apart from any engagement with Tillich. Conversation with Tillich only serves to bring it to the fore. Such tensions are, at any rate, an unavoidable part of the robust efflorescence of pentecostal theology so richly on display in this volume. Any vital and undomesticated movement will be marked by such creative difference.

I suspect that readers of this volume will be convinced that this diversity will enrich Christian theology in general and not just interested Tillichians.

That said, Tillich and those who stand in his lineage will find themselves especially indebted to this volume's contributors for multiple reasons. Almost to a person, our authors recognize Tillich as a theologian of the spirit and hence part of the larger community of pneumatological theologians. Not one pronounces Tillich dead and offers eulogies over his corpus; the Tillich presented herein remains very much alive and a vitalizing conversation partner. Finally, the authors of this volume not only generate rich interpretive work about Tillich; rather they proceed further by employing Tillich's work for constructive theological ends. Who could have predicted that pentecostal theologians would be the ones to make so energetic a case for Tillich's enduring promise for contemporary theology?

This positive reception notwithstanding, Tillich is not treated here with mere deference and kindliness. The authors of this volume press Tillich on many fronts: they contend that Tillich's theology of God must do more justice to the personal dimensions of the divine life even as it rightly urges us to remember that God is suprapersonal. Tillich's eschatology remains lacking, at least to pentecostal readers, who long for a stronger account of hope than Tillich appears able to offer (Peter Althouse). And Tillich's discourse about God must be chastened and revised in a postmodern era in which we think of God as beyond and without being (Rhys Kuzmič). Even Tillich's sacramentalism—one is hard pressed to think of a more sacramental modern protestant theologian—is found wanting (Andreas Nordlander). These are just some of the provocative and compelling challenges put to Tillich in this volume.

In what follows, I will trace both the strongly felt *positive* pneumatological resonance between Tillich and pentecostal theology as well as the unresolved question of a *negative* interference generated by the problem of supranaturalism. The constraints of space will not permit me to treat these issues in every chapter; rather, I hope to trace these themes as they find exemplification in just some of the authors in this rich volume.

In many ways, the challenge that Pentecostals face in supranaturalism is most strikingly presented and perhaps even partially resolved in the chapter by Wolfgang Vondey. Vondey rightly recognizes the central challenge as ontological in nature. Pentecostal theology abides in an unresolved dualism of spirit and nature. So long as this dualism abides, so long as spirit stands above and apart from nature, a supranaturalist picture of the spirit's intrusion into nature seems all but inevitable. That supranaturalism also threatens to leave Pentecostals with an impoverished, mechanistic account of the natural world. With acuteness of insight, Vondey looks to Tillich's synthesis of Schleiermacher's and Schelling's nondualism (the term nondualism is mine and not Vondey's) of nature and spirit as a crucial resource for pentecostal reflection. Vondey's name for what Tillich has accomplished is exactly right: "pneumatological ontology."[4]

Appealing to this fecund notion and phrase, Vondey contends that "Pentecostalism is no stranger to ecstasy but has failed to make the ecstatic a defining moment for a pneumatological ontology."[5] But is Pentecostalism alone on this front? How many have even recognized that what Tillich has to offer is just precisely a pneumatological ontology? And where else might such an ontology be found, inside or outside Pentecostalism? Vondey confirms and reaffirms what Kärkkäinen asserted, namely the need for wedding Spirit to life, a process that Vondey believes requires nothing less than an ecstatic ontology. Vondey's chapter offers an invaluable account of the enduring promise of Tillich's ontology, one I dare to venture has been underappreciated even by some Tillichians.

Rhys Kuzmič's further chapter on the question of ontology is stimulating in the extreme. The chapter manages somehow to treat a wide array of daunting topics with remarkable efficiency: Can Pentecostals take ontology seriously without becoming captive to being-itself discourse? Can a theology of God as being-itself survive the postmodern turn? Might Pentecostals help Tillich to address meaningfully the unresolved tensions between personal and suprapersonal dimensions of the divine life in Tillich's theology? Kuzmič manages to do all this while also appealing to and expounding the peculiar Christian philosophy of Jean-Luc Marion. The chapter can, of course, only announce a theological program, but it manages to do so splendidly.

For my part, I remain unconvinced that every appeal to being or being-itself discourse renders one captive to ontotheology. The term *being* becomes elusive when associated with the term *God*, and despite Tillich's questionable assertion in ST 1 that "God is being-itself" is a "literal" assertion—something he walked back in ST 2—being never functions in ontotheological fashion in Tillich's theology. Being is already shaped and inflected by pneumatology, a point that Vondey has made so well and one that Kuzmič also recognizes. Being is peculiarly mobile and dynamic in Tillich's imagination. It is by no means static and substance-like. Nor is being meant to serve as an answer to the question "Why is there something rather than nothing?"—a question that Tillich believes, at any rate, to point to the mystery of being and the threat of nonbeing, and not to a conception of God as *prima causa* and *causa sui*, which Heidegger contends is the hallmark of ontotheology.[6]

For these reasons, I believe that there is a greater resonance between Marion and Tillich than one might expect to find. If being-itself is already enspirited in Tillich's thought, then Tillich's discourse about God as being-itself is, even without Marion's assist, already a pneumatological ontology. Still, Kuzmič is right to press Tillich and Tillichians on the question of being-itself. More must be said on these matters than Tillich himself has said, and certainly the contemporary challenge that being might itself be an instance of conceptual idolatry is one that must now be met.

But there is also a challenge that Kuzmič and perhaps also Vondey must meet: how can a rich polyvalent theological symbol like "Spirit" serve as the basis for any ontology? Kuzmič is right to suggest that Pentecostals need a robust ontological grounding and that Tillich can help in this regard, but can Spirit play that conceptual role? Is not Spirit too rich a word, too motile, too elusive and expressive to function as a term in any ontology, which requires at least a considerable measure of conceptual precision? Symbolic terms—and no term is ever *only* a symbol for Tillich—are too powerful and hermeneutically fecund to serve as the basis of ontology, which is at any rate, a far humbler labor than the quest to speak of God. And would not Spirit too suffer semantic loss when it leaves the precincts of the sacred? Would it cease to serve as an icon and so in turn also become an idol? This too, unsurprisingly, is a danger that Kuzmič appreciates, but we must await further shared labor between Pentecostals and Tillichians to see how this danger might yet be met. The future of any pneumatological ontology hinges on such labor.

Frank Macchia's chapter on Tillich's pneumatological theology appreciates and demonstrates that the whole of Tillich's theology can be productively read as a theology from the third article of the creed. Having recently taught the entire system, I was already persuaded that this was the case, and I have been saying as much to my students. Those who are new to Tillich's theology are perhaps unavoidably overimpressed by what is distinctive in it, and that is, of course, the claim of a theology of God as ground of being or being itself. Captured by that discourse and its abstraction, readers often fail to understand what Macchia and indeed also Vondey and Kuzmič understand: Tillich's theology is thoroughly pneumatological.

Tillich, right from the beginning, wishes to assert that not any old doctrine of God as ground of being will do. He is aware that he stands in a broader being-itself tradition when he makes his ontological claim, but he also takes great care to distinguish his position from that of Thomas Aquinas. God cannot be pure actuality (*actus purus*), because a God who is pure actuality cannot be a living God. To emphasize this point, Tillich asserts that God must be both power as well as structure, or to use the old medieval language, both will and intellect. This double assertion, which is his wedding of John Duns Scotus and Aquinas, also grounds his understanding of Sprit as meaning bearing power. Thus, pneumatological considerations are at work in this theology already, from the first volume. Contrary to some (mis)readings, Spirit is not a late-arriving guest in Tillich's project.

Macchia understands all this rather well, presenting Tillich's system with care, fidelity, and even appreciation as pneumatological through and through. He has persuaded at least this reader that the conversation between Tillich and Pentecostals on the doctrine of the Spirit can be rich and fruitful, and that its full potential has yet to be tapped. I was particularly intrigued by Macchia's claim that even some of his reservations about Tillich mirror internal pentecostal debates, more specifically the conversations between oneness Pentecostals and Trinitarian Pentecostals. Hence, at least some of the debates that Pentecostals will have with Tillich are likely to have the character of a family squabble rather than a clash of alien intentions and systems. On this particular point, I am convinced that Studebaker has it right: Tillich's vision places him in greater proximity to Trinitarian Pentecostals than to Oneness Pentecostals.

In his final section, Macchia articulates a variety of worries about and objections to Tillich's theology. These concerns are very much worth articulating and exploring with great care. As someone who works in Tillich's lineage without seeking to replicate his insights, I am deeply grateful for Macchia's carefully articulated objections. Specifically, Macchia believes that it will not do to imagine divinity as meaning-bearing power. He wants a richer conception of divine action, action understood as causal, something that Tillich does not want. Once again the looming threat of supranaturalism presents itself. If God is to be a causal agent, must not God become a being among beings, a being who stands apart from the world with which he interacts in causal fashion? What are we to do with this radical difference between Tillich and at least this particular articulation of Pentecostalism?

In the work of Andreas Nordlander, we return again to the power and promise of pneumatological ontology, but this time for cultivating a deeper sacramental imagination. At the heart of Nordlander's chapter is a claim that pentecostal theology is out of tune and out of keeping with the implicit sacramentalism of pentecostal experience, rich with laying on of hands, of anointing with oil, with the sheer earthy bodilyness of the signs of the Spirit's ecstatic presence. Echoing many of the themes articulated by Vondey, Nordlander contends that Pentecostals can find in Tillich a holism of participation in the divine life that is the necessary precondition for a robust sacramentalism.

But there is something missing in Tillich, Nordlander contends. Tillich's sacramentalism falls short because of a critical fault in his doctrine of creation. Tillich's theology is (in)famous for his contention that there is a point of identification between creation and fall. If creatures are to be free, they must stand outside of and not be kept within the divine life. Moreover, to be a free creature is also to be a fallen creature; hence, there is a point of identity between the doctrines of creation and fall. This moment of inevitable separation is writ into creation and is only breached in the soteriological moment when we are ecstatically grasped by the power of the Spirit.

While Nordlander appreciates Tillich's affirmation of ecstasis, he rightly finds Tillich's vision problematic and pneumatologically insufficient. He writes that Spirit must be present not only at the moment of salvation but also in, with, and through creation. As he puts it, Nordlander wants a vision of creation in which "simply to be is already to be under the impact of the Spirit, who is the breath of God, giving life to all."[7] Affirming the Spirit's robust presence in creation, Nordlander contends, will offer a deeper sacramentalism than Tillich could offer. Nordlander's pneumatological supplementation of Tillich is precisely the sort of gift that this Tillichian was hoping to discover in this volume. Nordlander's critique of Tillich, although it can be nuanced, is on point, and his proposed corrective is also persuasive. Creation itself, and not just salvation, is the work of the Spirit. This, I believe, is a gift that Tillichians can and must gladly receive.

The quest for a deeper sacramentalism continues in the work of Lisa Stephenson. Stephenson's chapter is a grand undertaking. It presents itself as a bilateral conversation between pentecostal theology and Tillich, but it really aims at creating a tripartite conversation between pentecostal spirituality, feminist thought, and Tillich's sacramental theology. Stephenson's chapter seeks to create a conversation that will enrich each of these three partners. She writes as a feminist Pentecostal, but I was most excited to see that Stephenson believes that feminist Pentecostals can not only learn from Tillich but have much to teach Tillich as well. As I am a Tillichian who seeks to extend rather than merely reduplicate his theological project, it is particularly this feature of Stephenson's chapter that most captivated my interest.

Stephenson believes that there is an odd and peculiar omission in Tillich's otherwise deeply sacramental theology. For Tillich, she notes, anything whatsoever can become a sacrament because everything participates in God, who is the ground of being. Any reality can become transparent to that ground in which it participates. Spiritual presence can become manifest in a rock, a stream, a hill just as readily as in bread and wine.

But there is, Stephenson rightly notes, a profound omission in Tillich: the body. Can the bodies of men and women become sites of sacramentality? One can imagine that Tillich would be compelled by the logic of his own system to say, "Yes, absolutely!" And yet, Tillich does not himself envisage this possibility. It remains a curious omission. Stephenson's recognition of and proposal to correct for this omission is an important and rich gift given to Tillichian theology. Tillichians stand ready to receive this gift as no radical revision of his ontology is necessary for the reception.

Stephenson's chapter, however, appears to leave one question unresolved. How does her call for a feminist pentecostal sacramentality stand in relation to her claim that pentecostal spirituality remains committed, and positively so, to a certain otherworldliness? Why valorize pentecostal otherworldliness? What does Stephenson mean when she holds that for Pentecostals, "The 'real' world is the eternal one, not the earthly one?"[8] Do we have here the return of the problem of supranaturalism?

Stephenson attenuates the threat of supranaturalistic otherworldliness by reading this pentecostal notion through a Tillichian eschatological imagination, one in which the fullness of spiritual presence is not fully and finally given in the here and now. The kingdom of God is not in some other world but is yet to come and so not yet here. That kingdom is said to be "otherworldly" only in order to guard against any premature thisworldliness in which the sacramental is taken to be fully and finally realized. For Stephenson, this otherworldliness is to be understood in temporal categories rather than spatial ones. The other world is not *elsewhere* but *elsewhen*. As a careful Tillich scholar, she knows well that for Tillich the kingdom is coming and does not reside supranaturally above the world. Can the same claim be made about popular forms of pentecostal otherworldliness? Or must spatialized conceptions of otherworldliness in pentecostal piety be reformed under the pressure of Tillich's distinctive eschatological vision and feminist accounts of sacramentality?

Nimi Wariboko's chapter is a rich feast of an offering that speaks of African pentecostal theology as a whole and yet somehow manages to give the reader an ethnographic sense of the particularities of African cosmologies. His attentive and patient description of nonentitative conceptions of power in African contexts is subtly done. Power is not just juridical power, he tells us, but is also richly entangled with notions of magical powers, spectral realities, demonic powers, and the biopolitical. Wariboko's discussion of power and the political is influenced by a variety of sources in contemporary political theology drawn from continental thought—Nancy and Foucault inform the discussion, for example—but throughout one gathers by way of resonance that Tillich's construal of the political is, in its own way, as broad and encompassing as the more recent thinkers that Wariboko treats. Wariboko shows that by writing the political into the ontological, Tillich too thinks far beyond the political as juridical.

Wariboko's discussion also raises difficult matters for the encounter with Tillich that we have been tracing throughout this volume: What is the relationship between African pentecostal theology's openness to the spectral and the magical and Tillich's reservations about supranaturalism? Macchia's chapter rightly notes that Tillich is open to the legitimacy and authenticity of exceptional and extraordinary phenomena, including speaking in tongues, but these occurrences are subject to naturalistic interpretation. They cannot constitute violations of the natural order. Yes, Tillich's capacious conception of the political is certainly resonant with the political as it emerges in African religious experience, but is this resonance necessarily limited given the ecstatic naturalist cosmology within which Tillich operates? These questions are but various formulations of one overarching question: How robust a resource can Tillich really be for African Pentecostals given the very different cosmology which informs African pentecostal theology? And would Wariboko be prepared to naturalize his account of spectral realities in the way that Bradnick does later in this volume?

Bradnick's chapter on the demonic offers compelling evidence of mutual learning and transformation. Just demonstrating, as he does, that a rich conversation between Pentecostals and Tillichians on the question of demonology is both possible and profitable is a tremendous service. One of the joys of this volume is the thrill of such unexpected discoveries and alliances. Bradnick raises the question of demonology, as does Wariboko, but in a distinctive fashion. When both voices are taken together, we are given to believe that the demonic is as central to Pentecostals as it is to Tillichians, if not more so.

But Bradnick attempts to resolve a question that Wariboko does not. Bradnick's emergentist demonology refuses more traditional superaturalist accounts of demonic beings and refuses also any sort of substance dualism. He does not believe that demons are "conscious, independent spiritual entities,"[9] and neither does Tillich. But Bradnick wants to go further than Tillich is prepared to go by suggesting that the demonic has a power that extends beyond the anthropological. The demonic is not just a function of the human spirit. It is worth presenting his own words on the matter:

> In this case, the demonic is not a distinct spiritual substance but a product of evolutionary processes. This allows the demonic to supervene and exert its influence upon the created order. And rather than fallen angels, the demonic is a derivative phenomenon that emerges subsequently to living creatures. Furthermore, in regard to human beings, the demonic, as emergent, cannot be reduced to human agency alone. The human condition participates in giving rise to the demonic, but the demonic is not confined to humanity.[10]

How far is Tillich's own vision of the demonic in keeping with this vision? Might Tillich and Tillichians be prepared to accept this emergentist vision of the demonic as meaningful and genuinely non-supranaturalist? It is too soon to say without further discussion. What cannot be gainsaid is the creativity of Bradnick's position, a position that strives mightily to keep faith with both Tillich's core intuitions and his own community's deeper sense of the demonic agency.

Peter Althouse offers a compelling juxtaposition of two ecstatic eschatologies in Tillich and Catch the Fire Pentecostalism (CTF). He makes a persuasive case that we do not have here a case of apples and oranges, but of two visions of the Spirit's grasping presence. The test of validity for both Tillich and Pentecostals remains the Spirit's creation of love. Both hold to a proleptic eschatology: the Spirit's presence heralds the coming kingdom. This much is shared.

But what of that coming kingdom? What shape will it take? Here matters become muddied. Tillich does not expect a literal terminus to history. Do the CTF Pentecostals? That remains less than clear in Althouse's chapter. He does note that there is no consensus on this front within pentecostal communities. But to the extent that Pentecostals do expect the conclusion of history to be brought about by dramatic divine intervention, we would then have a moment of qualitative incommensurability between Tillichians and CTF Pentecostals on account of supranaturalism. There is no simple resolution to this tension. But what Althouse succeeds in demonstrating is that the conversation between Pentecostals and Tillichians does not have to be brought to an abrupt halt because of this particular point of conflict. Participation in the divine life, healing encounters with the divine spirit that might be named mystical, ecstatic fervor subject to the test of love, a robust sense of the coming of God's kingdom—all this can be shared and celebrated by both Tillich and Pentecostals. We can learn from Althouse that the question of supranaturalism does not have to be a conversation stopper despite the serious challenge that it repeatedly presents.

In the final pentecostal chapter of this volume, Pamela Holmes offers a compelling account of the promise of the encounter between Pentecostalism and Tillich. She notes that Tillich's warning against confusing ecstasy with mere enthusiasm or overexcitement must be received by Pentecostals. But, more excitingly, she holds that early Pentecostals understood the social, and indeed socialist, dimensions of the Spirit's presence. Pentecost creates a community in which all share. This Lukan account of the Spirit, Holmes suggests, might help to revivify Tillich's early religious socialism, which she believes became domesticated in Tillich's American writings, especially his systematic theology.[11] Moreover, both contemporary Tillichians and Pentecostals stand in need of the secular prophetic temper of the Frankfurt school. This claim in particular strikes me as productive and provocative, a sign of the deep promise of this conversation for Tillichians. The idea that ecstasy and religious socialism can be wedded together can hardly be news for those who have read Luke–Acts. And yet, a compelling case can be made that both Tillichians and Pentecostals have failed to fully appreciate the intimate and even inseparable connection between ecstasy and social equity.

I wish to conclude this conversation by turning to a chapter that I have not yet discussed, namely Tony Richie's chapter on theology of religions. Richie makes an eloquent plea that Pentecostals have much to learn from Tillich's careful and guarded christocentric inclusivism. Time does not permit a rehearsal of the entire argument. The crucial point is that Tillich is able to affirm that the Spirit is broadly at work in the world. The Spirit's operation cannot be confined within the walls of the church, but Richie notes that Christ remains ever the central and decisive manifestation of God in history and the criterion by which all other manifestations are to be measured. For these reasons, Richie argues, Tillich can remain a positive resource in ways that later pluralist theologians cannot be. Tillich keeps faith with core pentecostal intuitions in ways that the latter do not.

Of course, deep resonance and even agreement between Tillich and Pentecostals is not itself a confirmation of the validity and rightness of their shared theological position. Consider, for example, Tony Richie's affirmation that, for Tillich, "there can be only one ultimate manifestation of the Spiritual Presence and that is Jesus as the Christ. Pentecostals agree."[12] Yes, Pentecostals do, and Richie reads Tillich accurately on this score. But is this judgment that there can be only one ultimate manifestation warranted? A strong counterclaim might be made that there is nothing in the structure of Tillich's theology, nor is there anything in the logic of the Spirit's working, that requires that the Spirit can have one and only one "ultimate manifestation."

Consider Tillich's speculative ruminations about the theological ramifications that would follow upon the discovery of sentient beings on other planets. Tillich notes that if such beings were to be found, and if those beings too experienced themselves as caught up in a predicament, as fallen creatures, then they too would stand in need of New Being. We can then, Tillich contends, expect to find in such "other worlds" the presence of other Spirit-generated disclosures of New Being. The Spirit may be hovering not only above earth's blue-green waters but over other oceans and other peoples on other planets. But if in other worlds, why not also in other religious worlds? On this question, it may be the case that both Tillichians and Pentecostals stand in need of further reflection and development.

Within the chapters of this book a lively intra-pentecostal conversation has taken place about the uses to which Tillich might be put and what can and ought to be learned from him. Moved along by the Spirit that is leading us into all truth, pentecostal theologians have constructed in this volume correlationalist engagements between church and world that are every bit as robust as Tillich himself called for and exemplified. Little wonder, then, that this volume is as rich and rewarding as it is! The book's authors have sought to deepen and broaden the pentecostal tradition in and through conversation with Paul Tillich. Hence, Tillichians are sure to be instructed and inspired by these labors.

But I am confident that the work accomplished herein is of far broader interest and import. After all, these authors write not for their tradition alone. They write for the future of the entire church. In the process, pentecostal theologians are in admirable fashion challenging not only each other but also the church as a whole, in profound ways. Hence it is hardly surprising that this book generates in this reader a certain visceral conviction that pentecostal theology is the site of some of the most exciting theological construction happening in the present moment. Tillichians are fortunate to be a part of this conversation and have at least as much to receive and learn therefrom as they have to give.

Notes

1. See p. 48.
2. See p. 148.
3. See p. 78.
4. See p. 30.
5. See p. 38.
6. On Tillich, Heidegger, and the question of ontotheology, see my essay "Tillich and the Postmodern," in *The Cambridge Companion to Pentecostalism,* Russell Re Manning, ed. (Cambridge: Cambridge University Press, 2009), 288–301.
7. See p. 110.
8. See p. 116.
9. See p. 161.
10. See pp. 162-163.
11. It is important to note that Mark Lewis Taylor, who is the other respondent to this book, argues that religious socialism (or socialist-spirit) was the guiding framework for Tillich's thought, or at least the enduring force in his view of Spirit even in his North American years.
12. See p. 147.

CONTRIBUTORS

PETER ALTHOUSE (PhD, University of St Michael's College at the University of Toronto, Canada) is Professor of Religion and Theology at Southeastern University, Lakeland, Florida, author of *Spirit of the Last Days: Pentecostal Eschatology in Conversation with Jürgen Moltmann* and *The Ideological Development of Power in Early American Pentecostalism: An Historical, Theological and Sociological Study*, and coeditor (with Michael Wilkinson) of *Winds from the North: Canadian Contributions to the Pentecostal Movement* and *Catch the Fire: Soaking Prayer and Charismatic Renewal*.

DAVID BRADNICK (PhD candidate, Regent University, Virginia Beach, Virginia) is an adjunct professor at Stevenson University, Stevenson, Maryland, and Harrisburg Area Community College, York, Pennsylvania, and has published scholarly articles in *Zygon: The Journal of Religion and Science* and *Theology and Science*.

TERRY L. CROSS (PhD, Princeton Theological Seminary, New Jersey) is Professor of Systematic Theology and Dean of the School of Religion at Lee University, Cleveland, Tennessee, and the author of *Dialectic in Karl Barth's Doctrine of God*.

PAMELA HOLMES (PhD, University of Toronto, Canada) teaches in the areas of theology, spirituality, and field education at Queen's School of Religion, Queen's University, Kingston, Ontario, Canada, has published various book chapters, and is completing *God Works in Mysterious Ways! Women within the Pentecostal Assemblies of Canada, 1919–2010*.

VELI-MATTI KÄRKKÄINEN (Dr.Theol.Habil., University of Helsinki, Finland) is Professor of Systematic Theology, Fuller Theological Seminary, Pasadena, California, and Docent in Ecumenics, University of Helsinki, Finland, and the author and editor of many books, including *The Spirit in the World: Emerging Pentecostal Theologies in Global Contexts*.

RHYS KUZMIČ is a PhD candidate in Philosophy of Religion and Theology at Claremont Graduate University, Claremont, California, and has published "Beruf and Berufung in Karl Barth's Church Dogmatics: Toward a Subversive Klesiology," in the *International Journal of Systematic Theology*, among other articles.

FRANK D. MACCHIA (D.Theol., University of Basel, Switzerland) is Professor of Systematic Theology at Vanguard University, Costa Mesa, California, and author of numerous books on pentecostal theology, including *Justified in the Spirit: Creation, Redemption, and the Triune God.*

ANDREAS NORDLANDER (PhD, Lund University, Sweden) is senior lecturer in theology, philosophy of religion, and ethics at the University of Gothenburg, Göteborg, Sweden, and is currently at work editing a collection of essays in philosophical theology to appear in Swedish; he has published on the doctrine of creation in *Modern Theology* and has previously written on Augustine and Aquinas.

TONY RICHIE (PhD, London School of Theology) is Adjunct Professor of Historical and Doctrinal Theology at Pentecostal Theological Seminary, Cleveland, Tennessee, and author of many scholarly articles and two books: *Speaking by the Spirit: A Pentecostal Model for Interreligious Encounter and Dialogue,* and *Toward a Pentecostal Theology of Religions: Encountering Cornelius Today.*

LISA P. STEPHENSON (PhD, Marquette University, Milwaukee, Wisconsin) is Associate Professor of Systematic Theology at Lee University, Cleveland, Tennessee; she has articles published in *Scottish Journal of Theology, Journal of Church and State, Pneuma, Pax Pneuma: The Journal of Pentecostals,* and *Charismatics for Peace and Justice, Religions,* and in a number of edited volumes, and is the author of *Dismantling the Dualisms for American Pentecostal Women in Ministry.*

STEVEN M. STUDEBAKER (PhD, Marquette University, Milwaukee, Wisconsin) is Associate Professor of Systematic and Historical Theology and Howard and Shirley Bentall Chair in Evangelical Thought, McMaster Divinity College, McMaster University, Hamilton, Ontario; he has authored or edited *Jonathan Edwards' Social Augustinian Trinitarianism in Historical and Contemporary Perspectives, Defining Issues in Pentecostalism: Classical and Emergent,* and *From Pentecost to the Triune God,* among other books.

MARK LEWIS TAYLOR (PhD, University of Chicago, Illinois) is Maxwell M. Upson Professor of Theology and Culture at Princeton Theological Seminary, New Jersey, and the author or editor of many books, including *Paul Tillich: Theologian of the Boundaries,* and, most recently, *The Theological and the Political: On the Weight of the World.*

JOHN J. THATAMANIL (PhD, Boston University, Massachusetts) is Associate Professor of Theology and World Religions at Union Theological Seminary, New York City, past president of the North American Paul Tillich Society, and the author of *The Immanent Divine: God, Creation, and the Human Predicament. An East-West Conversation* and *The Hospitality of Receiving: The Promise of Religious Diversity,* among other publications.

WOLFGANG VONDEY (PhD, Marquette University, Milwaukee, Wisconsin) is Professor of Systematic Theology at Regent University School of Divinity, Virginia Beach, Virginia, and the author and editor of a number of books, including *Beyond Pentecostalism: The Crisis of Global Christianity and the Renewal of the Theological Agenda* and *Pentecostalism: A Guide for the Perplexed.*

NIMI WARIBOKO (PhD, Princeton Theological Seminary, New Jersey) is Walter G. Muelder Professor of Social Ethics, School of Theology, Boston University, Massachusetts, and the author of many books, four of which have used Tillichian frameworks for various philosophical-theological, social, and economic analyses: *The Depth and Destiny of Work: An African Theological Interpretation, God and Money: A Theology of Money in a Globalizing World, The Principle of Excellence: A Framework for Social Ethics,* and *The Pentecostal Principle: Ethical Methodology in New Spirit.*

AMOS YONG (PhD, Boston University, Massachusetts) is Professor of Theology and Mission at Fuller Theological Seminary, Pasadena, California, and the author and editor of more than three dozen books.

INDEX

CPSIA information can be obtained
at www.ICGtesting.com
Printed in the USA
LVHW012302131222
735141LV00003B/369